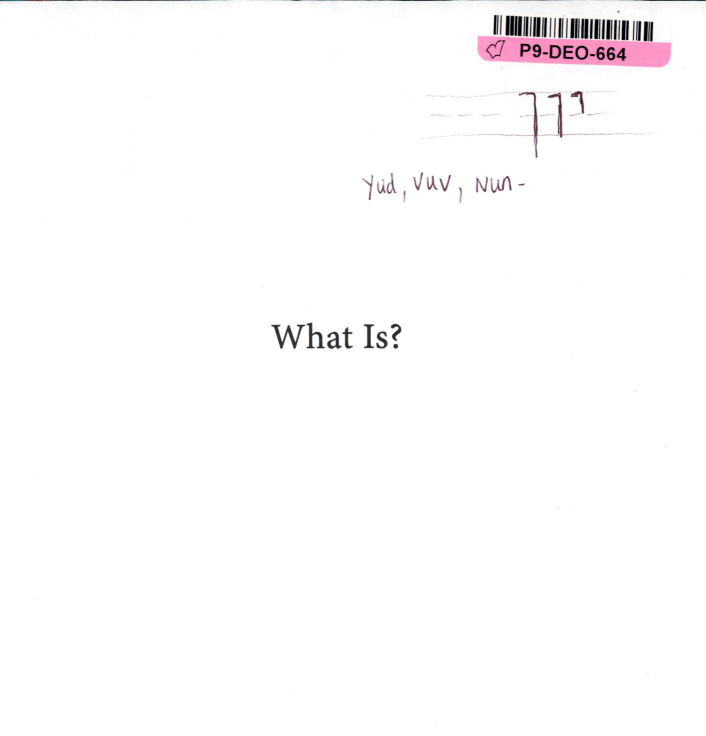

Yud, Vuv, Nun-

What Is?

EDITOR
Rabbi Yanki Tauber

CURRICULUM DEVELOPMENT
Rabbi Lazer Gurkow
Rabbi Yisrael Rice
Rabbi Benyomin Walters
Rabbi Yosi Wolf

EDITORIAL BOARD
Rabbi Sholom Raichik
Mrs. Rivkah Slonim
Rabbi Ari Sollish
Rabbi Shraga Sherman

COORDINATORS
Mrs. Mushka Minsky
Mrs. Rivki Mockin

ADMINISTRATOR
Mrs. Chana Dechter

Cover Art: Ciel-Terre *(detail), Hai Ja Bang,*
2011, pigment on paper. (Korean Art
Museum Association)

(888) YOUR-JLI/718-221-6900
WWW.MYJLI.COM

what is?

RETHINKING EVERYTHING WE KNOW ABOUT OUR UNIVERSE

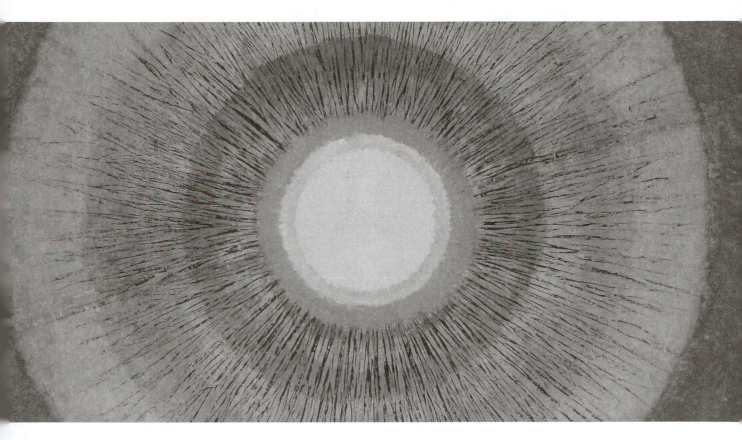

JLI

JEWISH LEARNING INSTITUTE

STUDENT TEXTBOOK

THE ROHR JEWISH LEARNING INSTITUTE

gratefully acknowledges
the pioneering and ongoing support of

George and Pamela Rohr

Since its inception,
the Rohr JLI has been
a beneficiary of the vision, generosity,
care, and concern
of the Rohr family.

In the merit of
the tens of thousands of hours of Torah study
by JLI students worldwide,
may they be blessed with health,
Yiddishe nachas *from all their loved ones,*
and extraordinary success
in all their endeavors.

Endorsements

We live in a practical age. But the quest for meaning in life is even more important than ever. The course *What Is?*, based on profound Chabad Chasidic teachings, is a wonderful resource to help modern man and woman tackle questions that are at the core of human existence. It includes topics such as Reality, Time, G-d, Self, and Freedom. This exciting course, explored in six sessions, will help participants know more clearly who they are as individuals and the global opportunities that face them day by day.

NAFTALI LOEWENTHAL, PHD
Author of *Communicating the Infinite: The Emergence of the Habad School*

Not all of us like small talk. Some of us prefer "big talk." We ask questions like "Who am I?" "Where did I come from?" "Where am I going?" "What for?" and "Why?" Well, this is a course of Jewish Big Talk for those of us who need to explore the profound questions of life. Many other courses are certainly interesting or informative. But this course is *important*. (And the author of the course, Rabbi Yanki Tauber, is extraordinary.)

ARTHUR KURZWEIL
Author, *Kabbalah for Dummies* and ten other titles

Jews are intelligent people who ask intelligent questions. This is the course that asks the questions that sit at the very core of our understanding of life and its meaning.

RABBI TZVI FREEMAN
Senior Editor, Chabad.org
Author, *Bringing Heaven Down to Earth*

We each have a purpose in this world. While an emotional feeling for Judaism is a great motivator to try to discern our particular purpose, *Chasidut* teaches that an intellectual understanding of how to achieve that goal is essential. As a guiding maxim of *Chasidut* puts it, *moach shalit al halev*, the mind should rule the heart. Being well educated in the foundations of Judaism is key to understanding our universe and our place in it. As a professional in the field of psychology and mental healing, I have found the Chasidic perspective on Torah Judaism to be the most effective means to self-awareness and self-mastery. In JLI's fascinating new *What Is?* course, Rabbi Tauber will apply this perspective to elucidate Torah fundamentals in an intellectually satisfying and emotionally fulfilling way.

MIRIAM YERUSHALMI, M.S.
Author, *Reaching New Heights* Self-Help Series

In a culture that promotes the religion of the self and hyper-individualism, one wherein the notions of truth and objectivity have been pushed aside by moral relativism, many of us are left floundering. *What Is?* offers a bedrock of knowledge on which to build a life of meaning and joy, and a sense of well-being and safety. From the ground zero question as to whether we are here at all, to the questions of whether time, G-d, evil, the self, and choice exist, it promises to release us from a truth-for-me reality into a world of truth and purpose.

SHIMONA TZUKERNIK
The Kabbalah Coach
Author, *The Method for Self-Mastery* course

Existential questioning is part and parcel of our development as deep-thinking and spiritually-seeking human beings. Yet the questions are endless—and can become overwhelming—unless one finds fertile responses. The new JLI course, *What Is?* cultivates those responses. The course explores the kabbalistic and Chasidic approach to key questions such as who we are, why we are here, and what we are meant to accomplish, providing participants with impactful insight and understanding.

RABBI ASHER CRISPE
Co-Director, Interinclusion.org

No serious discussion about faith, morality, values, or belief can take place without a basic appreciation for the subjects treated in this course. It is gratifying to think about the level of discourse that *What Is?* will enable students to engage in long after they have completed the course.

RABBI SHAIS TAUB
Author, *God of Our Understanding: Jewish Spirituality and Recovery from Addiction*

JLI's new course, *What Is?* will teach you some profound, mind-hacking wisdom and create a positive, permanent shift in your thinking. It masterfully delivers some of Judaism's most empowering ideas and will guide you to many personal and professional triumphs.

RABBI CHAIM MILLER
Author, *The Practical Tanya, The Gutnick Chumash,* and seven other titles

Profound questions arise for profound souls. And because every Jew possesses a questing and searching inner core, *What Is?* may well be the most eye-opening and brainstorming experience you will ever experience. Innately, we all sense there is more to the radical act of living than mere survival. To ask, at least once in one's life, the "Big Questions" of life, is not only an imperative, but it is also a prerequisite to quantum-leaping into the heart of existential meaning. And what's more, this course not only has the courage to raise and articulate the questions, it also provides answers!

RABBI DR. LAIBL WOLF
Author of *Practical Kabbalah*
Dean and Founder, Spiritgrow—The Josef Kryss Holistic Centre, Australia

Contents

Lesson

1

IS THE WORLD REAL?

Everything that we experience, we experience inside our heads, leading to the intriguing question: Maybe there is no existence outside of our minds? But perhaps a more fundamental question would be: What practical difference does it make if the world is real or not?

The Flammarion Engraving (detail), from Camille Flammarion's *L'Atmosphère: Météorologie Populaire* (The Atmosphere: Popular Meteorology). (Paris, Fr.: Librairie Hachette et Cie., 1888)

TEXT 1

DONALD SIMANEK AND JOHN HOLDEN, *SCIENCE ASKEW: A LIGHT-HEARTED LOOK AT THE SCIENTIFIC WORLD* (BOCA RATON, FLA.: CRC PRESS, 2001), P. 209

Is reality real? Such confusion!
Can it be that it's all just illusion?
Philosophers cogitate;
Scientists speculate.
But none of them reach a conclusion.

DONALD SIMANEK
1936–

Physicist. Simanek is emeritus professor of physics at Lock Haven University of Pennsylvania. His areas of expertise include conceptual development in physics, history and philosophy of science, photography, and visual illusions.

JOHN HOLDEN

Geologist, geophysicist, and paleontologist. Holden studied geology at S. Diego State University and paleontology at the University of California at Berkeley. He served as a marine geologist and geophysicist for the U.S. Coast and Geodetic Survey (USC&GS) and National Oceanic and Atmospheric Administration (NOAA). He has published a number of works, including *Science Askew: A light-hearted look at the scientific world.*

Observatory at Alexandria, from Camille Flammarion's *L'Astronomie Populaire* (Popular Astronomy), artist unknown. (Paris, Fr.: C. Marpon et E. Flammarion, Éditeurs, 1880)

TEXT 2

GENESIS 1:1

‌   בְּרֵאשִׁית בָּרָא אֱלֹקִים אֵת הַשָּׁמַיִם וְאֵת הָאָרֶץ.   **‌**

In the beginning God created the heavens and the earth.

TEXT 3

DEUTERONOMY 4:35

‌   אַתָּה הָרְאֵתָ לָדַעַת כִּי ה׳ הוּא הָאֱלֹקִים אֵין עוֹד מִלְבַדּוֹ.   **‌**

You have been shown to know that God is God; there is
none else besides Him.

Figure 1.1

Definition of "Reality"

reality

NOUN

1 The state of things as they actually exist, as opposed to an idealistic or notional idea of them.

2 *Philosophy* Existence that is absolute, self-sufficient, or objective, and not subject to human decisions or conventions.

Real is Outside of ME!

OXFORD ENGLISH DICTIONARY   *inside of me is opinion, etc.*

✱perception vs. fact

wired to mis read reality

Figure 1.2a

Which Box Is Darker—A or B?

EDWARD H. ADELSON, PROFESSOR OF VISION SCIENCE AT MIT, 1995

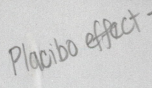

Figure 1.2b

Optical Illusion Exposed: A and B are the Same Shade

Cover the right and left sides of the image with two sheets of paper (or other objects), leaving only the two bars and the space between them exposed. This will show even more clearly that the two squares are the same color.

EDWARD H. ADELSON, PROFESSOR OF VISION SCIENCE AT MIT, 1995

Reality + Perception is blurred,

Figure 1.3

Preliminary Conclusions

we all agree with this...

1 Reality doesn't change based on our perception of it.

2 Therefore, we must conform to reality.

3 Success in life depends on learning effective strategies within the confines of reality.

TEXT 4

RABBI NISSIM GERONDI, *DERASHOT HARAN*, 8:63A

שֶׁחֶפֶץ ה' יִתְבָּרֵךְ וּרְצוֹנוֹ לְקַיֵּם מִנְהָגוֹ שֶׁל עוֹלָם בְּמַה שֶׁאֶפְשָׁר. וְשֶׁהַטֶּבַע
יָקָר בְּעֵינָיו, לֹא יְשַׁנֵּהוּ אֶלָּא לְצוֹרֶךְ הֶכְרֵחִי.

RABBI NISSIM GERONDI
1320–1376

Talmudist, halachic authority, and philosopher. Rabbi Nissim was born in Barcelona and lived in Girona. He was one of the last of the great Spanish medieval Talmudic scholars. He did not hold any rabbinic post, but served as a physician in the royal palace. His works include commentaries on Rabbi Yitschak Alfasi's code, responsa literature, and a collection of sermons that elucidate fundamentals of Judaism.

God's desire and will is to maintain the "way of the world" wherever possible. Nature is precious in God's eyes, and He does not change it unless it is absolutely necessary.

TEXT **5**

TALMUD, AVODAH ZARAH 54B

הֲרֵי שֶׁגָּזַל סְאָה שֶׁל חִטִּים [וְהָלַךְ] וְזָרְעָהּ בַּקַּרְקַע, דִּין הוּא שֶׁלֹּא תִּצְמַח? אֶלָּא עוֹלָם כְּמִנְהָגוֹ נוֹהֵג וְהוֹלֵךְ, וְשׁוֹטִים שֶׁקִּלְקְלוּ עֲתִידִין לִיתֵּן אֶת הַדִּין . . . הֲרֵי שֶׁבָּא עַל אֵשֶׁת חֲבֵירוֹ, דִּין הוּא שֶׁלֹּא תִּתְעַבֵּר? אֶלָּא עוֹלָם כְּמִנְהָגוֹ נוֹהֵג וְהוֹלֵךְ, וְשׁוֹטִים שֶׁקִּלְקְלוּ עֲתִידִין לִיתֵּן אֶת הַדִּין.

BABYLONIAN TALMUD

A literary work of monumental proportions that draws upon the legal, spiritual, intellectual, ethical, and historical traditions of Judaism. The 37 tractates of the Babylonian Talmud contain the teachings of the Jewish sages from the period after the destruction of the Second Temple through the fifth century CE. It has served as the primary vehicle for the transmission of the Oral Law and the education of Jews over the centuries; it is the entry point for all subsequent legal, ethical, and theological Jewish scholarship.

Suppose a person stole a measure of wheat and went and sowed it in the ground; should it be decreed that it not grow? Rather, the world follows its natural course, and the fools who acted wrongly will be held accountable. . . . Suppose a person has relations with his neighbor's wife; should it be decreed that that she should not conceive? Rather, the world follows its natural course, and the fools who acted wrongly will be held accountable.

QUESTION FOR DISCUSSION

What are the problems with a deterministic view of the world?

Relativity, M.C. Escher, lithograph, The Netherlands, 1953. (The Museum of Modern Art, New York)

TEXT 6

PSALMS 115:4–9

עֲצַבֵּיהֶם כֶּסֶף וְזָהָב, מַעֲשֵׂה יְדֵי אָדָם. פֶּה לָהֶם וְלֹא יְדַבֵּרוּ, עֵינַיִם לָהֶם וְלֹא
יִרְאוּ. אָזְנַיִם לָהֶם וְלֹא יִשְׁמָעוּ, אַף לָהֶם וְלֹא יְרִיחוּן. יְדֵיהֶם וְלֹא יְמִישׁוּן,
רַגְלֵיהֶם וְלֹא יְהַלֵּכוּ, לֹא יֶהְגּוּ בִּגְרוֹנָם. כְּמוֹהֶם יִהְיוּ עֹשֵׂיהֶם, כֹּל אֲשֶׁר בֹּטֵחַ
בָּהֶם. יִשְׂרָאֵל בְּטַח בַּה', עֶזְרָם וּמָגִנָּם הוּא.

Their idols are silver and gold, the handiwork of man. They have a mouth but they do not speak; they have eyes but they do not see. They have ears but they do not hear; they have a nose but they do not smell. They have hands but they do not feel; they have feet but they do not walk; they do not communicate with their throat. Like them shall be those who make them, all who trust in them. Israel [however,] trusts in God; He is their help and protector.

Figure 1.4

The Nine-Dot Challenge*

What you thought was impossible is possible.

J. TRAVERS, *THE PUZZLE-MINE: PUZZLES COLLECTED FROM THE WORKS OF THE LATE HENRY ERNEST DUDENEY.* (LONDON, U.K.: THOS. NELSON, 1951)

pg. 234

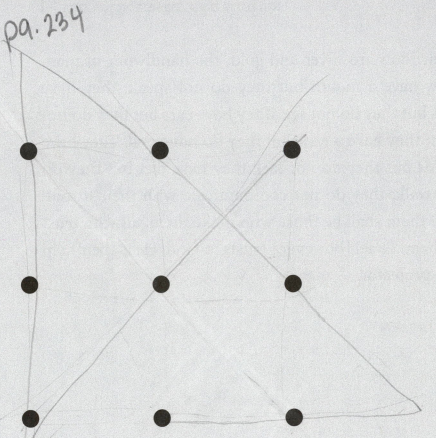

* Solution on p. 234

Figure 1.5a

Four Models of Reality—Take One

	REALITY MODEL	IS THE WORLD REAL?
1	Worldly Reality	The world is real because its limits are absolute.
2	Creation Reality	
3	Godly Reality	
4	Unified Reality	

TEXT 7 *godly reality has NO limits.*

NACHMANIDES, *COMMENTARY ON THE TORAH,* GENESIS 1:1

הַקָּדוֹשׁ בָּרוּךְ הוּא בָּרָא כָּל הַנִּבְרָאִים מֵאֲפִיסָה מוּחְלֶטֶת. וְאֵין אֶצְלֵנוּ בִּלְשׁוֹן הַקּוֹדֶשׁ בְּהוֹצָאַת הַיֵּשׁ מֵאַיִן אֶלָּא לָשׁוֹן "בָּרָא".

God created all creations out of absolute nothingness. The only word that we have in Hebrew to describe the creation of "something from nothing" is *bara.*

Reality is what was made.

RABBI MOSHE BEN NACHMAN (NACHMANIDES, RAMBAN) 1194–1270
Scholar, philosopher, author, and physician. Nachmanides was born in Spain and served as leader of Iberian Jewry. In 1263, he was summoned by King James of Aragon to a public disputation with Pablo Cristiani, a Jewish apostate. Though Nachmanides was the clear victor of the debate, he had to flee Spain because of the resulting persecution. He moved to Israel and helped reestablish communal life in Jerusalem. He authored a classic commentary on the Pentateuch and a commentary on the Talmud.

things are the way the are because god chose them to be that way

The People and the Sea, from *Haggadah: The Passover Story,* illustrated by Gérard Garouste. (New York, N.Y.: Assouline, 2001)

TEXT 8

RABBI SAMSON RAPHAEL HIRSCH, *COMMENTARY ON THE TORAH,* GENESIS 17:17
(ENGLISH EDITION BY ISAAC LEVY, LONDON, 1963)

The birth of Isaac was, of course, an absolute absurdity. The notion that a 100-year-old man and his 90-year-old wife, who have never had a child in the course of their long married life, should bear a son, and to place the hopes of the whole future of mankind on this child!

According to all natural conditions of cause and effect, the entire existence of the Jewish people, its history, its hopes, its expectations, must appear as the most laughable pretension. It makes sense only when it reckons on the deeply infringing, completely free almighty will of the Almighty God.

That was why God waited for the first seed of this nation to be laid until the "absurd" old age of its ancestors; that was why He waited to fulfill His promise until all human hopes for its realization had ended. For it was a question of creating a nation which, from the very beginning of its existence, was to be in opposition to all the ordinary laws of history—an intimation of God in the midst of mankind.

RABBI SAMSON RAPHAEL HIRSCH
1808–1888

Born in Hamburg, Germany; rabbi and educator; intellectual founder of the *Torah Im Derech Eretz* school of Orthodox Judaism, which advocates combining Torah with secular education. Beginning in 1830, Hirsch served as chief rabbi in several prominent German cities. During this period he wrote his *Nineteen Letters on Judaism,* under the pseudonym of Ben Uziel. His work helped preserve traditional Judaism during the era of the German Enlightenment. He is buried in Frankfurt am Main.

Our foundation trancends nature, laws of nature
but never trapped within nature
world reality
Creative reality

Figure 1.5b

Four Models of Reality—Take Two

	REALITY MODEL	IS THE WORLD REAL?
1	Worldly Reality	The world is real because its limits are absolute.
2	Creation Reality	The world is real because God created it.
3	Godly Reality	
4	Unified Reality	

TEXT 9

RABBI MENACHEM MENDEL OF LUBAVITCH, *DERECH MITZVOTECHA*, 94B

וְהָעִנְיָן דִּכְתִיב "אֵ-ל דֵעוֹת ה'" (שְׁמוּאֵל א ב' ג'). שֶׁכּוֹלֵל ב' דֵעוֹת.

הָא' הַדֵּעָה שֶׁלְּמַעְלָה הוּא הַיֵּשׁ הָאֲמִיתִּי, וְכָל מַה שֶׁלְּמַטָּה כֻּלָּא כְּלָא חָשִׁיב, כִּי הוּא רַק הֶאָרָה בְּעָלְמָא, וְנִקְרָא אַיִן. וּכְמוֹ שֶׁכָּתוּב מִצְוָה תי"ז פֶּרֶק ג' בְּפֵירוּשׁ אֵין עוֹד כוּלֵי. וְזוֹהִי הַדֵּעָה שֶׁלּוֹ דְּהַיְינוּ כְּמוֹ שֶׁהוּא קַמֵּי' יִתְבָּרֵךְ.

הַב' הִיא כְּמוֹ שֶׁנִּרְאֶה לְגַבֵּי הַנִּבְרָאִים. שֶׁנִּדְמֶה לָהֶם שֶׁהֵם בְּחִינַת יֵשׁ וְדָבָר. וְאוֹמְרִים שֶׁהַבְּרִיאָה "יֵשׁ מֵאַיִן". וְרוֹצֶה לוֹמַר שֶׁהָאֱלֹקוּת הוּא בְּחִינַת אַיִן עַל שֵׁם שֶׁאֵינוֹ מוּשָּׂג, וְהַנִּבְרָאִים הֵם בְּחִינַת יֵשׁ וְדָבָר נִרְאֶה לָעַיִן . . .

RABBI MENACHEM MENDEL SCHNEERSOHN OF LUBAVITCH (TSEMACH TSEDEK) 1789–1866

Chasidic rebbe and noted author. The *Tsemach Tsedek* was the third leader of the Chabad Chasidic movement and a noted authority on Jewish law. His numerous works include halachic responsa, Chasidic discourses, and kabbalistic writings. Active in the plight of Russian Jewry, he worked to alleviate the plight of the cantonists, Jewish children kidnapped to serve in the Czar's army. He passed away in Lubavitch, leaving seven sons and two daughters.

It is written (1 SAMUEL 2:3), "God is the God of minds." This implies the existence of two "minds" [i.e., perspectives on reality].

The first "mind" is that God is the true reality, and all that is here below is regarded as naught, as it is nothing but a reflection [of God's reality]. It is therefore called "nothing," as was explained [in an earlier discourse] regarding the meaning of the verse, "there is none else." This is God's "mind"—how it is from God's perspective.

The second "mind" is how it appears from the perspective of the creations. To them, it seems that they are real and "something." They describe the creation [of the world] as "something from nothing"—meaning that Godliness is "nothing," as it is not graspable, and the creations are real and "something."

* Samuel Annoited King Saul

can only grasp things with limits

G_d is way beyond our

nothing out of something ~

TEXT 10

RABBI SHNE'UR ZALMAN OF LIADI, *TANYA,*
SHAAR HAYICHUD VEHA'EMUNAH, CHAPTER 3

וּמַה שֶׁכָּל נִבְרָא וְנִפְעָל נִרְאֶה לָנוּ לְיֵשׁ וּמַמָּשׁוּת, זֶהוּ מֵחֲמַת שֶׁאֵין אָנוּ מַשִּׂיגִים וְרוֹאִים בְּעֵינֵי בָּשָׂר אֶת כֹּחַ ה' וְרוּחַ פִּיו שֶׁבְּנִבְרָא. אֲבָל אִילוּ נִיתְּנָה רְשׁוּת לָעַיִן לִרְאוֹת וּלְהַשִּׂיג אֶת הַחַיּוּת וְרוּחָנִיוּת שֶׁבְּכָל נִבְרָא הַשּׁוֹפֵעַ בּוֹ . . . לֹא הָיָה גַּשְׁמִיוּת הַנִּבְרָא וְחוּמְרוֹ וּמַמָּשׁוֹ נִרְאֶה כְּלָל לְעֵינֵינוּ.

**RABBI SHNE'UR ZALMAN OF LIADI
(ALTER REBBE) 1745–1812**

Chasidic rebbe, halachic authority, and founder of the Chabad movement. The Alter Rebbe was born in Liozna, Belarus, and was among the principal students of the Magid of Mezeritch. His numerous works include the *Tanya,* an early classic containing the fundamentals of Chabad Chasidism, and *Shulchan Aruch HaRav,* an expanded and reworked code of Jewish law.

The fact that every creation and event appears to us as "something" and as tangible is only because we do not grasp and see with our eyes of flesh the divine energy and the divine utterances within each creation. But if the eye were allowed to see and apprehend the [divine] vitality and spiritually being infused into every creation . . . the physicality, materiality, and substance of that creation would be utterly invisible to us.

TEXT 11

RABBI MENACHEM MENDEL OF LUBAVITCH, *DERECH MITZVOTECHA*, 94B

וְהִנֵּה אָנוּ אוֹמְרִים, "מוֹדִים אֲנַחְנוּ לָךְ" (דִּבְרֵי הַיָּמִים א כ"ט י"ג). פֵּירוּשׁ, שֶׁאֲנַחְנוּ מוֹדִים שֶׁהָאֱמֶת כְּמוֹ שֶׁהוּא קַמֵּי' יִתְבָּרֵךְ . . . וּמַה שֶׁהָעוֹלָם וּמְלוֹאוֹ נִרְאָה לְיֵשׁ וְדָבָר, זֶהוּ מִצַּד הַצִּמְצוּמִים וְהַהֶעְלָמִים, כְּדִכְתִיב, "אֵ-ל מִסְתַּתֵּר" (יְשַׁעְיָ' מ"ה ט"ו). שֶׁעַל יְדֵי צִמְצוּם זֶה נִרְאָה הַנִּבְרָא לְיֵשׁ, וְעַל פִּי צִמְצוּמִים אֵלוּ הוּא הַדֵּעָה הַב' . . . וּבֶאֱמֶת הַצִּמְצוּמִים אֵינָן אֶלָּא לְפָנֵינוּ, אֲבָל קַמֵּי' יִתְבָּרֵךְ אֵין הַצִּמְצוּמִים אֲמִיתִּיִּים כְּלָל. וְנִמְצָא הָאֱמֶת כְּמוֹ שֶׁהוּא קַמֵּי' בְּדֵעָה הָעֶלְיוֹנָה. וְעַל זֶה אוֹמְרִים מוֹדִים כוּלֵי.

Now we say (1 CHRONICLES 29:13), "We concede to You." Meaning, we concede that the truth is how it is from God's perspective. . . . The fact that the world and all it contains appears to be real and "something," this is only due to the "constrictions" (*tsimtsumim*) and concealments, as it is written (ISAIAH 45:15), "God hides Himself." It is by means of this constriction that a created thing appears to be "something," and these constrictions generate the "second mind." . . . Yet the constrictions are only from our perspective. From God's perspective, the constrictions are not real at all. Hence, the truth is as it is from God's perspective, which is the higher "mind." Thus we say: "We concede . . . ."

The truth is from G-d's perspective

From G-ds perspective, Reality is NOT Real.

Figure 1.5c

Four Models of Reality—Take Three

	REALITY MODEL	IS THE WORLD REAL?
1	Worldly Reality	The world is real because its limits are absolute.
2	Creation Reality	The world is real because God created it.
3	Godly Reality	The world is not real.
4	Unified Reality	

Creative Reality is the <u>front end</u>
G-d's Reality is the back end
        or Created

Figure 1.6

Back End / Front End Duality

	BACK END	**FRONT END**
Computer Application	A software developer has the freedom to design an app do whatever they want.	A user can only download the apps they find in the app store and use them for their designed purposes.
Electronics	Someone expert in electronics can make their own circuit boards and repair broken ones.	Electronics often state "no user-serviceable parts inside." The average user can only buy ready-made products, and must pay to repair or replace them if broken.
Medicine	Doctors prescribe treatments, and researchers invent new cures.	Patient cannot self-prescribe, and may only "use as directed."
Books, Stage, and Film	Writers, directors, and actors	Readers and audience
Food	Chefs invent recipes, because they understand the fundamentals.	Consumers eat prepared food or follow recipes.
Education	Educators create curricula and teaching methods.	Students follow their syllabi and the rules of their institutions. Their grades reflect these standards.
Human Being	Subconscious	Behavior

unified reality perspective.

TEXT 12

RABBI MENACHEM MENDEL OF LUBAVITCH, *DERECH MITZVOTECHA*, 94B

שֶׁהֲרֵי הוּא לְמַעְלָה מִן הַצִּמְצוּמִים, וְגַם הוּא הַמְצַמְצֵם הַצִּמְצוּמִים.
וְנִמְצָא הוּא כּוֹלֵל ב' הַדֵּעוֹת. וְזֶהוּ שֶׁכָּתוּב "אֵ-ל דֵעוֹת ה'."

God is beyond the *tsimtsumim* [the self-concealments and "constrictions" that generate the Creation Reality], and God is also the source of the "constrictions." So in the end result, God includes both "minds." Hence the verse states, "God is the God of minds."

Godly expression

The World is a devine Communication

Drawing Hands, M.C. Escher, lithograph, The Netherlands, 1948. (National Gallery of Art, Washington, D.C.)

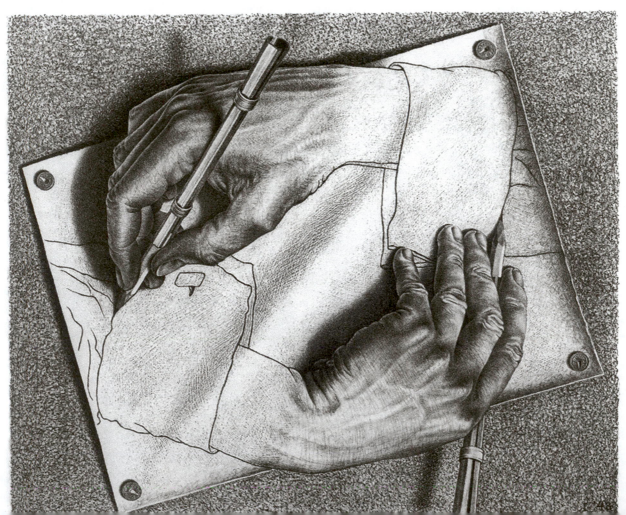

The Created Reality is the Parable for the Godly Reality [23]

TEXT 13

RABBI SHALOM DOVBER OF LUBAVITCH, *SEFER HAMAAMARIM* 5657, P. 48

אַךְ הָעִנְיָן יוּבַן עַל דֶּרֶךְ מָשָׁל . . . כְּמוֹ חָכָם גָּדוֹל שֶׁצָּרִיךְ לְהַשְׁפִּיעַ שֵׂכֶל לִמְקַבֵּל קָטָן בְּשֵׂכֶל, שֶׁלֹּא בְּעֶרֶךְ הַמַּשְׁפִּיעַ כְּלָל . . . שֶׁאִם יְגַלֶּה לוֹ עוֹמֶק וְרוֹחַב חָכְמָתוֹ בְּהַדָּבָר מוּשְׂכָּל כְּמוֹ שֶׁהוּא אֶצְלוֹ, יִתְבַּלְבֵּל חוּשֵׁי הַמְקַבֵּל, וְלֹא יוּכַל לְקַבֵּל כְּלָל. כִּי אִם בְּהֶכְרֵחַ שֶׁיְּצַמְצֵם וְיַעֲלִים כָּל עוֹמֶק וְרוֹחַב חָכְמָתוֹ . . . וְאַף גַּם זֹאת מַלְבִּישׁ וּמַעֲלִים בַּמָּשָׁל. שֶׁהַמָּשָׁל הוּא דָּבָר זָר לְגַמְרֵי מֵהַנִּמְשָׁל, וַהֲרֵי הוּא מְכַסֶּה וּמַעֲלִים עַל הַשֵּׂכֶל, כְּמוֹ הַלְּבוּשׁ שֶׁמְכַסֶּה עַל אֵיזֶה דָּבָר . . . אָמְנָם עַל יְדֵי זֶה יִתְפּוֹס בְּהַנִּמְשָׁל וְיָבִין אוֹתוֹ, לִהְיוֹתוֹ מְכֻוָּן אֶל הַנִּמְשָׁל . . .

RABBI SHALOM DOVBER SCHNEERSOHN (RASHAB) 1860–1920

Chasidic rebbe. Rabbi Shalom Dovber became the fifth leader of the Chabad movement upon the passing of his father, Rabbi Shmuel of Lubavitch. He established the Lubavitch network of *yeshivot* called Tomchei Temimim. He authored many volumes of chasidic discourses and is renowned for his lucid and thorough explanations of kabbalistic concepts.

This will be understood by way of example . . . of the case of a great sage who needs to transmit an idea to a minor student, whose intellect is many levels lower than that of the teacher. . . . If the teacher were to reveal the depth and breadth of the idea as he has it, the student's faculties would be confused, and he would not be able to receive anything at all. So the teacher needs to contract and conceal the full depth and breadth of his wisdom in this idea . . . and to dress it and conceal it within a parable. The parable is something that is completely foreign to the idea, so it covers it and conceals it, like a garment covers that which is within it . . . But it is by the means of the parable that the student will grasp the idea and understand it, because the parable corresponds to the idea.

G-d is the best parable maker in the world. Our finite world is like a parable that communicates the infinite truth of g-d.

God is the ultimate parable maker

? QUESTIONS FOR DISCUSSION

1   Parable examples: What are your favorite examples of the parable as a communication tool?

2   The advantages in using a parable: What are the advantages in using a parable to communicate an idea, as opposed to simply explaining the idea?

3   Parable dos and don'ts: Imagine that you are creating a parable. What are the ingredients of an effective parable? What are the pitfalls to avoid?

Learning Talmud,
Zalman Kleinman,
acrylic on canvas, 1984.

TEXT **14**

RABBI SHALOM DOVBER OF LUBAVITCH, *SEFER HAMAAMARIM* 5657, P. 49

הִנֵּה כָּל צִמְצוּם וְהֶעְלֵם הַנִּזְכָּר לְעֵיל הוּא רַק לְגַבֵּי הַמְקַבֵּל, וְלֹא לְגַבֵּי
הַמַּשְׁפִּיעַ. שֶׁהֲרֵי גַּבֵּי הַמַּשְׁפִּיעַ מֵאִיר בְּגִילוּי כָּל עוֹמֶק שִׂכְלוֹ וְחָכְמָתוֹ
בְּהַשֵּׂכֶל הַמְצוּמְצָם, כְּמוֹ שֶׁהָיָה קוֹדֶם שֶׁנִּתְצַמְצֵם . . . שֶׁגַּם בְּהַמְשָׁלִים
הֲרֵי הוּא רוֹאֶה כָּל פְּרָטֵי הַנִּמְשָׁל כְּמוֹ שֶׁהוּא אֶצְלוֹ כְּשֶׁהָיָה מוּפְשָׁט מִכָּל
לְבוּשׁ וְצִמְצוּם וְהֶעְלֵם.

Now, this entire constriction and concealment is only for the student, not for the teacher. For the teacher, the full depth of his idea and wisdom shines forth within the "constricted" idea, as it did before it was constricted. . . . Also within the parables [that he devises], the teacher sees all the details of the idea as they existed within his own mind, when it was still completely abstracted of all garments, constrictions, and concealments.

TEXT 15

RABBI SHALOM DOVBER OF LUBAVITCH, *SEFER HAMAAMARIM* 5657, P. 49

וּבֶאֱמֶת גַּם לְגַבֵּי הַמְקַבֵּל אֵין זֶה הֶעְלֵם אֲמִיתִּי . . . כִּי בִּלְעֲדֵי הַצִּמְצוּם
וְהַהֶסְתֵּר לֹא הָיָה מֵאִיר לוֹ אוֹר הַשֵּׂכֶל כְּלָל כַּנִּזְכָּר לְעֵיל. שֶׁאִם הַמַּשְׁפִּיעַ
הָיָה מְגַלֶּה לוֹ כָּל עוֹמֶק חָכְמָתוֹ כְּמוֹ שֶׁהוּא אֶצְלוֹ, הָיָה מִתְבַּלְבְּלִים חוּשָׁיו
לְגַמְרֵי כּוּלֵּי. וְעַל יְדֵי הַצִּמְצוּם וְהַהֶסְתֵּר מֵאִיר לוֹ אוֹר הַשֵּׂכֶל. אִם כֵּן אֵין
זֶה הֶסְתֵּר אֲמִיתִּי.

In truth, for the student, too, this isn't a true concealment. . . . Because without this constriction and concealment, the light of the idea would not have reached
him at all. For as we said, if the teacher were to reveal
to the student the full depth of his wisdom as he has
it, the student's faculties would be completely confused.
But by means of these "constrictions," the light of the
idea illuminates the student's mind. So it is not a true
concealment.

The concealment is the real [27].
" " is a limited revelation
" " is a full revelation

TEXT 16

RABBI SHALOM DOVBER OF LUBAVITCH, *SEFER HAMAAMARIM* 5657, PP. 49–50

וּבֶאֱמֶת גַּם עוֹמֶק פְּנִימִיּוּת הַשֵּׂכֶל שֶׁל הַמַּשְׁפִּיעַ מֵאִיר וּמִתְגַּלֶּה לְהַמְקַבֵּל . . . שֶׁהֲרֵי אָמְרוּ זִכְרוֹנָם לִבְרָכָה, "לֹא קָאֵים אִינָשׁ אַדַּעְתֵּי' דְרַבֵּי' עַד אַרְבְּעִים שְׁנִין"–אֲבָל לְאַחַר אַרְבָּעִים שְׁנִין קָאֵים כּוּלֵּי . . .

וְהָעִנְיָן דְּהִנֵּה נִתְבָּאֵר לְעֵיל דְּהַגַּם שֶׁמַּשְׁפִּיעַ לוֹ בְּדֶרֶךְ קְצָרָה, מִכָּל מָקוֹם יֵשׁ בָּזֶה בְּהֶעְלֵם כָּל עוֹמֶק חָכְמָתוֹ. רַק מַה שֶּׁמִּתְגַּלֶּה לְהַמְקַבֵּל הוּא בְּחִינַת הָאָרָה חִיצוֹנִית מֵחָכְמָתוֹ, וְעֶצֶם חָכְמָתוֹ נוֹתֵן לוֹ הַמַּשְׁפִּיעַ בְּהֶעְלֵם בְּהָעִנְיָנִים וְהַדִּקְדּוּקֵי תֵּיבוֹת כּוּלֵּי. וּלְזֹאת הַמְקַבֵּל, לְאַחַר שֶׁמְּקַבֵּל הַהַשְׁפָּעָה וּמִתְיַישֶּׁבֶת אֶצְלוֹ, הִנֵּה כְּשֶׁמְּדַקְדֵּק אַחַר כָּךְ בְּהָעִנְיָנִים וְדִקְדּוּקֵי הַתֵּיבוֹת וּמְיַיגֵּעַ אֶת עַצְמוֹ בָּזֶה עַל פִּי מַה שֶׁקִּיבֵּל בְּהִתְגַּלּוּת כּוּלֵּי, הֲרֵי הוּא בָּא לְעוֹמֶק פְּנִימִיּוּת כַּוָּנָתוֹ וְעֶצֶם חָכְמָתוֹ כְּמוֹ שֶׁהוּא אֵצֶל הָרַב מַמָּשׁ קוֹדֶם שֶׁצִּמְצֵם אֶת עַצְמוֹ לְהַשְׁפִּיעַ כּוּלֵּי.

Ultimately, also the inner depth of the teacher's idea is revealed to the student . . . For as the sages said, "A person does not attain his teacher's mind until forty years," implying that after forty years, he does attain it. . . .

The reason for this is that, as we explained, although the teacher transmits a condensed form of the idea to the student, it nevertheless contains, in hidden form, the full depth of his wisdom. It is only that what is revealed to the student is its external aspect, while the essence of the wisdom is hidden by the teacher within the details and the wording. Therefore, after the student receives the teaching and absorbs it, when he later examines the details and the wording and toils with this, guided by what he received in a revealed way, he will reach the depth of the inner intent and the essential wisdom as it was in the teacher's mind, before the teacher constricted it for the purpose of teaching it.

The concealment ultimately reveals everything

Figure 1.5d

Four Models of Reality—Take Four

	REALITY MODEL	IS THE WORLD REAL?
1	Worldly Reality	The world is real because its limits are absolute.
2	Creation Reality	The world is real because God created it.
3	Godly Reality	The world is not real.
4	Unified Reality	The world is real because it communicates the divine reality.

Figure 1.7

Hiding in Plain Sight[**]

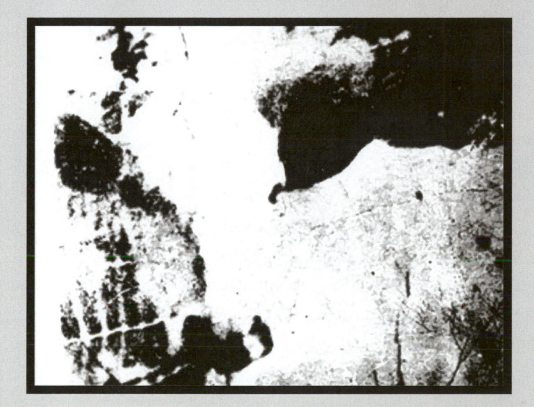

KEY POINTS

1 The question, "Is the world real?" has four different answers, because there are four different perspectives on reality: the *Worldly Reality*, the *Creation Reality*, the *Godly Reality*, and the *Unified Reality*.

2 From the perspective of the *Worldly Reality*, the world is real because its limitations are real and immutable. This leads to the conclusion that success in life depends on learning effective strategies within the dictates of nature and society.

3 From the perspective of the *Creation Reality*, the world, and the laws that govern it, are real not because they possess any inherent reality of their own, but only because God created them, and they exist solely to serve God's purpose in creation.

4 The divine act of creation is commonly described as "something from nothing," because the world is definitive and tangible ("something"), and God is infinite and intangible ("nothing") to our finite minds. But from the perspective of the *Godly Reality,* the opposite is true: the world is "nothing from something," as its finite and conditional existence is nothing in comparison to the infinite and absolute divine reality.

5 The *Unified Reality* reveals that the Creation Reality and the Godly Reality are two sides of the same truth, in the same way that a parable is only a finite and "digestible" incarnation of the abstract concept it communicates. The world, therefore, is real because it communicates the reality of God.

6 The moral and spiritual challenges that the world presents to us are plot twists in the "parable," woven into it to empower us to discover the truth of God in the workings of creation.

Additional Readings

MAAMAR VEYADAATA

BY RABBI SHALOM DOVBER SCHNEERSOHN

"And you shall know today and take it unto your heart, that *Havayah*[1] is the *E-lohim*[2] in the heavens above and the earth below; there is nothing else."[3]

The verses which precede this statement concern the exodus from Egypt and the entry [of the Jewish people] into *Eretz Yisrael*.[4] [Since sequence is significant in the Torah,] there is a need for explanation: What is the connection between the exodus from Egypt and the entry [of the Jewish people] into *Eretz Yisrael* and the verse, "And you shall know . . ."?

[To resolve this question,] it is first necessary to explain the phrase, "that *Havayah* is the *E-lohim*." In this context, the *Zohar*[5] states, "*Havayah* and *E-lohim* are all one." On the surface, it is difficult to comprehend how [these two names] can be "all one." It is well known that *Havayah* is the source for revelation and is [associated with] the attribute of mercy (as explained in the *Midrash*[6] and the *Zohar*[7] in several places). I.e., it reflects revelation in a manner characterized by kindness and mercy without any limitation at all. For all limitation stems from the name *E-lohim*, as will be explained, while the name *Havayah* is [associated with] revelation that is utterly boundless in nature.

[By contrast,] the name *E-lohim* is [associated with] the quality of judgment and contraction, to limit and to conceal the revelation of light. Thus it is the source for the manifold division [which exists among the creations of the world]. As such, the plural form is used in regard to the name *E-lohim* as in the verse,[8]

RABBI SHALOM DOVBER SCHNEERSOHN (RASHAB), 1860–1920

Chasidic rebbe. Rabbi Shalom Dovber became the fifth leader of the Chabad movement upon the passing of his father, Rabbi Shmuel of Lubavitch. He established the Lubavitch network of *yeshivot* called Tomchei Temimim. He authored many volumes of chasidic discourses and is renowned for his lucid and thorough explanations of kabbalistic concepts.

E-lohim Kedoshim. [This emphasizes that] the manifold division [which exists within our world] stems from the [manner in which the infinite Divine light] is limited and concealed [through the influence of the name *E-lohim*].

[To elaborate slightly on the latter concept: The name *E-lohim* is the medium through which the infinite Divine life-force is meted out to the creations. Since this life-force is to be enclothed and internalized within the creations, it must undergo a process of self-contraction and limitation. Hence, judgment is necessary to determine precisely the degree of limitation necessary for the light to enclothe itself within a particular creation. And it is this process of limited revelation that allows for the possibility of diverse creations to come into existence.]

In *Kabbalistic* terminology,[9] [we find a parallel explanation]. [G-dly light and influence is conveyed and revealed by the *Sefiros*, which have two dimensions, the *oros* ("lights") and the *keilim* ("vessels").] The name *Havayah* is the source for the *oros*, while the name *E-lohim* is the source for the *keilim*.[10] The light is simple, above all possibility for division, and is unlimited in nature. For the light is representative of the source of light (since it is *davuk* in its source, i.e., it has no independent identity of its own as explained in other sources,[11] using the analogy of the sun and the light and radiance [it produces]). Accordingly, just as the source of light is simple, totally above all possibility for division or qualification, and is unlimited in nature, so too, the light and the revelation which emanate from it resemble its source and are simple, above division, and infinite [in nature].

In contrast, the name *E-lohim* is the source for the vessels which contract, limit, and conceal the light, causing it to be expressed in different qualities, [e.g., the attribute] of wisdom or that of kindness. This process of qualification comes as a result of the vessels.

It is true that the vessels of the ten *Sefiros* reveal the light which is enclothed within them. [To use an analogy from the human realm,] the brain reveals the light of the intellect which is enclothed within it. Similarly, the eye reveals the spiritual power of sight and the heart reveals the emotions. Similarly, [in the analogue] in the spiritual realms, the attribute of *Chochmah* ("wisdom") resembles the brain and the attribute of *Chesed* ("kindness") resembles the right hand.[12] I.e., it is these [vessels] which reveal the lights. Indeed, this is the entire purpose of the vessels to reveal the lights and to cause the lights to influence [our world] as is well known and as is clear from the analogy to the human body mentioned above.

In truth, however, both are true. [The vessels] reveal the light, and they also conceal and veil the light. The light which they reveal is the light which is on the level of the worlds;[13] i.e., the vessels of the world of *Atzilus* shine forth and reveal light in the world of *Atzilus*. And through the medium of the *parsa*[14] which divides between *Atzilus* and *Beriah*, they reveal the light within the world of *Beriah*; and from *Beriah*, [the light descends] to *Yetzirah*.

This is not, however, a revelation of the light as it exists in its own right. For, as explained above, the light is representative of the source of light and is truly simple and infinite in nature. Thus, in essence, the light is not on the level of the worlds; for [by definition,] a world must exist as a separate and limited individual entity. Even within the world of *Atzilus*, the *heichalus*[15] of *Atzilus* are separate and limited individual entities as stated in *Tanya, Iggeres HaKodesh, Ihu ViChaiyeihu Chad*.[16] Surely, this applies in the worlds of *Beriah, Yetzirah,* and *Asiyah*, which are limited in nature.

Since limitation and infinity are by definition different, [G-d's infinite] light is not at all on the level of these [finite] worlds. Thus we can appreciate that the light which the vessels reveal in the worlds is not the essence of the light, but rather an external ray of the light.[17] Indeed, the essence of the light remains hidden within them, concealed by them. And it is through concealing the essence of the light that they are able to reveal the external dimensions of the light and cause it to effect change in the world.

Thus both concepts are true; [the vessels] conceal the essence of the light and reveal its external dimensions. These two concepts are interrelated; it is because they conceal the essence of the light that they are able to reveal its external dimensions.

An analogy to the concept that the vessels do not reveal the essence of the light can be drawn from the letters of speech. [The relationship of] the letters of speech to the content and ideas they express [parallels the relationship between the lights and the vessels]. In this instance as well, [the letters of speech] reveal only the external dimensions of the ideas and not their inner [power]. For this reason, we find that when the judges of a *Sanhedrin* [a Jewish High Court would rule on a case involving capital punishment], they would stay up the entire night debating the case, lest they forget the motivating principle [for their argument overnight].[18] There were two court scribes who would record the opinions of those arguing on behalf of acquittal and those arguing on behalf on conviction. [It was, nevertheless, necessary for the judges to discuss the case the entire night to keep the ideas fresh in their minds, because] to quote *Rashi*[19] "a person cannot write down the convictions of another's heart." One's true and inner intent cannot be expressed through words; they are merely an external [representation of the idea].

Similarly, to refer to the analogue in the spiritual realms, the vessels reveal only the external dimensions of the light, while the inner, essential light is concealed within them. [To further illustrate this concept, it is possible to employ the analogy of] the powers of the soul as they are enclothed within the limbs of the body, e.g., the power of intellect [which enclothes itself] in the brain to conceive [ideas] or the power of sight [which enclothes itself] in the eye to see.

In truth, the power of intellect exists within the soul before it enclothes itself in the brain, and the power of sight exists before it enclothes itself in the eye. Indeed, these [powers] exist within the soul on a much higher plane than they exist after they are enclothed within the limbs. Nevertheless, at that level, the power of sight does not cause another entity to be seen, i.e., it does not function as [we know] it functions.

Similarly, the power of intellect does not function as it does after it becomes enclothed within the brain, but rather functions on a higher plane.

These concepts are interrelated. The power of intellect as it exists within the soul before it is enclothed within the body is an essential light which is [far above] the level on which it can conceive of concepts that are at all physical in nature or involve material things. Instead, it perceives spiritual matters, e.g., the concepts revealed in *Gan Eden* and the like. Similarly, [at that incorporate level,] the power of sight sees spiritual matters. It is only as these [powers] enclothe themselves in the limbs of the body that this essential light becomes hidden and its external dimensions become revealed [causing these powers] to function in relation to other entities.

This leads to a general principle of greater scope: A revelation of the essence brings about concealment for others. [For they are not on the same level as the essence, and hence, cannot perceive it.] Conversely, a concealment of the essence brings about revelation for others. [For when the essential light is hidden, the aspects which the others can perceive are revealed.]

From this, we can understand how, in the spiritual realms, the vessels of *Atzilus* conceal the essence of the light and reveal only its external dimensions. And indeed, it is because they conceal the inner, essential light, that they are able to reveal the external dimensions of the light and thus perform [various] functions as explained within the context of the analogy to the soul.

Therefore, [the vessels] are identified with the name *E-lohim*, which relates to the attribute of judgment and [the power of] contraction, for it limits and veils the light. Similarly, all the veiling and concealing processes in the world stem from the name *E-lohim*. These refer to the *parseos*, the curtains,[20] which separate each and every world. Similarly, within the worlds themselves, there may be *parseos*, [for example,] in [the world of] *Atzilus*, there is a *parsa* between the *mochin* (the intellectual attributes of that realm) and the *middos* (the emotional attributes). There is a *parsa* which separates *Atzilus* and *Beriah*, and within *Beriah* itself there are *parseos*. Similarly, there are *parseos* between the worlds of *Beriah* and *Yetzirah* and between

Yetzirah and *Asiyah*, and within each of these worlds, there are also *parseos*.

This [entire process of] limitation stems from the name *E-lohim*, while all [the potential for] revelation within the worlds stems from the name *Havayah*.

Thus the two names *Havayah* and *E-lohim* are opposite in nature; one is the source for revelation, and the other, the source for concealment. [And so, we return to the original question:] How can it be said that [these two names] "are all one"?

[This concept can be explained by developing the analogy of the expression of the soul's powers through the limbs of the body] as reflected in the verse,[21] "From my flesh, I will perceive G-dliness." ([Since] man was created in the image of the spiritual realms above as it is written,[22] "Let us make man in our image and in our form," from [an analysis of the operation of] the powers of the soul, we can perceive the makeup of the spiritual realms.)

Within [each of] the powers of the soul, there is also a potential for revelation and a potential for limitation and concealment. For example, the power of intelligence which conceives ideas is drawn down from the essential power of intellect[23] within the soul, which is an unbounded potential for all types of intellectual revelations; they all have their source in the essential power of intellect.

[Thus, we see that] the essential power of intellect contains the potential for revelation, [the capacity] to conceive and express any intellectual concept. It also possesses the power of limitation, to confine the scope of any concept. [This is of fundamental importance.] Every idea and concept must have a limit to its scope; it may be extended to a particular point, but no further. For if one [thinks abstractly and] extends the scope of an idea beyond its limits, one will begin to deviate and lose sight of the truth.

Similarly, [when one desires to come to a decision regarding a particular matter] and [there are conflicting opinions, i.e.,] there are several perspectives which lean towards a ruling that it is permitted and others which lean toward a ruling that it is forbidden, it is impossible to reach a final decision unless there is a clear definition and limit [to these ideas]. In the same manner, it is impossible to study a [Talmudic] passage with the intent of arriving at a *Halachic* decision unless one defines and limits one's ideas. When [these limits are established], one can see the advantage one idea has over another one, and thus one can perceive the truth and reach a decision.

Similarly, [in the communication of an idea from] a *mashpia* [teacher, lit. source of influence] to a *mekabel* [student, lit. recipient]: It is necessary for the *mashpia* to condense, veil, and limit the concept [he is teaching] so that it can be grasped by the *mekabel*. Were the *mashpia* to reveal the essence of his appreciation of an idea, it would be impossible [for the *mekabel*] to comprehend it. Instead, it is necessary for him to conceal the essence of his appreciation of the idea and reveal only what is on the level [of the *mekabel*]. Similarly, it is necessary [for the *mashpia*] to limit the scope of his appreciation of the idea so that it does not extend beyond the appropriate limits of the *mekabel's* ability to grasp it. For if it extends beyond those limits, it will not be on the level that can be grasped by the capacities of the *mekabel*.

Thus we see there is a power of limitation which defines concepts. This power of limitation also has its source in the essential power of intellect itself. Just as that power is the source for the revelation of intelligence, to conceive of all intellectual ideas, so too, is it the source for the power of limitation that defines the ideas. These are the potentials of *Chesed* ("kindness") and *Gevurah* ("might") in the essential power of intellect. The attributes of *Chesed* are the source for the potential to reveal ideas, and the attributes of *Gevurah* are the source for the potential to limit and define.

[We are forced to say that both of these potentials have their source in the essential power of intellect. For the only way we can put limits on an intellectual idea or bring a concept down to a lower level of understanding is through the use of our minds. Our other potentials, our wills and our feelings, can spur or inhibit our thinking processes; they cannot, however, effect a change within them. Such change can only be a result of an intellectual power, albeit a power of a different nature from the power of conceptualization.]

The analogue to this concept can be understood in regard to the two names *Havayah* and *E-lohim*. They represent the power of revelation and the power of limitation, and they are both drawn down from the essence of the *Or Ein Sof*, G-d's infinite light. The power of revelation, which is identified with the name *Havayah*, is drawn down from the essence of the *Or Ein Sof* ([for] the light is at one with the source of light and is [therefore] representative of the source of light as explained in other sources[24]). Similarly, the power of limitation and contraction which is identified with the name *E-lohim* is drawn down from the essence of the *Or Ein Sof*. This is its potential for limitation, for as the *Avodas HaKodesh*[25] writes:

The *Or Ein Sof* is the perfection of all things. Just as it contains an infinite potential, it also contains a finite potential. For were one to say that it contains an infinite potential, but does not contain a finite potential, one would detract from its perfection. Instead, just as it contains an infinite potential, it also contains a finite potential.

This [finite potential], the power of limitation within the essence of the *Or Ein Sof*, is identified with the name *E-lohim*. Since the name *E-lohim* is actually [an expression of] the *essence* of the *Or Ein Sof*, as is the name *Havayah*, it, therefore, can be understood that the name *E-lohim* does not conceal the name *Havayah*.

An *essence* cannot conceal itself, as a person cannot conceal himself with [another portion of] his own [body]. This is reflected in [the decision of] the *Shulchan Aruch (Orach Chayim* 91:4) in regard to the laws of covering one's head: It is not sufficient to cover one's head with one's hand (although it is acceptable if a colleague covers one's head with his hand), because an essence cannot cover itself. Similarly, in the spiritual realms, the name *E-lohim,* which is [an expression of] the essence of the *Or Ein Sof,* does not veil or conceal the name *Havayah*.

This is the meaning of "*Havayah* and *E-lohim* are all one," that they are both [expressions of] the essence of the *Or Ein Sof*. Thus, they are not opposites at all. Although the name *E-lohim* is [identified with] the power of limitation, it does not limit or conceal the name *Havayah* at all.

The above is, on the surface, difficult to understand, and requires explanation. The entire purpose for the name *E-lohim* is to limit and to conceal. How is it possible for both to be true, that it conceals and yet, it does not conceal?

[To clarify the question: As mentioned in the beginning of the *maamar*, an inner, essential light is at times, concealed so that its external dimensions can be revealed. In that pattern, however, the concealment is genuine; that inner light is indeed held back from the recipient. In contrast, in the process of limitation and concealment associated with the name *E-lohim*, there is outwardly a degree of limitation, for indeed we see a downward progression of spiritual realms in which each receives a lesser revelation of G-dly light. Nevertheless, the *maamar* is saying that this concealment is only an external phenomenon. In truth, there is a complete and total transmission of G-dliness from one level to another with no limitation. It is the nature of this process that requires explanation.]

This concept can also be understood by [expanding our explanation] of the analogy to [the functioning of] human [intellect] as reflected in the relationship between a *mashpia* and a *mekabel*. When the *mekabel's* level is far removed from that of the *mashpia*, e.g., when a great sage is required to communicate a concept to a recipient whose intellectual potential is far less than his, he is required to limit and conceal the essence of his comprehension and conception of the idea.[26] Were he to reveal to him the depth and breadth of his conception of the idea as it exists within his own mind, the *mekabel's* powers [of comprehension] would become confused, and he would not be able to grasp the concept at all. Rather, it is necessary for him to limit and conceal the entire depth and breadth of his own conception of the concept and reveal to [the *mekabel*] only an external glimmer of the idea in a concentrated form which is appropriate to the *mekabel's* level of comprehension.

Furthermore, even this point must be enclothed and hidden in an analogy. [The term "hidden in an analogy" is used, because] an analogy is an utterly different matter from the analogue and indeed, it covers up and conceals the concept itself. To [explain this very concept by] use of an analogy, an analogy is like a garment which is used to cover an object. [Although] the garment [in which a person or object is clothed serves as a means of presentation,] it is, [nevertheless,]

a separate entity. Similarly, an analogy is a separate and different matter from the analogue, and indeed, it covers up the analogue.[27] It does, however, serve as a medium to allow [the student] to grasp and comprehend the analogue. (For [the analogy] parallels the analogue as a garment fits the person who wears it. Since the analogy is closer [to the *mekabel's*] level of understanding, it allows him to comprehend the analogue.)

This [process] is implied in our Sages' teaching,[28] "A person should always teach his students in a concise form." I.e., [a teacher] should not reveal to [a student, i.e.,] a *mekabel*, the depth and breadth of his own conception of the idea which is not on the level of the *mekabel*. Instead, he should find a concise form which does not reveal the entire inner appreciation of the idea, i.e., the depth and breadth of his own conception, but merely that which is on the level of the *mekabel*. And it is this [perception of the idea] which he can reveal [to the *mekabel*] on his own level. Nevertheless, the intent in teaching a student in such a concise form is not that the inner dimensions and the essence of [the teacher's] conception be withheld. Were that to be the case, the concept he would be communicating would not be a "concise form" [of his original idea], but rather a different idea entirely.

The intent is that he should teach the *mekabel* the essence of his conception of the idea, but that he should do so in a concise form, i.e., the concept which he communicates should contain in a hidden manner, all the depth and wisdom of his conception of this [original] idea. [Nevertheless, this depth] should be entirely hidden in the subject matter, in the precise choice of the wording and the like. In these matters, he conveys in a hidden way his inner wisdom concerning the matter.

An example of this process is the *Mishnah* composed by [Rabbi Yehudah HaNasi,] our holy teacher. This is a concise form of the extensive didactic reasoning of the Sages of that era. Rabbi Yehudah HaNasi capsulized the full length and breadth of their perception of the subject in an extremely concise, [but yet precise] form in the *Mishnah* so that it would be on a level [which an ordinary person could comprehend]. Nevertheless, within the *Mishnah* is contained all the depth, length, and breadth of their inner, essential wisdom as reflected in the *Gemara's* exposition in depth, length, and breadth of the [implications of] the particular wording [used by] the *Mishnah*. This is all contained in the *Mishnah*, but in a hidden manner.

A similar process is reflected in a *mashpia's* communication of concepts [to a *mekabel*]. He conceals the entire depth of his wisdom within the concepts he transmits. [Nevertheless, at the outset,] it is hidden from the *mekabel,* and it is only the external dimensions of the concept that are on the *mekabel's* level of conception that are openly revealed.

As explained above, the potential for the *mashpia* to contract and conceal his essential conception of the matter comes from the power of limitation that exists within the essential power of the intellect. [This leads to a further concept, that] the limitation and concealment is perceived only by the *mekabel*, but not by the *mashpia*. For the *mashpia*, the entire depth of his wisdom and comprehension shine openly within the concept as exists in its concise form as it did before this process of concentration.

Similarly, within the analogies he gives, he appreciates all the depth contained within the concept, i.e., within the analogies, he sees all the particulars as they exist within his abstract conception of the analogue, as it is above being enclothed, limited, and concealed [in the analogy].

For example, our material earth is an analogy for the *Sefirah* of *Malchus* (Kingship). Its particulars that it is thick, round, heavy, and that it has the potential to cause vegetation to grow all serve as analogies for the manner in which *Malchus* of *Atzilus* brings into being the creations of the worlds of *Beriah, Yetzirah,* and *Asiyah, ex nihilo,* as explained in other sources.[29]

[When a sage of this nature uses this analogy,] he sees how all the particular qualities of the physical earth are analogous to *Malchus* of *Atzilus*. (Through this process, he also sees how this physical earth is not at all a separate entity, divorced from its root and source. Instead, [he grasps] how it is the higher level which, through [G-d's] infinite power, has become manifest in a material form.)

In truth, an analogy and its analogue are the same exact entity, except that one is spiritual and the other is material. Therefore, it is possible for [such a person] to see all the particulars of the analogue in the analogy. And this [brings him to] the direct appreciation of G-dliness. (This is the new dimension [of perception] that the power of limitation contributes to the *mashpia*. Through enclothing his conception in garments where it is [on an apparent level] concealed, he comes to an actual [almost palpable] appreciation of a G-dly concept.)

Thus, for the *mashpia*, this process does not involve any concealment at all; the concealment is felt only by the *mekabel*. For only the external dimensions of the concept have been revealed to him; its inner, essential dimensions remain hidden.

[Furthermore,] in truth, this [process] cannot truly be considered as concealment, even for the *mekabel*. For through [this process,] the light of intellect is revealed for him. And were there not to have been [a process of] limitation and concealment, the light of intellect would not have been revealed for him at all. As explained above, were the *mashpia* to reveal to him the depth of his own conception of the idea in its entirety, [the *mekabel's* thinking] processes would have become confused. In contrast, through this process of contraction and concealment, the light of intellect is revealed for him. Thus, [these limitations] cannot truly be considered as concealment [of the idea].

Furthermore, even the inner depth of the *mashpia's* conception of the idea shines forth and is revealed to the *mekabel* through the influence conveyed to him. As our Sages said:[30] "A person does not appreciate [the full dimension of] his teacher's knowledge until forty years have passed." [This also implies, however,] that after forty years, it is possible for him to grasp his teacher's knowledge, and indeed, perceive his inner, essential intent.

[To explain, when a person teaches, there is a concept which is communicated on an obvious level, and also, there is a deeper and more innerfelt intent.] Thus, our Sages said about Rabbi Meir,[31] "The Sages could not appreciate his ultimate intent." *Rashi*[32] interprets this as referring to "the essence of his intent," [i.e., they understood the outward meaning of his message, but they could not comprehend the core of the concept he desired to communicate. Similarly, in every teacher-student relationship, when communicating to his students, a teacher conveys] an inner, essential intent, and this is what a student can grasp after forty years.

As mentioned above, although a *mashpia* communicates a concept in a concise form, in a hidden way, [that concept] also contains the full depth of his wisdom. [At the outset,] only an external reflection of his wisdom is revealed to the student, while the essence of his wisdom is concealed in his precise choice of wording and other similar methods.

[For this reason, the student's appreciation of the subject matter also comes in stages.] After he receives the content [of the *mashpia's* lesson] and allows it to settle within his [mind], he then carefully analyzes the precise choice of wording and the other techniques [used by the *mashpia*] and devotes himself tirelessly to this [analysis, guided by the germ of] the concept which was revealed openly to him. In this way, he approaches the depth of the *[mashpia's]* inner intent and the essence of his wisdom, [conceiving of the idea] as it existed within his teacher's [mind] before he condensed it to convey it [to the student].

Similarly, he sees the teacher's inner wisdom enclothed in the analogies, [perceiving how each particular reflects the analogue] as the teacher does himself. [To elaborate,] first, he understands the analogue through the analogy, i.e., from an in-depth appreciation of the particulars of the analogy, he develops an in-depth appreciation of the particulars of the analogue, comprehending the inner intent with all its depth and meaning. And then all the particulars of the analogue become illuminated by the analogy, thus granting him a direct perception and feeling for the G-dly concept [conveyed].

Thus through this process, an equivalence between the *mekabel* and the *mashpia*, is established even in regard to the comprehension and grasp of the inner intent. For the *mashpia*, however, this comes according to the pattern of *or yashar* ("a direct light"), i.e., first he knows the depth of the analogue, and then he draws it down and enclothes it in an analogy, and through this process he comes to an actual perception of the G-dly concept.

In contrast, the *mekabel's* [understanding works] according to the pattern of *or chozar* ("a rebounding light"), i.e., he approaches the inner intent through the medium of the analogy and the external dimension of the intellect which is conveyed to him.

From the [analysis of the above process], we can appreciate how the *mashpia's* power to limit his conception to a concise form, conceal it, and convey it through analogy, is not true concealment. For it does not conceal at all; through the concept conveyed to him, the *mekabel* receives the totality of the *mashpia's* inner conception of the matter.

Thus, the "concealment" is not really concealment, but rather a medium through which the *mekabel* can receive the subject matter. Were the *mashpia* to reveal his conception of the idea without [it undergoing this process of] concealment, the *mekabel's* process of conception would become confused, and he would not be able to receive even the external dimension of the idea, and surely not [the *mashpia's*] inner intent. And conversely, it is through the process of veiling and concealment that, at the outset, the external dimensions of the concept are revealed for [the *mekabel*], and ultimately, [this process enables] him to come to the appreciation of his teacher's inner intent.

Thus the process of concealment brought about by the *mashpia* does not truly really conceal. On the contrary, its entire objective is to reveal. In this manner, it communicates the light of the *mashpia's* understanding, including the inner dimension and essence of his wisdom, to a lower level. Thus this process of "concealment" allows for the *mashpia's* light to shine forth and be revealed on a plane [where by nature such ideas could not be revealed].

[The possibility is generated for] a *mekabel* of small potential, who is not at all on the *mashpia's* level, to comprehend and grasp the *mashpia's* light, and indeed, the depths of the inner dimension and the essence of his wisdom. Thus this process is not one of concealment at all; quite the contrary, it is a means of conveying light to a lower level.

The comprehension of the analogue to the above concept in the spiritual realms [sheds light on the relationship between] the names *Havayah* and *E-lohim*. The name *E-lohim* represents the attribute of limitation and concealment, which limits and conceals the light of the name *Havayah* to allow for the worlds to come into being.

For as explained above, the name *Havayah* is the source of revelation, revealing light which is infinite. Because this light is *davuk* in its source [and has no identity of its own], it is representative of the source of light. Thus, since the source of light is infinite, the light is also infinite. And so, this light is not at all on a level [on which it can relate to] the worlds. For all the worlds are separate, limited entities, while the *Or Ein Sof*, G-d's infinite light, is infinite in nature. And limitation and infinity are surely not on the same level. Nevertheless, [this light is the source of our existence], for the only medium through which it is possible for the worlds to come into existence is [the power of] revelation within the *Or Ein Sof*. For, as is well known, every activity comes about through the expression of an active potential. [Although the power of limitation conveys energy to the lower levels, it does not generate this energy itself. It merely shapes and controls the nature of the revelation from the power of revelation. Herein, however, lies a difficulty, for as explained above,] the power of revelation of the *Or Ein Sof* is infinite, entirely above the level of the worlds.

[The possibility for this infinite light to shine within a finite frame of reference is generated by] the name *E-lohim* which limits, conceals, and veils the light of the name *Havayah*, causing only an external ray of that name to shine forth. This ray enclothes itself in the vessels of the ten *Sefiros* of *Atzilus*, thus [bringing about the existence of] different attributes wisdom, kindness, and the like.

[Thus the light becomes qualified in a manner that] compares [to the limitation that characterizes] the worlds, and a point of interrelation between them is established. [To refer to the analogy mentioned previously:] This resembles the concise form of the concept presented by the *mashpia* which is on the *mekabel's* level.

Afterwards, through the medium of the *parsa* which divides between the world of *Atzilus* and the worlds of *Beriah, Yetzirah*, and *Asiyah* (see the explanation of the concept of a *parsa* in *Torah Or, Parshas*

Vayeira, in the *maamar* beginning *Pasach Eliyahu*, which relates [that a *parsa*] resembles an analogy) is drawn down a light which is on the level of the limited worlds [with the intent of] bringing into being the worlds of *Beriah, Yetzirah*, and *Asiyah*. Nevertheless, this entire process of veiling and concealment brought about by the name *E-lohim* does not create any concealment for the essence of the *Or Ein Sof* itself. As explained above, [the process of limitation] does not conceal [the idea] from the *mashpia*. Indeed, the full depth of his conception and wisdom shines in the concise form of the concept and in the analogies [which are employed].

Similarly, in the spiritual realms, there is no limitation and concealment at all for the *Or Ein Sof*. [On the contrary,] the *Or Ein Sof* is found in the place of the vacuum after the *tzimtzum*[33] exactly as it was before the *tzimtzum*, as it is written:[34] "I fill the heavens and the earth," and it is written:[35] "Will a person hide in concealed places without My seeing him?" Despite the entire process of veiling and concealment, the light of the *Ein Sof* is found in all places; "there is no place where He is not."[36] As it is written:[37] "If I ascend to heaven, You are there; if I make my bed in the netherworld, You are present."

Even in the netherworld, "in a parched land, in the shadow of death,"[38] in the ultimate of concealment, the *Or Ein Sof* is found. The concealment affects only the creations, who do not perceive the revelation of the light of the *Ein Sof*. But for the *Or Ein Sof* itself, there is no concealment or veiling at all.

Furthermore, even for the creations, this [process] cannot be considered as genuine concealment. (The two concepts are interrelated: Were the concealment to be genuine for the *mashpia*, it would also be genuine for the *mekabel*. Conversely, since there is no genuine concealment for the *mashpia*, there is no true concealment for the *mekabel* either. The difference between them is only whether their appreciation comes in the manner of *or yashar* [a direct light] or *or chozar* [a rebounding light].) On the contrary, [this process] conveys and reveals the light to lower levels.

To explain: From the name *Havayah* itself, it is impossible for the worlds to come into being, for [*Havayah*] is unlimited [and cannot bring into being limited existence]. Through the medium of the name *E-lohim*, the light of the name *Havayah* is drawn down and revealed within the worlds to bring them into being and to give them life.

Thus, the creation stems from the name *Havayah*. Although it is written:[39] "in the beginning, *E-lohim* created," this means that creation came about through the medium of the name *E-lohim*. The essential power for creation, however, stems from the name *Havayah*. Indeed, the very letters of the name *Havayah* (י-ה-ו-ה) relate to the word *mehave* (מהוה), which means "bring into being."

[*Havayah* must be the motivating force behind the creation,] because every activity comes about through the expression of an active potential, [in this instance,] the name *Havayah*. For the name *Havayah* is associated with revelation.

On this basis, we can comprehend the phrase,[40] "G-d is King; G-d was King; G-d will be King," expressing His Kingship within the framework of time, using past, present, and future tenses. [This framework stems] from the name *E-lohim*. Nevertheless, it is *Havayah* who reigns in the past, present, and future. [Similarly,] all existence has its source in the name *Havayah* as expressed through the medium of the name *E-lohim*. In this manner, the name *Havayah* is drawn down and shines within each world, [and more specifically,] within each creation, bringing it into being and giving it life.

[The influence of the name *Havayah* is expressed] in the life-force, for every creation feels that it is alive. The life energy within every creation is the light from the name *Havayah* as expressed through the medium of the name *E-lohim*.

[To refer to the analogy employed above the communication of a concept by] a *mashpia* to a *mekabel*: [Through this process,] the light of the concept can be received and can become settled within [the mind of] the *mekabel*. It is true that there has been a process of limitation and concealment of the essential light of the *mashpia*, and [the concept] has been enclothed in analogies. Nevertheless, the [end result] is that the light of the *mashpia's* conception [has been communicated,] and it shines forth and becomes settled [within the *mekabel's* mind. Thus, even at the outset, the *mashpia's* efforts to conceal and limit his thoughts produce communication, albeit to a limited degree. For the *mekabel* has been given a concept which he could otherwise not have conceived of. Beyond this, as will be explained, the potential is granted to grasp the *mashpia's* inner intent.]

Similarly, [in the spiritual analogue,] the light and the life-energy which shines within the inner dimension of every creation to give it life, is the light of the name *Havayah* which is drawn down through the medium of the name *E-lohim*. [This light] shines and enclothes itself within every creation. [I.e., there is a direct and immediate result equivalent to the student's immediate perception of the concept from the transmission of this G-dly influence.]

(There is a dimension of concealment in this as well, for [although the creation feels alive,] he does not feel that his life-force is G-dliness. In truth, however, this is not true concealment, for [the life-force] is G-dliness and a person can perceive this, when he focuses his attention on doing so.)

Thus the concealment produced by the name *E-lohim* is not genuine concealment. On the contrary, it conveys and reveals the light on a lower level; i.e., to creations which are limited and not on the level of the light of the name *Havayah*. [In this manner,] the light of the name *Havayah* shines to them as well.

Behold, as explained above, in the analogy of [the relationship between] a *mashpia* and a *mekabel*, [not only does] the *mekabel* [receive a limited perception of the *mashpia's* wisdom in the analogue, he also] has the potential to come to an appreciation of his teacher's inner and essential wisdom, i.e., the [complete] grasp of his teacher's knowledge which he achieves after forty years.

Similarly, in the analogue, in truth, it is possible for every person to appreciate a revelation of the inner dimensions and essence of the *Or Ein Sof*, that the name *Havayah* will shine in a revealed manner within his soul. This is accomplished through *avodah*, Divine service, toiling with both body and soul to remove the concealments and veils until one comes to a revelation of the inner dimension and the essence of the *Or Ein Sof*, which is above the external level that serves as a source for the worlds to come into being.

[I.e., in the analogy, it is not merely the passage of forty years of time, but rather forty years of strenuous labor, dedicated to discovering the inner meaning of the teacher's wisdom which is hidden in the allegories he used. Similarly, regarding our *avodah*, we must dedicate ourselves to the task of trying to appreciate the nature of the mediums with which G-d fashioned our framework of existence. By perceiving of them as channels through which G-d conveys His light, we can merit the revelation of a light which transcends this entire limited framework.]

To explain [the nature of the *avodah* required to perceive the *Or Ein Sof* as manifest within our world], it is necessary first to explain the concept of challenges [that arise in our service of G-d]. It is written:[41] "For G-d, your L-rd, is challenging you;" i.e., a person is confronted with challenges which he must overcome. We must understand: What is the Divine intent [in having man face] such challenges?

In other sources,[42] it is explained that the descent of the soul into the body is a descent of great proportions. As explained in the *Chassidic* interpretation of the statement of the *Mishnah*,[43] "[Know] from where you came." Before [the soul] descended into the body, the soul existed in the spiritual realms, in the lower *Gan Eden* or in the upper *Gan Eden*. There it perceived G-dliness [openly] and [as a result of this perception] stood in love and fear and was overcome with [utter] *bittul* ["self-nullification"] to G-d.

[This concept is reflected in the *Chassidic* interpretation[44] of the phrase,[45] "As the G-d, whom I have stood before, lives…." [It is explained that the Prophet Eliyahu made this statement in reference to his soul's existence in the spiritual realms.] There the concept of standing [must be interpreted as an allegory] referring to a state of *bittul*,[46] (for [in the spiritual realms, all corporal activities including] standing and sitting [in a literal sense] do not exist).

[From these peaks, the soul] descended to "hidden clefts [behind] the steps,"[47] to this physical world, where it is drastically distant from G-d's light. [In the physical world, however] it does not perceive the light as it did in the spiritual realms, because the Divine light which shines in these lowly worlds is limited and concealed to an ultimate degree. Only an external reflection of a ray [is revealed], and even this is perceived in an unrefined manner; i.e., we conceive of [G-dliness within the scope of] our materially oriented thinking processes.

Thus [such perception] cannot be compared at all to the incorporeal perception of the Divine light which the soul enjoys in the spiritual realms. The difference is twofold: a) [In the spiritual realms], a higher quality of Divine light is revealed; and b) [this light] is perceived with fewer material trappings, i.e., the perception is refined and spiritual in nature.

Because of [this difference in perception], the love and fear of G-d which the soul experiences on the earthly plane cannot at all be compared to the love and fear it experiences in the spiritual realms. The descent [of the soul] is also characterized by *hester ponim*,[48] a process of veiling which hides Divine light and conceals its holiness. [And for this reason,] a person must labor greatly until he perceives Divine light. Thus the descent of the soul is very great.

The ultimate purpose of this descent comes to the fore through the challenges which confront a person, when he faces *hester ponim*, e.g., a removal of vitalizing influence, where one's health or income is held back. This conceals the light of G-d, creating obstacles from within and from without for a person who desires to come close to G-d through his *avodah* of prayer and Torah study. [The intent is that] the person withstand these challenges, and stand firm in the face of all obstacles and hindrances. This was the purpose of the soul's descent and through this process, it reaches a revelation of a higher light.

On the surface, an explanation is required as to why it is through such a process that the soul comes to a revelation of a higher light. [Why must the ascent be preceded by such a descent?]

The concept can be explained in the following manner: Challenges come from the concealment of the truth. Were a person to know the truth, the situation would not constitute a challenge at all.[49] When does a situation constitute a challenge? When the truth is hidden and despite this concealment, a person withstands the challenge [and proceeds with determination]. And in this manner, the person appreciates the [underlying] truth of the matter.

[To cite a classic example,] when Avraham confronted the challenge [presented to him by Nimrod] in Ur Kasdim and was thrown into a burning fire,[50] he did not know that he would not be consumed by the fire. [On the contrary,] had he known that he would not be consumed by the fire, [his unwillingness to worship the idols] would not have been a challenge. Avraham, however, was not aware [that a miracle] would take place. Quite the contrary, he was sure that he would be consumed, for this is fire's natural property.

[The properties and laws of nature are a product of the Divine process of self-limitation described in the first portion of this *maamar*.] Indeed, the Hebrew term meaning "the nature," הטבע, is numerically equivalent to the name *E-lohim* (א-להים).[51] Implied is that the natural tendencies existing in the world are garments and veils stemming from the name *E-lohim*. For it is the name *E-lohim* which imparts the many different tendencies [that exist in the world, establishing specific] definitions [for each entity], causing fire to burn and water to extinguish [fire], making the nature of one warm, and the other, cold.

In contrast, from the perspective of *Havayah*, which is unlimited, there is no [conflicting] definition or difference between fire and water at all. It is possible that water will not quench a fire and that a fire will not burn. As the Talmud relates,[52] "He who ordered that oil will burn, [can] order that vinegar burn." And fire and water need not quench each other as our Sages relate,[53] commenting on the verse,[54] "Dominion and fear are with Him. He establishes peace on high." ["On high," i.e., in the spiritual realms, there are angels with different tendencies:] Michoel is the angel of water; Gavriel is the angel of fire. [G-d "establishes peace" between them, causing them] not to extinguish each other. [Moreover, we find that] at times, fire will consume water as [in the confrontation between] Eliyahu [the Prophet, and the prophets of Baal].[55]

All of these occurrences, which reflect how nature can be transcended, have their source in the *Or Ein Sof*, which is unlimited and which is not confined by the limits of nature at all. In contrast, the pattern of existence of the world at large depends on the definite limits established by the name *E-lohim*. The name

Havayah is the source for the world's coming into being. For an entity can only come into being through the revelation of an active force as explained at length above within the context of the verse, "*Havayah* is king." Nevertheless, the manner [in which the world comes into being] involves the shining of the light of the name *Havayah* through the medium of the name *E-lohim*, thus [causing this infinite light to be] concealed and hidden and [to descend] within the context of limitation. [Among these limitations] are [the different properties endowed to fire and water,] that water extinguishes [fire] and that fire burns.

Avraham did not think that the order that transcends nature would be revealed on his behalf. On the contrary, he thought that the natural order would continue to prevail and that the fire would consume…. Nevertheless, he withstood the challenge not to separate himself from G-d despite the obstacles and hindrances presented by Nimrod and his supporters who desired to have him burnt to death.

[For Avraham,] these were the veilings and concealments of the natural order. They did not budge him in the slightest [from his resolve. On the contrary,] he stood fast in the face of all these obstacles, though it meant being consumed in the fiery furnace rather than separate himself from G-d in the slightest.

And a miracle was wrought for him and he was delivered. [What is the nature of this sequence?] He removed all the veilings of nature, the enclothing and the concealment which stem from the name *E-lohim*, and therefore, the *Or Ein Sof* which is absolutely unlimited shone forth for him. And from the perspective of this infinite light, fire does not necessarily consume. For it is only within the confines of the garments of nature that fire consumes; from the perspective of G-d's infinite light, this need not be so. For [on this sublime level,] there are no limits nor any definition at all.

It was through withstanding a challenge that Avraham came to the revelation of this unlimited light. Otherwise, the conduct [of the world at large] would have been controlled by the revelation of the name *Havayah* as it passes through the medium of the name *E-lohim*, i.e., a mere external ray from the name *Havayah*.

To merit the revelation of the true and infinite dimension of the name *Havayah* which transcends the name *E-lohim*, it is necessary to confront challenges [as Avraham did]. And by standing firm in the face of the challenges and confronting the constraints that arise because of the veiling and concealment that stem from the name *E-lohim*, it is possible to come to a revelation of the infinite qualities of *Or Ein Sof* which transcend the limits of nature.

It has already been explained that were the infinite dimensions of the name *Havayah* to be revealed as they truly are, without the medium of the name *E-lohim*, this revelation could not be received within the world, i.e., there would be no possibility for the existence of entities which are limited and self-conscious, [*yesh* in Chassidic terminology]. This can be made possible only by the name *Havayah* enclothing itself in the name *E-lohim*, so that [outwardly], only an external ray of the name *Havayah* is revealed, as explained above.

This process, however, makes it possible to come to a revelation of the inner, essential, and infinite dimension of the name *Havayah*. As explained above, through confronting challenges, as illustrated in the example of Avraham our Patriarch, [a higher dimension of G-dliness is revealed]. A similar process, albeit in microcosm, occurs whenever a person confronts a challenge presented by the natural order of the world, [as reflected in] the obstacles and concealment that hinder and hold back [a person from advancing] in Torah study and in *avodah*.

When one stands fast in the face of every obstacle and hindrance, refusing to become separated from G-d, and involving oneself in Torah study and the service of G-d [despite these challenges], each person according to his individual capacity, one reaches a revelation of a higher light which transcends the natural order.

[The challenges referred to are not only those of a life or death nature, but those which a person confronts within his day-to-day existence. This process of confrontation] is the purpose of the descent of the soul to a physical body on this earthly plane, where it is limited within the confines of the natural order. On the surface, the demands of the natural order would make it appear that one should follow a specific course of behavior. For example, in the business world, [it may appear necessary] to leave home early, return late, and devote one's entire day to one's business. [According to this perspective,] taking off time for oneself to pray or to study will surely bring a loss.

Similarly, it might appear that it is necessary to employ certain crafty techniques in one's business, and that it is impossible to follow the path of truth, for in the latter manner seemingly, one will incur losses rather than profit. [This entire conception, however, is false.] It is only a product of the process of enclothement and veiling [described above], which in essence do not conceal [the fundamental truth].

[What is] the ultimate intent? That a person should stand firm despite all the obstacles and hindrances, praying in a proper manner, devoting himself to Torah study each day according to the fixed schedule which he has outlined for himself. [Following the Torah's guideline[56]] "Keep distance from falsehood," he should steer clear of all craftiness, and instead, proceed with a forthright and honest approach, making sure there is not even the slightest trace of a prohibition in any of his business dealings.

When a person confronts a challenge in these matters, he comes to a revelation of a higher light that transcends nature. In simple terms, he sees that even when he conducts himself according to the Torah and its *mitzvos* and involves himself in Torah study and the service of G-d, he will not lose anything at all despite the fact that [his approach] runs contrary to the norms outwardly prevalent in the world. In direct proportion to the extent of his service and effort, he ascends level by level [in connection with G-d].

This is the intent of the challenges of which it is said, "And G-d your L-rd is challenging you" that one should come to the revelation of the *Or Ein Sof* which transcends nature. This level was revealed in the challenge which confronted Avraham. And similarly, it is revealed in all the challenges confronted by every individual Jew.

From the above, we can appreciate [the nature] of the entire lifework of man, [to reveal] the unity of the names *Havayah* and *E-lohim*, to truly know that in reality the name *E-lohim* does not conceal the name

Havayah. For the name *E-lohim* is an expression of the essence of the *Or Ein Sof* as is the name *Havayah,* and one expression of the essence cannot conceal another expression of the same essence.

Havayah is [the dynamic source] which brings into being all the creations. [Although the light of *Havayah* shines through the medium of the name *E-lohim,*] all the garments and veils of the name *E-lohim* do not truly conceal. On the contrary, they convey the light to a lower level, [allowing] the light of *Havayah* to be drawn down to creations which are limited in nature, to bring them into being and to grant them life. At whatever level [a created being is], the light of *Havayah* is drawn down to it [through the medium of the name *E-lohim*].

As will be explained, [the awareness of this concept should prompt a person] to cling to the Divine light and life-energy which is drawn down to him, and not to the mediums and veils [through which it is conveyed,] as they exist within their own right. When a person achieves this, (he clings [to G-d] and unites with Him). Through [confronting] a challenge, he comes to the revelation of a higher level of light, the revelation of the *Or Ein Sof* which transcends nature.

On the basis of the above, we can understand the connection between the verse "And you shall know… that *Havayah* is *E-lohim,*" and the preceding verses which mention the exodus from Egypt and the entry into *Eretz Yisrael.* For it is through the exodus from Egypt and the entry into *Eretz Yisrael,* that one can come to the awareness that "*Havayah* and *E-lohim* are all one."

To explain: The *Pri Eitz Chayim,*[57] states that the Jews who endured servitude in Egypt were a reincarnation of the generation which constructed the Tower of Babel. Through their hard labor with mortar and bricks, they expiated the sin of "And the brick took the place of stone for them, and clay, the place of mortar."[58]

To understand this, it is necessary to understand the nature of the sin of the generation of the Tower of Babel, described as *dor haflagah,* "the generation of the division," in Torah literature. This name implies that their sin was one of division and separation. [The intent is not that they were divided in the realm of personal relations,[59]] but rather that they conceived of the existence of separation and division between the name *Havayah* and the name *E-lohim.* I.e., [they conceived] that the name *E-lohim* actually conceals the name *Havayah,* Heaven forbid, and therefore, everything which occurs in the world is governed by the name *E-lohim* alone (as will be explained within the context of the interpretation of the verse,[60] "*Havayah* has forsaken the earth.")

This [mistaken] conception leads one to consider the veils and concealments [of G-dliness that exist within the world] to be entities of fundamental importance. [Similarly,] it causes one to give oneself over to the norms outwardly prevalent in the world which hold back and prevent [a connection with] G-dliness.

This is the direct opposite of the unity between the names *Havayah* and *E-lohim,* [which leads to the awareness] that there is no [genuine] concealment at all. [On the contrary,] all the [apparent] concealments are for the sake of revelation, to convey the light to an even lower and far-removed level, as explained above using the analogy of how a teacher conveys [an idea] to a student. [As mentioned, the teacher] communicates the concept in a concise form and also enclothes it in analogies which are foreign to the concept itself. Nevertheless, the purpose of this entire process is to reveal the light of the teacher's intellect to the student (and ultimately to allow the student to penetrate to the depth of the teacher's wisdom as explained).

A similar motif applies, in the spiritual sense, in regard with to the two names *Havayah* and *E-lohim.* Thus [although] the Divine light [is enclothed and veiled in the material entities of this world,] it is [the fact that this light] is conveyed through these garments and veils that is of primary importance and to [this light], a person should cling and unite through his observance of the Torah and its *mitzvos.*

[A person must realize that] there is nothing separating or holding him back from G-dliness. (If there are obstacles which confront him and [appear to] prevent his [observance of] the Torah and its *mitzvos,* he should face the challenge and not allow them to block him or hold him back at all. And through such [efforts], he will come to a revelation of a higher quality of light as explained above.)

Division to separate [between *Havayah* and *E-lohim*] reflects a directly opposite approach. Thus commenting on the verse[61] mentioned in connection with the *dor haflagah*, "Let us make ourselves a name," *Bereishis Rabbah* 38:8 relates, "Rabbi Yishmael taught: The sole meaning of the word *shem* ('a name') is the worship of false divinities." I.e., the sin of the *dor haflagah* was the worship of false divinities.

The concept can be explained as follows: As explained above, it is impossible for an entity that sees itself as independent from G-d, a *yesh*, to come into existence from the name *Havayah* as it exists in its own right. For were the light of the name *Havayah* to shine forth [without any concealment], the worlds would not be able to receive this light, i.e., there could be no conception of limited and independent existence. To refer to the analogy of communicating an idea mentioned above were the teacher to reveal his essential conception of the idea as it is for himself, the *mekabel* could not accept it. [Indeed,] his thinking processes would become totally confused (this represents the nullification of his vessels, as is well known).

Similarly, in the analogue in the spiritual realms, were the light of the essence of the name *Havayah* to be revealed, the worlds could not exist as a *yesh*. Thus, the *Eitz Chayim* states:[62] "At the outset, when there was a simple, sublime light encompassing all existence, there was no place to establish the worlds." The expression "there was no place" [does not refer to physical place], but rather to the concept that the revelation of the "simple, sublime light" as it existed for itself prevented the existence of [limited] worlds.}

This is possible only through the medium of the name *E-lohim*, as reflected in the verse:[63] "In the beginning, *E-lohim* created." [*E-lohim*] represents the attribute of self-limitation and concealment which limits the light of the name *Havayah*, enclothing it in several garments until an existence which is *yesh* can come into being.

In this context, we can understand our Sages' statement:[64] "There is no blade of grass on this earthly plane which does not have a *mazal* striking it and commanding it to grow." Each and every blade of grass (and similarly, each and every individual created being) has a particular *mazal*, i.e., a source of [spiritual] influence from which [it receives] its life-force.

These *mazalos* [receive their vitality from a higher] source, the angels of the spiritual realms, [who themselves receive from a higher source] as implied by the verse:[65] "for there is one who is higher, who watches those which are high." And the source for all the angels is the name *E-lohim*. For this reason, the angels themselves are called *elohim*[66] or *b'nei haelohim*.[67] These represent the mediums through which [Divine] light and life-energy are drawn down to all the material entities in this world.

This can be explained on the basis of a principle stated above: that material existence can come into being only through the limitation and concealment of the light [which is the source for its being]. This is accomplished by enclothing [the light] in garments and veils. Thus as the light passes through the mediums of the angels and the *mazalos*, [on an apparent level,] it becomes reduced until [there is the potential for] material existence to come into being. (The extent of the material nature of the entity determines the multitude of mediums [through which the light must pass] until [this material entity] can come into existence.) Nevertheless, the essential [potential for] creation comes from the name *Havayah*; it is *Havayah* which is the creative [force for all existence]. However, the light of *Havayah* passes through the medium of the name *E-lohim*, so that it can bring into being an entity which conceives of itself as a *yesh*, and so that the light of *Havayah* can shine within that created being according to its nature to bring it into existence and to grant it life.

Thus the essence is the light of the name *Havayah*, and that light has been drawn down through the medium of the name *E-lohim* [and through the angels, *mazalos*, and other mediums (which all have their source in the name *E-lohim*)], until it is possible for there to be the actual creation of a material entity from the [infinite] G-dly light.

When this is understood, it becomes apparent that the medium is nothing in its own right, for it is not the source of influence or vitality. It is merely a medium to convey the creative [force], the Divine light to the created entities. And therefore, no importance at all should be attached to the medium [in its own right].

Thus it is written,[68] "Shall an axe boast over the one who hews with it?" Although [trees are] hewn with an axe, the one responsible is the man who does the hewing, and not the axe. The axe, in and of itself, does nothing; rather, the action is performed by the person using the axe.

Thus, no one would ever say, "What a beautiful building the axe built!" or "How praiseworthy is the axe for constructing such a magnificent building!" It is the person who constructed the building; he is praised and the building is attributed to him. The axe [or any other tools he used] are not connected with the building at all. For they are merely instruments with which the building was constructed; they are not the builders. I.e., these tools had no choice [whether or not the building would be] constructed, nor was it in their power alone to build it. On the contrary, a man was the builder; [he made the decision to build it and he was the power manipulating the tools].

Similar concepts apply in regard to the intermediaries in the spiritual realms; they are nothing more than an axe in the hands of a chopper. The influence passes through them, but it is not produced by their power, nor do they have choice in passing on this influence or not. Rather the source of the influence is G-dliness; He gives forth this influence as a result of His will. And [then] this influence passes through the mediums mentioned above so that physical entities can be brought into being and so that influence, light, and life energy can be conveyed to them in a physical form on their level.

[The above relates to a concept] explained in other sources[69] within the context of the interpretation of the verse,[70] "And G-d will bless you in all that you do." [The verse] implies that man must "do," i.e., he must involve himself in activity in the material [world], e.g., commercial enterprise, since it is necessary to receive one's life-force from [G-d's] light and life-energy [as they have descended to the level of] materiality. Were the person to be able to derive his life-energy from spiritual light, e.g., intellectual pleasure or the like, he would not have to become involved in business or other material pursuits.

([We see, in contrast, that] the souls in *Gan Eden* receive their life-energy from their conception of G-dliness as reflected in the statement,[71] "sitting and benefiting from the radiance of His presence." Similarly, concerning [the era of] the Future [Redemption],[72] our Sages commented,[73] "There will be no eating and drinking in the World to Come.... Instead, the righteous will sit with their crowns on their heads and derive benefit from the radiance of His presence." Just as we derive life-energy from physical food and drink, in [the era of] the Future [Redemption], life-energy will be derived from the pleasure of being in the radiance of His presence.)

Since, [at present,] it is necessary for us to receive our life-force in a material form, the influence must pass through the medium of commercial activity in this material world, i.e., the influence must descend to the material level on which we operate. Nevertheless, the influence itself is Divine in origin.

This influence passes through several mediums, the angels, the *mazalos*, and even one's commercial activity with material entities. And it enclothes itself in bread and other physical [foods] from which a person derives his vitality. These mediums [are, however, no more than pathways for] the Divine light which is enclothed and drawn down through them.

When a person comprehends and assimilates these ideas, as a matter of course, he will not be [overly] concerned with worldly affairs and will not be disturbed about them at all. Instead, G-d will be the entire focus of his attention [and this will be expressed in a commitment] to prayer and to Torah study. Involvement in the matters of this world will not upset him, nor prevent him from serving G-d.

[This approach will be possible] because he has a thorough knowledge that the essence is G-dliness and that G-d endows him with his vitality. [He realizes how] all the mediums and similarly, all the material entities in which this influence is enclothed, e.g., one's commercial activity, and similarly, the bread he eats, are all nothing in and of themselves. They are not the essential source of his vitality. The essence is the Divine light which endows one with life and all the material entities are merely mediums and vessels to enclothe the Divine light so that this vitality can be expressed within the material plane, on the level appropriate for [each entity].

Therefore i.e., since a person realizes that material affairs are not of fundamental concern it is inconceivable that they will disturb him and prevent him [from concentrating] on prayer and Torah study. For [he is aware] that the essence is G-dliness and that he should cling to G-d and His Torah.

[This approach will also affect the nature of] his business dealings. He will not employ craftiness, nor will he be overinvolved in his business to the extent that it prevents him from occupying himself with Torah study and prayer at the opportune times. On the contrary, he will seek involvement in an appropriate level of commercial activity which will not prevent or hamper him from praying at the proper time or studying Torah every day. And he will trust G-d who endows him with vitality to grant his livelihood[74] as it is written,[75] "For it is He who grants you the power to prosper."

Surely, [such a perspective] will cause a person to show careful concern for his soul and make sure that he conducts his business dealings without the slightest violation [of Torah law]. Since he knows that his commercial activity is merely a medium and a vessel in which the Divine light and life-energy which grants him life is enclothed, [he appreciates how] it must be a vessel which is worthy of the Divine light. And if there is the slightest trace of a violation of a prohibition, heaven forbid, [in one's dealings,] they are not a fit vessel for the light. It is only when there is no trace of sin or the violation of a prohibition in one's dealings that they can serve as a medium to draw down the G-dly light and life-energy which endows one with life.

[Such an approach is dependent on] the unification of the names Havayah and E-lohim, i.e., that one appreciates that the name E-lohim does not conceal the name Havayah at all and that Havayah is the source for all creation, and [that creative energy] is directed through the medium of the name E-lohim.

This leads to the awareness that all the mediums i.e., the angels and the mazalos are of no importance in their own right. They are merely agents to convey the influence and [can be compared to] an axe in the hands of a chopper. Similarly, [all] material entities are merely vessels in which Divine power is enclothed, and therefore, they should not be at all considered of fundamental importance. What is of fundamental importance is the Divine power which is conveyed through them. Therefore, the person should apply himself and make efforts [to insure that his business is conducted] as befits a vessel which receives G-dly light. Hence, he will not employ craftiness, nor will he become overinvolved in his affairs. [His business] will not trouble or disturb him, nor will it hold him back from Torah study, prayer, or service of G-d.

This is particularly true, since these entities cannot, in and of themselves, prevent one from serving G-d, for they do not represent [nor is there a possibility for] genuine concealment [of G-d's light] as explained above in detail. On the contrary, the function of all these mediums is to convey the G-dly influence [to a lower level]. How could they prevent one from serving G-d?

It is only a person with underdeveloped knowledge who is bound to superficial things who will forget G-dliness and consider the physical entities to be important and give himself over to them. And when this happens, they will hold him back and hinder [his spiritual activity]. But when he focuses his mind and heart on the oneness of G-d, [realizing] that it is He alone who "grants you the power to prosper," that all the mediums are merely pathways for [Divine] influence, and that G-d is of fundamental importance, then no factor whether internal or external will hold him back or hinder him.

He will cling to G-d alone. (His involvement in his business dealings will involve [only] the superficial dimensions of his will. [Indeed, he will seek such activity] only because, as explained above within the context of the verse, "And G-d your L-rd will bless you in all that you do," it is necessary that [the Divine influence] pass through [the medium of physical] activity. And therefore, he will conduct his business dealings in a desired manner as explained above. And primarily, he will cling to G-dliness). And in this manner, he will attain fulfillment [in his relationship with] G-d, His Torah, and His service.

In contrast, [there are those who,] heaven forbid, separate between *Havayah* and *E-lohim*, who think that the name *E-lohim* truly conceals the name *Havayah*, heaven forbid, and that all the events which occur within the world stem from the name *E-lohim* in its own right. It follows that they also consider the mediums of primary concern, viewing them as the source of their vitalizing influence.

[To describe this approach, one can borrow] the verse, "*Havayah* has forsaken the earth," i.e., they say [that G-d does not manifest direct influence over this earth]. Instead, the influence on this material plane comes from the *mazalos* who endow [this earth] with influence by their own power. And because [such a person sees these mediums as genuine] sources of influence, he considers them as important. (This, in turn, leads him to consider the material entities as likewise important and involve himself with them totally, using his full power and capacity in order to increase his wealth.) This is the source of the worship of the stars and the *mazalos*[76] [in previous generations]. People would bow down to them because they considered them important entities and sources of influence.[77]

On the basis of this explanation, [we can understand one of the points raised initially in this *maamar* the connection between the entry into *Eretz Yisrael* and the unity between the names *Havayah* and *E-lohim*. To explain,] our Sages stated:[78] "A Jew living in the diaspora serves false divinities with purity." On the surface, this statement requires explanation: Most of the Jewish people live in the diaspora. How can it be said that they serve false divinities, heaven forbid?

This concept can be resolved as follows: In a physical sense, worshipping a false divinity involves bending one's head and bowing to the stars, the constellations, the sun, the moon, and the like. Why? Because one considers them important and a source of influence, as might be construed from the verse:[79] "the sweetness of the sun's yield and the sweetness of the moon's crop."

([In truth, the intent of the verse is not that they are the source of this influence,] but that they are merely mediums, like an axe in the hand of the chopper. [The individuals mentioned above, however,] err and

consider [these mediums] as important entities, as if the influence they convey is generated by their own power, heaven forbid.)

In a more abstract sense, the worship of false divinities entails attaching importance to the material entities that receive influence from the sun, the moon, the stars and the constellations, and considering them as the source for one's livelihood. Just as in a physical sense, one bows one's head in the worship of false divinities, in an abstract sense, this means bending and [even] subjugating one's thinking process to the entities which receive influence from the stars and the constellations.

Such a person will concentrate his thoughts and his feelings on his material concerns and will be worried about earning a livelihood. For this reason, he will carry out his commercial affairs in a crafty manner, thinking that this will bring him profit, forgetting that it is G-d, blessed be He, who grants him "the power to prosper." If he loses money, heaven forbid, he will not take notice that it was G-d who caused this to happen in reciprocation for his [unworthy] conduct. Instead, he will assume that his loss resulted from his own business errors and were he to have taken another course of action, he would have profited.

With this approach, he considers his business efforts in the material world as fundamentally important and devotes his thoughts to them, constantly employing different crafty tactics. Day in and day out, his mind and his thought are concerned only with his business. And these thoughts disturb and distract him in the midst of prayer and prevent him from [involving himself] in Torah study and *avodah*.

[In an abstract sense,] this is the worship of false divinities. [Indeed,] it bears a very close resemblance to the worship of false divinities in an actual physical sense. And this is the intent of the statement that "A Jew living in the diaspora serves false divinities with purity." For the great preoccupation with business activity [that is prevalent in the diaspora] and the craftiness [people employ], forgetting G-d and thinking that "it is my power and my strength that made me prosper,"[80] is tantamount to the worship of false divinities. Nevertheless, this service of false divinities is described as being "with purity," i.e., there is room to justify these individuals' conduct, for they live in the diaspora. And in the diaspora, the Divine light is enclothed in the garment of *Asiyah*, which is a very coarse garment, as explained in other sources,[81] which conceals and hides the spirituality of [G-d's] light to the extent that it cannot be seen.

And yet, they are called "worshipers of false divinities," for they must know that in truth there is no concealment or hiddenness, as explained above. (The coarse garment of *Asiyah* causes the Divine light to be revealed on the material plane and thus conceals the spirituality of the light to the extent that it is not obvious and cannot be seen. Nevertheless, in truth even the most coarse garments do not actually conceal [the light]. On the contrary, they convey the [Divine] light and life-energy [to a lower level] as explained above. It is merely that [on this material plane], the [Divine] life-energy is expressed as material energy.) In truth, one should be able to feel G-dliness even in the midst of one's business activities.

The reason why, in contrast, one bends one's head to the [material] entities which receive their influence from the stars and the constellations is because one separates the name *E-lohim* from the name *Havayah*, thinking that [the name *E-lohim*] generates genuine concealment, heaven forbid. And therefore one thinks that the mediums, whose source are in the name *E-lohim* which serves as the immediate source to bring every entity into existence are of importance, and therefore he bows down to them. Similarly, he views as important all the [material] entities which receive this influence and grants them prominence, bending his head and his mind to them. This is the concept of "worshipping false divinities in purity," as explained above.

In contrast, when one unites [the names] *Havayah* and *E-lohim*, i.e., appreciating the truth that, as explained above, the name *E-lohim* does not conceal the name *Havayah* and on the contrary, brings the revelation of the name *Havayah* to the lowest levels, one will know with certainty that all the mediums are merely an axe in the hands of the chopper, i.e., they exist solely to convey Divine influence. Thus such a person will not attach importance to them in their own right. Similarly, he will not grant prominence to

material pursuits at all. Instead, he will appreciate that the essence is G-dliness, "for He is your life,"[82] and "He grants you strength to prosper."

Thus [even when such a person] is involved in business dealings with material entities, he will remain at one with G-d, and will thus be precise in his observance of [both] the positive commandments and the negative commandments; he will pray as one should, and study Torah according to the level appropriate for him. And thus, he will be complete [in his devotion] to G-d, his Torah study, and his *avodah*.

Based on the above, we can understand the previous statements cited concerning the *dor haflagah*, the verse "Let us make ourselves a name," and our Sages' comment that "The sole meaning of the word '*shem* (a name)' is the worship of false divinities." The people of this generation separated the name *E-lohim* from the name *Havayah,* and this led to their considering the mediums of primary importance. This is [the essence of] the worship of false divinities, as explained above.

Through the slavery in Egypt, [the Jews] corrected the sin of the *dor haflagah*. Their enslavement and hard labor with mortar and bricks corrected the sin of "And the brick took the place of stone for them,"[83] as explained in other sources at great length.[84]

[Based on the above, we can now appreciate the connection between the exodus from Egypt and the verse, "And you shall know . . ." mentioned at the beginning of the *maamar*.] For it was the slavery in Egypt, which enabled [the Jews] to see [the miracles of the] exodus through which it was revealed that "*Havayah* and *E-lohim* are all one." The wonders and miracles of the Ten Plagues and the Splitting of the Red Sea, which went beyond the limits of nature, revealed a transcendent level of G-dliness on this earthly plane.

[This demonstrated that there was no separation between the names *Havayah* and *E-lohim*.] For were the concealment of the name *Havayah* brought about by the name *E-lohim* to be genuine, how could it be possible for there to be a revelation of transcendent G-dliness on this earthly plane?

This allows us to understand a teaching of our Sages (*Sanhedrin* 39a*)*:

A non-believer told Ameimer [a Talmudic Sage]: "Your upper half belongs to Hormiz; your lower half, to Hormin," (see the gloss of *Tosafos*).

[Ameimar] answered him: "If so, why does Hormin allow Hormiz to pass water through his territory.

([This interchange can be explained as follows: [According to the non-believer's mistaken belief,] there are two [godlike] powers,[85] heaven forbid. This relates to the concept that "*Havayah* has abandoned the earth" [mentioned above,] leaving it under the dominion of the stars and the constellations. "His glory is over the heavens,"[86] [i.e., it is only in the higher spiritual realms where it can be manifest]. And on the earthly plane, the sources of influence are the constellations which conceal G-dliness.)

[Ameimar's rhetorical question thus means:] According to your mistaken conception that the mediums bring about genuine concealment: how is it possible for G-dliness to be revealed in the world? And G-dliness has been revealed as evident from the miracles of the exodus from Egypt. At that time, it was openly seen that the name *E-lohim* does not conceal the name *Havayah* at all, and "*Havayah* and *E-lohim* are all one."

Similarly, and indeed to a greater extent, the unity between *Havayah* and *E-lohim* was revealed with the entry [of the Jewish people] into *Eretz Yisrael*. For as explained above, a Jew living in the diaspora "serves false divinities with purity." And this applies only in the diaspora, since it is in the diaspora that the Divine influence and light is conveyed through the garments of *Asiyah* which [at least outwardly] conceal [this G-dliness] to a great extent. In *Eretz Yisrael*, by contrast, the [Divine] influence is conveyed by the garments of *Yetzirah* [which are more refined]. Hence, there the concealment of G-dliness is not as great, and there to a greater extent, it is revealed how "*Havayah* and *E-lohim* are all one."

It is known that just as there is an actual, physical *Eretz Yisrael*, there is a spiritual conception of the Holy Land, namely, the observance of the *mitzvos*. For the Hebrew for "land," *eretz* (ארץ) is related to the word for "will," *ratzon*, (רצון). As our Sages said,[87] "Why was it called *eretz*? Because it desired (*ratztoh*) to fulfill the will of its Creator." In our Divine service,

this refers to the fulfillment of the *mitzvos* motivated by *kabbalas ol*, acceptance of G-d's yoke, as explained in other sources.[88] And it is [living in this spiritual counterpart of *Eretz Yisrael*,] i.e., fulfilling the *mitzvos* with *kabbalas ol*, which will bring one to the awareness that "*Havayah* and *E-lohim* are all one."

[To draw focus to this concept, the Torah] mentions the narrative of the exodus from Egypt and the entry [of the Jewish people] into *Eretz Yisrael* before the verse, "And you shall know today…." For it is through the exodus from Egypt and the entry into *Eretz Yisrael* that one comes to an awareness that "*Havayah* is the *E-lohim*,"i.e., one can unite *Havayah* and *E-lohim* and thus perceive how "*Havayah* and *E-lohim* are all one."

Translation by Rabbi Eliyahu Touger.
Reprinted with permission of Kehot Publication Society.

Endnotes:

[1] The term *Havayah* is derived from a rearrangement of the letters of the name י-ה-ו-ה which, because of its holiness, is not pronounced in the usual manner.

[2] Both *Havayah* and *E-lohim* (א-להים) are names which refer to G-d. As explained in the *Kabbalah* and in the *Midrash* (*Shmos Rabbah* 3:6), the different names of G-d represent different manifestations of G-d's attributes. Indeed, a major portion of this *maamar* is devoted to explaining the difference between the qualities expressed by these two names.

[3] *Devarim* 4:39.

[4] See *Devarim* 4:34-38, "Has G-d ever wrought miracles, bringing one nation out of another nation with such tremendous signs, wonders, and miracles . . . as G-d did for you in Egypt. . . . He will drive away nations that are greater and stronger than you . . . to bring you into their lands, and give them to you as a heritage."

[5] Vol. II, 26b.

[6] E.g., *Bereishis Rabbah* 12:15.

[7] *Zohar*, vol. 1, 173b, 251b.

[8] *Yehoshua* 24:19. Not only is the word *E-lohim* itself a plural form (in contrast to the word *E-loha*, which also serves as a name for G-d); the modifier *kedoshim* also uses a plural form. See also *Rashi*, *Bereishis* 20:13.

[9] *Torah Or, Yisro* 69d. See *Tanya, Shaar HaYichud VeHaEmunah*, ch. 6 and other sources.

[10] Thus the term "light" refers to the effusion of G-dly energy, while "vessel" refers to the particular qualities which give expression to that energy. (This explanation follows the thesis explained within this *maamar* that the lights are *peshutim*, "simple," above the level of distinction and differentiation. In contrast, there is another thesis within *Kabbalah* and *Chassidus* that the lights are *metzu'arim*, qualified in nature. According to that thesis, the explanations of the terms "lights" and "vessels" are slightly different.)

[11] *Sefer HaErchim-Chabad*, Vol. II, p. 458 and sources cited there.

12 *Tikkunei Zohar, Pesach Eliyahu.*

13 The concept of spiritual worlds refers to the existence of different planes of being. On each level, the G-dly light is manifest in a certain manner. The downward progression of spiritual existence allows for that light to become manifest on a lower plane, i.e., in a less refined frame of reference. And since the latter frame of reference is different from the first, it is considered as a different world.

14 The Hebrew word *parsa* means "curtain." It refers to a process of Divine self-contraction and veiling, which changes the very nature of the light revealed. Although the revelation of Divine light is reduced as it descends level by level within the world of *Atzilus*, the light revealed in all the *Sefiros* of that realm is essentially the same. In contrast, the *parsa* alters the nature of the light and thus causes *Beriah* to be considered as a different world than *Atzilus*.

15 The word *heichalos* literally means "palaces." This refers to the external manifestation of a particular world. The term can thus be understood within the context of the comparison of "lights" and "vessels" to the soul and the limbs of the body. Developing this analogy further, the *heichalos* can be compared to a person's house, that which, though apart from him, reflects his character.

16 Epistle 20, p. 130a.

17 Since the essence of the light is on a higher level than the worlds, the revelation of such a light would bring about a nullification of the worlds. In this manner, *Chassidus* (see *Likkutei Sichos*, Vol. X, p. 52 footnote 28 and sources cited there) explains our Sages' statement (*Sanhedrin* 38b), that "the Holy One, blessed be He took out His small finger and burnt" the angels who had been lax in the fulfillment of His will, i.e., G-d revealed a level of light slightly higher than which is normally revealed to them, and this caused their existence to be nullified.

18 *Sanhedrin* 40a.

19 *Ibid.*, 35a.

20 See note 11.

21 *Iyov* 19:26. The translation of this phrase which we have chosen fits the context of its use in this and other *Chassidic* sources. Within the context of the statements of *Iyov* in the original source, another translation would be more appropriate.

22 *Bereishis* 1:26.

23 The *maamar* is defining two levels in our intellectual potential; the *koach hasechel* כח השכל, translated as the "power of intelligence" and the *koach hamaskil*, כח המשכיל, translated as the "essential power of intellect." The difference between the two is that "intelligence" refers to our conscious potential for thought, the ability we have to conceive of ideas. "The essential power of intellect" refers to the source for this capacity, a level within the soul which is above conscious thought, and yet is the source from which all thought ultimately emanates.

24 See *Iggeres HaKodesh*, Epistle 20, p. 130a ff.; *Sefer HaMaamarim* 5662, p. 175.

25 Vol. I, the beginning of ch. 8.

26 This is one of the instances in which, not only the analogue which the *maamar* is trying to communicate is abstract and requires explanation, even the analogy itself is not readily comprehensible. Here we are not speaking of a normal teacher-student relationship in which the teacher merely knows more than the student, and hence, must work to prepare the presentation of the concepts so that they can be grasped by the student. Without minimizing the challenge involved in such a task, such a difficulty is not insurmountable, for

the student is on the same level as the teacher and is capable of understanding the material if presented to him in the proper manner. The *maamar*, by contrast, is speaking about a teacher and a student who are on two different levels of thought. The difference between them is not merely quantitative—the teacher knows more about the subject than the student—it is qualitative. The very nature of their thinking processes differ; their minds work differently. And for this reason, the process of communication is intricate and involved, as explained within the *maamar*.

27 To illustrate this concept: When a teacher tries to communicate an idea to a student through an allegory, the allegory will often make a powerful impression on the student. Even when the student comprehends the concept itself, he will always associate it with the allegory. For example, to communicate the principle that the Divine life-force which vitalizes creation must be constantly invested within the creation, for otherwise, the creation would return to its initial state, absolute nothingness, Chassidic thought uses the analogy of a stone which is thrown upward. As soon as the force which propels it upward is exhausted, it reverts to its initial tendency and falls downward. Often a student for whom this allegory was used to communicate this concept will forever comprehend it within the context of the allegory. As soon as he hears mention of the concept that the Divine life-force must be constantly invested in the creation, he begins to picture a stone being hurled upward.

Thus, on one hand, the allegory has enabled him to appreciate the concept. From a deeper perspective, however, the student has not been taught the concept itself, but rather has grasped a separate idea which merely represents the concept.

28 *Pesachim* 3b.

29 See *Iggeres HaKodesh*, Epistle 20.

30 *Avodah Zarah* 19b.

31 *Eruvin* 13b.

32 *Loc. cit.*

33 Using the following similes, the *Eitz Chayim* relates that before the entire spiritual cosmos came into being, the *Or Ein Sof* (G-d's infinite light) filled up all existence. In order to allow for the worlds to come into being, G-d placed this great light on the side, leaving an empty cavity, and into this cavity, revealed a short vector of light which became the source for the limited worlds. The process of "placing this light on the side" is identified with the first *tzimtzum*. On one hand, this *tzimtzum* was complete, leaving no vestiges of the original light at all (for only in this manner could a limited world be created). Nevertheless, the *maamar* is stipulating that this is true, only on the apparent level. Only the revealed dimension of the Divine light was "placed on the side," while its inner dimension, which transcends revelation, remains intact.

34 *Yirmiyahu* 23:24.

35 *Loc. cit.* The Hebrew wording of that verse is slightly different from that used by the *maamar*.

36 *Tikkunei Zohar, Tikkun* 57 (91b); quoted in *Tanya, Shaar HaYichud VeHaEmunah* ch. 7.

37 *Tehillim* 139:8.

38 *Yirmiyahu* 2:6.

39 *Bereishis* 1:1.

40 The daily liturgy.

41 *Devarim* 13:4.

42 Note the explanation of the above verse in *Likkutei Torah, Parshas Re'eh*, p. 19bff.

43 *Avos* 3:1.

44 *Likkutei Torah, Naso* 20:3.

45 *II Melachim* 5:15.

46 *Chagigah* 15a, *Mishneh Torah, Hilchos Yesodei HaTorah* 1:11.

47 Cf. *Shir HaShirim* 2:14.

48 Lit. "the hiding of [G-d's] face." *Ponim* also means "inner dimension." Thus, this term indicates an expression of the inner dimensions of G-dliness, albeit in a form in which they are not openly revealed.

49 To use a simple analogy: If a person knows a particular food is poison, refraining from eating it does not constitute a challenge, no matter how appetizing it appears.

50 *Bereishis Rabbah* 38:13.

51 *Pardes*, Section 12, Chapter 2.

52 *Taanis* 25a.

53 This is the form in which this passage is quoted in *Iggeres HaKodesh*, Epistle 12. In a slightly different form, it is found in *Midrash Tanchuma, Vayigash* 6, *Bamidbar Rabbah* 12:8.

54 *Iyov* 25:2.

55 *I Melachim* 18:38; note the manner in which this narrative is interpreted in *Yoma* 21b.

56 *Shmos* 23:6.

57 *Shaar Chag HaMatzos*, Chapter 1.

58 *Bereishis* 11:3.

59 See *Bereishis* 11:1 and commentaries.

60 *Yechezkel* 8:12, in regard to the interpretation of this verse, see *Sefer HaErchim-Chabad*, Vol. II, p. 274 ff.

61 *Bereishis* 11:4.

62 *Shaar* 1, *Anaf* 2.

63 *Bereishis* 1:1.

64 See *Bereishis Rabbah* 10:6; *Zohar*, Vol. I, 251a.

65 *Koheles* 5:7.

66 See *Bereishis* 32:31, *Tehillim* 82:6; *Mishneh Torah, Hilchos Yesodei HaTorah* 2:7.

67 See *Tehillim* 29:1, *Iyov* 1:6; *Mishneh Torah, Hilchos Yesodei HaTorah* 2:7.

68 *Yeshayahu* 10:15.

69 See *Likkutei Torah, Ki Seitzei* 37b ff., *Derech Mitzvosecha* 106a.

70 *Devarim* 16:18.

71 Cf. *Zohar Chodash* 21a.

72 More specifically, this refers to the second period in the Era of the Redemption. See the essay entitled "Two Periods in the Era of the Redemption" in *I Await His Coming Every Day*, Kehot, 5751.

73 *Berachos* 17a.

74 Cf. *Ta'anis* 8b.

75 *Devarim* 8:18.

76 Although as explained above, the word *mazalos* refers to the sources of influence in the spiritual realms, this is an uncommon usage. More commonly, the term is used to refer to the Zodiac constellation which were considered as sources of influence.

77 See *Mishneh Torah, Hilchos Avodas Kochavim*, Ch. 1, where the *Rambam* explains that the worship of the stars came about because the people conceived of them as intermediaries whom G-d entrusted with power and authority.

78 *Avodah Zarah* 8a.

79 *Devarim* 33:14.

80 *Devarim* 8:17.

81 See *Likkutei Torah, Masei* 89b.

82 Cf. *Devarim* 30:20. This represents an expansion of the literal meaning of the verse.

83 *Bereishis* 11:3.

84 See *Or HaTorah, Noach*, Vol. III, 664aff.

85 The commentaries identify these two deities with the Zoroastrian system of belief which speaks of a god of light and a god of darkness.

86 *Tehillim* 113:4.

87 *Bereishis Rabbah* 5:7.

88 See *Sefer Likkutim-D'ach Tzemach Tzedek, Erach Eretz*.

THE FAITH OF THE FARMER

BY RABBI YANKI TAUBER

To plant a seed, says the Talmud, is an act of faith.

After all, the farmer takes a supply of perfectly good grain and dumps it in the ground, where it will spoil and decompose. All in the hope that, months later, the earth will reward his toil and expense with a profitable return.

This is why, explains the Talmud, the first section of the Mishnah, which contains the Torah's agricultural laws, is associated with the concept of "faith." A person who sows a field, "believes in the One who sustains the world, and therefore sows."[1]

This, of course, begs the question: Are there no atheist farmers? The utility of plowing and sowing is a matter of experience: countless generations of farmers have sown and profited from their toil. Why does the act of farming demonstrate one's faith in G-d any more than the other endeavors, great and small, of human life?

The Veil

In creating the world, G-d established certain "laws" which delineate the manner in which it operates. The world, however, does not "operate" on its own: every event that transpires in it, from the birth of a child to a leaf turning in the wind, represents a direct and purposeful act of G-d.[2] So the laws of nature are not really laws at all, but divine "behavior patterns." The consistency of these behavior patterns—only rarely does G-d depart from them, and when He does we call the event a "miracle"—creates the illusion of "laws," as if there is some inherent necessity that things should continue to operate the way they have in the past. In

truth, there is no such inherent necessity, only the divine desire to continue acting upon the world in a manner consistent with these established patterns. If tomorrow the sun were to rise in the west and water were to begin to flow uphill, this would be no more or less "miraculous" than today's natural reality. The fact that G-d has thus far chosen to make the sun rise in the east and water flow downhill in no way compels that He continue to do so.

This, of course, is a believer's perspective, the perspective of one who perceives a deeper, more basic reality than what meets the eye, or can be dissected in the laboratory. To a more superficial eye, the laws of nature are axiomatic and immutable—laws that not only guarantee that a certain sequence of actions will produce grain or put a human being on the moon, but which are also the last word on what is, will, and ought to be in our world. Our mission in life is to "Know Him in all your ways."[3]—to recognize the divine *essence* of reality and to manifest this truth in everything we do. To live a life that is not subservient to the laws of nature but to their divine author: a life in which the natural reality is respected as the divine *modus operandi*, but is neither venerated nor awed; a life in which nature is not the dictator of life, but the facilitator of life's purpose to serve one's Creator.

By assuming this perspective and setting it as the guiding principle in everything we do, we penetrate the veil of nature and reveal the divine reality it conceals.[4] Our every deed becomes an exercise in the revelation of G-dliness, a demonstration of the subservience of nature and the all-pervasiveness of the divine.

Translucent Soil

Every person has their own path through life, their own particular aspect of the veil to penetrate.

For the veil is not uniform, but contains patches of greater and lesser opacity. The world of the businessman, for example, is far less predictable than that of the assembly-line worker. The product that succeeds

RABBI YANKI TAUBER, 1965–

Chasidic scholar and author. A native of Brooklyn, NY, Rabbi Tauber is an internationally renowned author who specializes in adapting the teachings of the Lubavitcher Rebbe. He is a member of the JLI curriculum development team, and has written numerous articles and books, including *Once Upon a Chassid* and *Beyond the Letter of the Law*.

against all odds, or the deal that is born out of a dozen incredible coincidences, can be explained in such prosaic terms as "market forces" and "statistical probability," but every businessman has encountered the hand of divine providence behind the monotony of natural law. By the same token, the brain surgeon's veil is more translucent than that of the dentist, and the physicist bores deeper than the civil engineer.

Therein lies the specialness of the faith of the farmer. The farmer's contact is with the thickest, most opaque part of the veil. The farmer is slave to the weather, the contours of the land, the chemistry of the soil; the farmer contends with nature in its rawest, most obstinate, most dictatorial incarnation. So when the farmer recognizes and acts upon the truth that it is the "One who sustains the world" who answers our toil with sustenance, this represents the ultimate triumph of faith, the ultimate penetration of spiritual vision through the material haze.

From *The Inside Story*, vol. III, to be published by the Meaningful Life Center, meaningfullife.com. Printed with permission of the publisher.

Endnotes

1 Talmud, *Shabbat* 31a; *Tosafot*, ad loc., citing the Jerusalem Talmud. The Mishnah consists of six "orders," each containing the tractates that deal with a specific area of Torah law. The six orders are alluded to by six key words in the verse (Isaiah 33:6), ". . . the *faith* of your *times*, a *stronghold* of *salvation*, *wisdom*, and *knowledge* . . ." The word "faith" refers to the order of *Zera'im* ("Seeds"), which includes the laws pertaining to the produce of the land.
2 As per the doctrine of *hashgachah peratit* ("particular divine providence") formulated by Rabbi Israel Baal Shem Tov. See *Likutei Sichot*, vol. 7, pp. 277–284, for a detailed discussion of the writings of the sages on the topic.
3 Proverbs 3:6.
4 The Hebrew word for "world," *olam*, means "concealment." Our world is a system of laws and axioms whose apparent consistency and predictability conceal its divine essence.

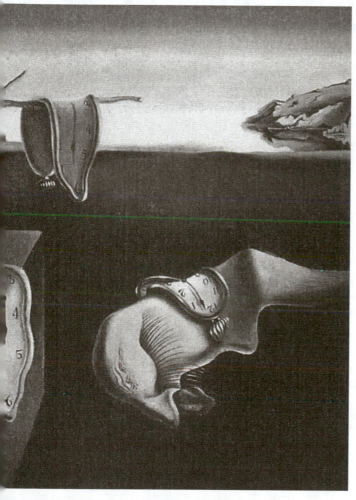

Lesson

IS TIME REAL?

Is time the engine that drives the whole of existence, or is it just a product of our subjective experience? If the future is impenetrable, the past irretrievable, and the present moment too fleeting to meaningfully inhabit, what part of our lives can we call our own?

La persistència de la memòria (The Persistence of Memory), Salvador Dali, oil on canvas, 1931. (Museum of Modern Art, New York)

TEXT 1

ECCLESIASTES 3:1, 11

לְכֹל זְמָן, וְעֵת לְכָל חֵפֶץ, תַּחַת הַשָּׁמָיִם ...
אֶת הַכֹּל עָשָׂה יָפֶה בְעִתּוֹ; גַּם אֶת הָעֹלָם נָתַן בְּלִבָּם, מִבְּלִי אֲשֶׁר לֹא יִמְצָא
הָאָדָם אֶת הַמַּעֲשֶׂה אֲשֶׁר עָשָׂה הָאֱלֹקִים מֵרֹאשׁ וְעַד סוֹף.

There is a time for everything, and a moment for every pursuit under the sun. . . .

He has made everything beautiful in its time; also the world He set in their hearts, yet without man being able to discover the work that God has done from beginning to end.

King Solomon wrote 3 Books.
Song of Songs - young
Kohellet - synacle + middle aged
Proverbs - old + Wise

TEXT 2

AUGUSTINE OF HIPPO, *CONFESSIONS*

What, then, is time? If no one asks me, I know what it is. If I wish to explain it to him who asks, I do not know.

**AUGUSTINE OF HIPPO
354–430**

Philosopher, theologian. Augustine of Hippo was a philosopher and Christian theologian who lived in the Roman province of Africa (present day Tunisia and Libya) in the fourth and fifth centuries CE. Among his most famous works are *The City of God* and *Confessions*.

Drawing depicting Euclid holding a sphere and dioptra observing the moon and stars and Hermanus holding an astrolabe. From *Liber Fortunae* (a.k.a. *Experimentarius*), Bernardus Silvester, parchment manuscript, England, late 14th century. (Bodleian Libraries, University of Oxford; Oxford, U.K.)

Learning Exercise 2.1

Rate your relationship with time on a scale of one to ten, "one" being "easy and satisfying," and "ten" being "difficult and frustrating."

EASY AND SATISFYING　　　　　　　**DIFFICULT AND FRUSTRATING**

Our relationship with time can be very scary

QUESTION FOR DISCUSSION

What are our difficulties with time?

Old Man with Hourglass, Antonio Cifrondi, oil on canvas, c. 1717.
(Fondazione Brescia Musei, Brescia, Italy)

TEXT 3

ATTICUS

Time is everything we have and don't.

Objects exist in space
experiences exist in time.
or events

ATTICUS
CA. 1999–

Poet. Contemporary online poet, born in coastal British Columbia, Canada. Renowned for his mystery, he uses "Atticus" as his pen name, and he wears a mask in public to remain anonymous. In 2016, he was called the "#1 Poet to Follow" by *Teen Vogue*. In 2017, Atticus reportedly signed a publishing deal with Atria Books (of Simon and Schuster Publishers) to release a collection of his work.

The Fastest Time on Record, Syracuse, New York, May 10, 1893. (Photo credit: A. P. Yates)

TEXT 4

MAR'EH MUSAR (PRAGUE, 1614), P. 6

הֶעָבַר אַיִן
וְהֶעָתִיד עֲדַיִן
וְהַהֹוֶה כְּהֶרֶף עַיִן
אִם כֵּן דְּאָגָה מִנַּיִן?

The past is gone
The future is yet to come
And the present is like the blink of an eye;
So what's to worry?

MAR'EH MUSAR

Mar'eh Musar was compiled by Rabbi Yehuda Zeligman Ulma Ginzberg. It was first printed in Prague in 1614. It is a compilation of approximately 515 Hebrew and Aramaic proverbs, from the Talmud, Midrash, Middle Ages literature, and folk sayings. A Yiddish translation follows each proverb.

TEXT **5**

RABBI YOSEF ALBO, *IKARIM*, 3:27

שֶׁהַזְּמַן הוּא דָבָר בִּלְתִּי נִמְצָא בְּפֹעַל. כִּי הֶעָבַר אֵינוֹ נִמְצָא, וְהֶעָתִיד לֹא
יָצָא עֲדַיִן אֶל הַפֹּעַל, וְהַהֹוֶה אֵינוֹ אֶלָּא הָעַתָּה הַקּוֹשֵׁר בֵּין הֶעָבַר וְהֶעָתִיד.
וְאוּלָם הָעַתָּה עַצְמוֹ אֵינוֹ זְמַן עַל דֶּרֶךְ הָאֱמֶת ... אֲבָל יַחַס הָעַתָּה אֶל הַזְּמַן
יַחַס הַנְּקוּדָה אֶל הַקַו. וְאִם כֵּן, אֵין הַזְּמַן נִמְצָא בְּפֹעַל. וְאַף עַל פִּי כֵן, הוּא
נוֹתֵן שְׁלֵמוּת הַמְצִיאוּת לְכָל הַדְּבָרִים הַנִּמְצָאִים בִּזְמַן.

Time is something that does not actually exist. For the past isn't here anymore, the future has not yet come into actuality, and the present is just the "now" that connects past and future. The "now" itself is not really a part of time . . . rather, its relationship to time is like the relationship of a point to a line. So time doesn't really exist. Yet time provides the full existence to everything that exists in time!

RABBI YOSEF ALBO
CA. 1380–1444

Spanish rabbi and philosopher. A student of Rabbi Chasdai Crescas, Albo is renowned for his philosophical work *Sefer Ha'ikarim* (*Book of Fundamentals*). The work stresses three fundamental aspects of Jewish belief: the existence of God, Torah from Sinai, and reward and punishment.

? QUESTION FOR DISCUSSION

Can anything exist outside of time?

TEXT 6

MAIMONIDES, *COMMENTARY ON THE MISHNAH,*
INTRODUCTION TO CHAPTER *CHELEK* 🔧

הַיְסוֹד הָרְבִיעִי: הַקַּדְמוּת. וְהוּא שֶׁנַּאֲמִין כִּי זֶה הָאֶחָד הָאָמוּר הוּא קַדְמוֹן
בְּהֶחְלֵט, וְכָל נִמְצָא זוּלָתוֹ בִּלְתִּי קַדְמוֹן בְּעֶרְכּוֹ אֵלָיו.

The Fourth Principle is [God's] primordiality. This is the belief that God is absolutely primordial, and all other existences are not similarly primordial.

God always existed.

**RABBI MOSHE BEN MAIMON
(MAIMONIDES, RAMBAM) 1135–1204**

Halachist, philosopher, author, and physician. Maimonides was born in Córdoba, Spain. After the conquest of Córdoba by the Almohads, he fled Spain and eventually settled in Cairo, Egypt. There, he became the leader of the Jewish community and served as court physician to the vizier of Egypt. He is most noted for authoring the *Mishneh Torah,* an encyclopedic arrangement of Jewish law, and for his philosophical work, *Guide for the Perplexed.* His rulings on Jewish law are integral to the formation of halachic consensus.

TEXT 7

RABBI OVADIAH SEFORNO, *COMMENTARY ON THE TORAH*, GENESIS 1:1

בְּרֵאשִׁית: בִּתְחִילַת הַזְּמַן. וְהוּא רֶגַע רִאשׁוֹן בִּלְתִּי מִתְחַלֵּק, שֶׁלֹּא הָיָה זְמַן קוֹדֶם לוֹ.

RABBI OVADIAH SEFORNO
1475–1550

Biblical exegete, philosopher, and physician. Seforno was born in Cesena, Italy. After gaining a thorough knowledge of Talmud and the sciences, he moved to Rome, where he studied medicine and taught Hebrew to the German scholar Johannes Reuchlin. Seforno eventually settled in Bologna, where he founded and directed a yeshiva until his death. His magnum opus is a biblical commentary focused on the simple interpretation of text, with an emphasis on philology and philosophy.

"In the beginning [God created]": Meaning, in the beginning of time. This is the first, indivisible moment, prior to which there was no time.

TEXT 8

RABBI SAADIA GA'ON, *MIPIRUSHEI SAADIA GA'ON LAMIKRA*, COMPILED BY YEHUDAH RATZAHVI (JERUSALEM: MOSAD HARAV KOOK, 2004), GENESIS 1:1

וְטָעֲנוּ הַכּוֹפְרִים בְּעִנְיָן בְּרִיאַת הָעוֹלָם וְאָמְרוּ: מִפְּנֵי מָה לֹא בְּרָאוֹ הַבּוֹרֵא
לִפְנֵי הַזְּמַן אֲשֶׁר בּוֹ בְּרָאוֹ? כִּי חָשְׁבוּ שֶׁיֵּשׁ מָקוֹם לִשְׁאֵלָה זֹג, וְהִתְחִילוּ
לְחַלֵּק אוֹתָהּ וְלֵאמוֹר: מִסִּבַּת הַמַּתָּנָה, אוֹ בִּגְלַל מוֹנֵעַ שֶׁמְּנָעוֹ? וְלֹא יָדְעוּ
שֶׁעֶצֶם הַשְּׁאֵלָה הִיא בִּלְתִּי אֶפְשָׁרִי, כִּי אָנוּ אוֹמְרִים שֶׁהוּא בָּרָא אֶת הַזְּמַן,
אֲשֶׁר בּוֹ נִכְנָסִים כָּל "לִפְנֵי" וְ"אַחֲרֵי". וּכְשֶׁהֵם מַצִּיעִים שֶׁיִּהְיֶה זֶה לִפְנֵי
הַזְּמַן הַהוּא, הֵם מַצִּיעִים... שֶׁיִּהְיֶה לֹא זְמַן, זְמַן.

RAV SAADIA GA'ON (RASAG) 882–942 CE

Rabbinic scholar, philosopher, and exegete. Rav Sa'adia Ga'on was born in Egypt and came to the forefront of the rabbinic scene through his active opposition to Karaism, a divergent sect that denied the divinity of the Oral Law. In 928, the exilarch David ben Zakai invited him to head the illustrious yeshiva in Sura, Babylonia, thereby bestowing upon him the honorific title "Ga'on." He is renowned for his works on the Torah, Hebrew linguistics, Jewish philosophy, and his redaction of a *siddur*.

The deniers dispute the creation of the world, arguing: Why didn't the Creator create it at an earlier time than He did? Thinking that their argument has a place, they analyze it further: Was it because God was waiting, or because something was preventing Him? They don't realize that their very question is a non sequitur. For we say that God created time, which includes all "before" and "after." To speak about what was "before" time is to apply . . . the characteristics of time to non-time.

TEXT 9

RABBI MENACHEM MENDEL SCHNEERSOHN OF LUBAVITCH,
DERECH MITZVOTECHA, 57B–58B

שֶׁהַזְּמַן הוּא נִבְרָא, וּמְחוּדָּשׁ מֵאַיִן לְיֵשׁ, כְּכָל הַבְּרוּאִים. וְהוּא יִתְבָּרֵךְ הָיָה לְבַד בְּלִי בְּחִינַת זְמַן . . . שֶׁהוּא לְמַעְלָה מִן הַזְּמַן לְגַמְרֵי וַאֲפִילוּ מִן הֶמְשֵׁךְ הַבִּלְתִּי מְשׁוֹעָר. . . אֶלָּא הוּא בִּבְחִינַת הֹוֶה תָּמִיד.

Time is a creation, something new brought into being out of nothingness, like all other creations. Only God is timeless. . . . For God is utterly beyond time, even of time as an incalculable expanse. . . . Rather, [the whole of time] is in the continual present [for Him].

God has! No Before, during OR after

RABBI MENACHEM MENDEL SCHNEERSOHN OF LUBAVITCH (*TSEMACH TSEDEK*) 1789–1866

Chasidic rebbe and noted author. The *Tsemach Tsedek* was the third leader of the Chabad Chasidic movement and a noted authority on Jewish law. His numerous works include halachic responsa, Chasidic discourses, and kabbalistic writings. Active in the plight of Russian Jewry, he worked to alleviate the plight of the cantonists, Jewish children kidnapped to serve in the Czar's army. He passed away in Lubavitch, leaving seven sons and two daughters.

Learning Exercise 2.2

Flipbook

The Student Book that you are using for this class is also a "flipbook." On the bottom right corner of page one (the cover page for Lesson One) is an image of a baby. Flip the pages of the book to watch the baby's progress through time.

Figure 2.1

Meaning of the Tetragrammaton: Past, Present, and Future in One

these 4 letters spell being

י-ה-ו-ה		
uniting the was, the is, and the will be		
היה	הוה	יהיה
was	is	will be

god is a combination of past, present & future.

transcends time & prevades time.
Inside + Outside at the same moment

TEXT 10

SIDDUR, DAILY MORNING PRAYERS, FIRST BLESSING PRECEDING THE *SHEMA*

הַמְחַדֵּשׁ בְּטוּבוֹ בְּכָל יוֹם תָּמִיד מַעֲשֵׂה בְרֵאשִׁית

Who in His goodness renews each day, constantly, the first act of creation.

SIDDUR

The siddur is the Jewish prayer book. It was originally developed by the sages of the Great Assembly in the 4th century BCE, and later reconstructed by Rabban Gamliel after the destruction of the Second Temple. Various authorities continued to add prayers, from then until contemporary times. It includes praise of God, requests for personal and national needs, selections of the Bible, and much else. Various Jewish communities have slightly different versions of the siddur.

Prière du Soir: La Bénédiction de la Lune (Evening Prayer: The Sanctification of the Moon [*kiddush levanah*]), Alphonse Jacques Lévy, oil on canvas, c. 1883. (Museum of Jewish Art and History, Paris, France)

TEXT 11

RABBI YESHAYAH HOROWITZ, *SHENEI LUCHOT HABERIT,*
ASARAH MAAMAROT, MAAMAR 1, 40B-41A

הִנֵּה סְבָרַת הָעוֹלָם הִיא. . . כָּךְ: הַבּוֹרֵא בָּרוּךְ הוּא חִידֵּשׁ הַכֹּל יֵשׁ מֵאַיִן
הַמֻּחְלָט. . . בְּרֵאשִׁית נָתַן הַקָּדוֹשׁ בָּרוּךְ הוּא לְצָבָא הַשָּׁמַיִם כֹּחַ וִיכֹלֶת
לְהַנְהִיג הָעוֹלָם. . . . הָעוֹלָם כְּמִנְהָגוֹ נוֹהֵג, וְכִבְיָכוֹל זָזָה יָדוֹ מֵהֶם; רַק אִם
לְעֵת מֵהָעִתִּים רוֹצֶה לְשַׁדֵּד אוֹתָם. וְכָל זְמַן שֶׁאֵינוֹ מְשַׁדֵּד, אָז מַנְהִיגָם
בְּכֹחַ שֶׁהוּשַּׂג לָהֶם בְּעֵת הַבְּרִיאָה.

אָמְנָם אֲמִיתַּת הָאֱמוּנָה. . . הִיא: הַשֵּׁם יִתְבָּרֵךְ מְחַדֵּשׁ בְּטוּבוֹ בְּכָל יוֹם
תָּמִיד מַעֲשֵׂה בְרֵאשִׁית, בְּכַוָּונָה מְכֻוֶּונֶת שׁוֹפֵעַ שִׁפְעוֹ. וְאִילוּ הָיָה מוֹנֵעַ
רֶגַע אֶחָד, הָיָה הַכֹּל כְּלֹא הָיָה, בָּטֵל הַמְּצִיאוּת. . .

**RABBI YESHAYAH HALEVI HOROWITZ
(*SHELAH*) 1565–1630**

Kabbalist and author. Rabbi
Horowitz was born in Prague
and served as rabbi in several
prominent Jewish communities,
including Frankfurt am Main and
his native Prague. After the passing
of his wife in 1620, he moved to
Israel. In Tiberias, he completed
his *Shenei Luchot Haberit*, an
encyclopedic compilation of
kabbalistic ideas. He is buried in
Tiberias, next to Maimonides.

A common perception . . . is that God created everything out of absolute nothingness . . . and that in the
beginning of creation, God imparted to the hosts of
heaven [i.e., the forces of nature] the power and ability
to run the world. . . . The world thus operates according
to its manner, as if God has let go of His creation; it is
only that occasionally God may desire to override [the
natural order]. But as long as God does not override it,
the world runs on the power it obtained at the time of
its creation.

But the true faith . . . is that God "in His goodness renews each day, constantly, the first act of creation," actively directing His flow of vitality. Should God cease
to do so for even an instant, all would be as naught; its
existence would be utterly nullified.

TEXT 12

RABBI SHNE'UR ZALMAN OF LIADI, *TANYA, SHAAR HAYICHUD VEHA'EMUNAH*, CH. 1

הִנֵּה כְּתִיב "לְעוֹלָם ה' דְּבָרְךָ נִצָּב בַּשָּׁמָיִם"... וְכֵן בְּכָל הַבְּרוּאִים שֶׁבְּכָל הָעוֹלָמוֹת עֶלְיוֹנִים וְתַחְתּוֹנִים וַאֲפִילוּ אֶרֶץ הַלָּזוּ הַגַּשְׁמִית וּבְחִינַת דּוֹמֵם מַמָּשׁ אִילוּ הָיוּ מִסְתַּלְּקוֹת מִמֶּנָּה לְרֶגַע חַס וְשָׁלוֹם הָאוֹתִיּוֹת מֵעֲשָׂרָה מַאֲמָרוֹת שֶׁבָּהֶן נִבְרֵאת הָאָרֶץ בְּשֵׁשֶׁת יְמֵי בְּרֵאשִׁית, הָיְתָה חוֹזֶרֶת לְאַיִן וָאֶפֶס מַמָּשׁ, כְּמוֹ לִפְנֵי שֵׁשֶׁת יְמֵי בְּרֵאשִׁית מַמָּשׁ.

RABBI SHNE'UR ZALMAN OF LIADI (ALTER REBBE) 1745–1812

Chasidic rebbe, halachic authority, and founder of the Chabad movement. The Alter Rebbe was born in Liozna, Belarus, and was among the principal students of the Magid of Mezeritch. His numerous works include the *Tanya*, an early classic containing the fundamentals of Chabad Chasidism, and *Shulchan Aruch HaRav*, an expanded and reworked code of Jewish law.

It is written (PSALMS 119:89), "Forever, O God, Your word stands firm in the heavens" . . . So it also is with all created things in all the supernal and lower worlds, even this physical earth and inanimate matter: If the letters of the "ten utterances" by which the world was created during the six days of creation were to depart from it but for an instant, God forbid, it would literally revert to naught and absolute nothingness, exactly as before the six days of creation.

TEXT 13

TALMUD, TAANIT 25A

חַד בֵּי שִׁמְשֵׁי חַזְיֵיהּ [ר' חֲנִינָא בֶּן דּוֹסָא] לִבְרַתֵּיהּ דַּהֲוַות עֲצִיבָא. אָמַר לָהּ: בִּתִּי, לְמַאי עֲצִיבַת? אָמְרָה לֵיהּ: כְּלִי שֶׁל חוֹמֶץ נִתְחַלֵּף לִי בִּכְלִי שֶׁל שֶׁמֶן, וְהִדְלַקְתִּי מִמֶּנּוּ אוֹר לְשַׁבָּת. אָמַר לָהּ: בִּתִּי מַאי אִיכְפַּת לָךְ? מִי שֶׁאָמַר לַשֶּׁמֶן וְיִדְלוֹק, הוּא יֹאמַר לַחוֹמֶץ וְיִדְלוֹק! תָּנָא: הָיָה דּוֹלֵק וְהוֹלֵךְ כָּל הַיּוֹם כּוּלוֹ, עַד שֶׁהֵבִיאוּ מִמֶּנּוּ אוֹר לְהַבְדָּלָה.

One [Friday] eve [Rabbi Chanina ben Dosa] saw that his daughter was sad. Said he to her: "My daughter, why are you sad?"

Said she to him: "I confused a vessel of vinegar for a vessel of oil, and I kindled the Shabbat light from it."

Said he to her: "My daughter, what are you concerned about? The One who said to oil that it should burn, shall say to vinegar that it should burn!"

We learned: The light continued to burn the whole day, until they brought from it light for *Havdalah*.

BABYLONIAN TALMUD

A literary work of monumental proportions that draws upon the legal, spiritual, intellectual, ethical, and historical traditions of Judaism. The 37 tractates of the Babylonian Talmud contain the teachings of the Jewish sages from the period after the destruction of the Second Temple through the fifth century CE. It has served as the primary vehicle for the transmission of the Oral Law and the education of Jews over the centuries; it is the entry point for all subsequent legal, ethical, and theological Jewish scholarship.

TEXT 14

RABBI MENACHEM MENDEL SCHNEERSOHN OF LUBAVITCH,
TORAH OR, INYANIM, PP. 111–112 🔖

שֶׁכְּשֶׁפּוֹעֵל הָאוּמָן כְּלִי, הִנֵּה הַכְּלִי מִתְקַיֵּים לְעוֹלָם, אַף שֶׁיָּדָיו מְסוּלָקוֹת הֵימֶנָה. מַה שֶּׁאֵין כֵּן כְּשֶׁזּוֹרֵק אֶבֶן לְמַעֲלָה בְּגוֹבַהּ, לֹא יִתְקַיֵּים הָאֶבֶן בָּאֲוִיר רַק מְעַט, וּמִיָּד יִפּוֹל כְּכְלוֹת הַכֹּחַ. וְהַיְינוּ, לְפִי שֶׁמִּטְבַּע הָאֶבֶן לֵירֵד לְמַטָּה בָּאָרֶץ. לָכֵן אִי אֶפְשָׁר שֶׁיִּתְקַיֵּים נֶגֶד טִבְעוֹ כִּי אִם עַל יְדֵי הַכֹּחַ הַמַּכְרִיחוֹ. וְלָכֵן כְּכְלוֹת הַכֹּחַ יִפּוֹל לָאָרֶץ. מַה שֶּׁאֵין כֵּן בַּעֲשִׂיַּית כְּלִי, שֶׁאֵינוֹ מְשַׁנֶּה טִבְעוֹ כְּלַל רַק הַצּוּרָה כוּלִי.

וְאִם כֵּן, כָּל שֶׁכֵּן בִּבְרִיאַת שָׁמַיִם וָאָרֶץ יֵשׁ מֵאַיִן בְּכֹחוֹ הַגָּדוֹל, שֶׁזֶּה הַכֹּחַ צָרִיךְ לִהְיוֹת נִמְשָׁךְ תָּמִיד . . . שֶׁהִתְהַוּוּת יֵשׁ מֵאַיִן הוּא יוֹתֵר הֵפֶךְ הַטֶּבַע מֵעֲמִידַת הָאֶבֶן בָּאֲוִיר כוּלִי.

When an artisan makes a utensil, that utensil will continue to exist also after the artisan disengages from it. In contrast, if a person throws a stone upward, the stone will remain aloft only for a short time, and will immediately fall down when the force [impelling it upward] ceases to act on it. This is because the stone's nature is to fall downward. Therefore, the stone will remain in a state that is contrary to its nature only as long as a [superior] force compels it; when the force ceases to act on it, it will fall to the ground. Not so with the [artisan's] fashioning of a utensil, which does not change the nature of [its material], only its form.

How much more so is it in the case of the creation of the heavens and the earth, as something from nothing, by the creative power of God, that this force must continually be exerted. . . . For the creation of something from nothing is more contrary to the natural state [of nothingness] than a stone remaining airborne. . . .

Horologia Ferrea (The Invention of Clockwork), Theodor Galle, engraving, c. 1590–1600. (Davison Art Center, Wesleyan University, Middletown, Conn.)

QUESTION FOR DISCUSSION

How does the knowledge that God creates the world out of absolute nothingness each and every moment affect the way we go about our daily lives?

QUESTION FOR DISCUSSION

How does the Doctrine of Perpetual Creation impact our time-related frustrations?

TEXT **15**

THE REBBE, RABBI MENACHEM MENDEL SCHNEERSON,
LIKUTEI SICHOT, VOL. 6, P. 88.

בְּהַמָּשָׁל דִּזְרִיקַת אֶבֶן, הֲרֵי גַם אַחַר כַּךְ שַׁיָּיךְ לוֹמַר שֶׁבַּתְּחִלָּה הָלַךְ מִלְּמַטָּה לְמַעֲלָה. מַה שֶׁאֵין כֵּן בְּהַנִּמְשָׁל. מִכֵּיוָן שֶׁגַם זְמַן עַצְמוֹ הוּא מְצִיאוּת נִבְרָא . . . וּבְהִסְתַּלֵּק (הַמַאֲמָר אֲשֶׁר בּוֹ מֵ)הָעֲשָׂרָה מַאֲמָרוֹת, יִתְבַּטֵּל גַם הַזְמַן. הֲרֵי בְּמֵילָא לֹא יִשָּׁאֵר שׁוּם רוֹשֶׁם כוּ' כְּלָל.

RABBI MENACHEM MENDEL SCHNEERSON
1902–1994

In the analogy of the thrown stone, after the stone ceases flying it can still be said that, earlier, it was moving upward. Not so in the analogue [of God's creation]. Because time is itself a created reality, . . . should the divine utterance cease to create, time will also cease to exist. So there would not remain anything of the world at all [not even its past existence].

The towering Jewish leader of the 20th century, known as "the Lubavitcher Rebbe," or simply as "the Rebbe." Born in southern Ukraine, the Rebbe escaped Nazi-occupied Europe, arriving in the U.S. in June 1941. The Rebbe inspired and guided the revival of traditional Judaism after the European devastation, impacting virtually every Jewish community the world over. The Rebbe often emphasized that the performance of just one additional good deed could usher in the era of Mashiach. The Rebbe's scholarly talks and writings have been printed in more than 200 volumes.

Portrait of Success, lithograph, 2007. (Wriston Art Center Galleries, Lawrence University, Appleton, WI)

TEXT **16**

THE REBBE, RABBI MENACHEM MENDEL SCHNEERSON,
SEFER HASICHOT 5749, VOL. 1, P. 190.

בְּגֶדֶר הַזְּמַן, שֶׁנֶּחְלַק לְעָבָר הֹוֶה וְעָתִיד, יֶשְׁנָם שְׁנֵי עִנְיָנִים: (א) כָּל רֶגַע
וְרֶגַע הוּא עִנְיָן בִּפְנֵי עַצְמוֹ, נְקוּדָה אַחַת שֶׁל זְמַן; (ב) כְּלָלוּת הֶמְשֵׁךְ הַזְּמַן.
וּכְמוּדְגָשׁ בִּכְלָלוּת עִנְיַן הַבְּרִיאָה . . . שֶׁיֵּשׁ בָּהּ שְׁנֵי עִנְיָנִים: (א) חִידוּשׁ
הַהִתְהַוּוּת מֵאַיִן וְאֶפֶס הַמֻּחְלָט בְּכָל רֶגַע וְרֶגַע . . . (ב) וּבְיַחַד עִם זֶה,
"לֹא יִשְׁבֹּתוּ", הַיְינוּ שֶׁהַהִתְהַוּוּת בְּרֶגַע זֶה הִיא בְּהֶמְשֵׁךְ לְהִתְהַוּוּת בְּרֶגַע
שֶׁלְּפָנֵי זֶה וְהַמְשָׁכָה בְּהִתְהַוּוּת בְּרֶגַע שֶׁלְּאַחֲרֵי זֶה בְּאוֹפֶן תְּמִידִי.

The reality of time, which consists of past, present, and future, has two aspects: (1) each and every moment is a distinct entity, a single point of time; (2) the overall continuum of time.

God's creation of the world . . . also incorporates these two aspects: (1) God's renewal of existence from absolute nothingness in each and every moment . . . a new creation solely for this single moment; (2) the divinely ordained principle that "[the cycles of nature] shall not be disrupted" (GENESIS 8:22)—meaning that the creation of this moment is a continuation of the previous created moment and continues into the creation of the following moment in an undisrupted way.

TEXT 17

TALMUD, YOMA 86B

אָמַר רֵישׁ לָקִישׁ: "גְּדוֹלָה תְּשׁוּבָה, שֶׁזְּדוֹנוֹת נַעֲשׂוֹת לוֹ כִּשְׁגָגוֹת"...
וְהָאָמַר רֵישׁ לָקִישׁ, "גְּדוֹלָה תְּשׁוּבָה שֶׁזְּדוֹנוֹת נַעֲשׂוֹת לוֹ כִּזְכִיּוֹת"?...
לֹא קַשְׁיָא: כַּאן מֵאַהֲבָה, כַּאן מִיִּרְאָה.

Said Reish Lakish: "Great is *teshuvah*, in that a person's deliberate sins become like mistakes." . . . But did not Reish Lakish say, "Great is *teshuvah*, in that a person's deliberate sins become like virtues"? . . . There is no contradiction: the latter case is when a person repents out of love; and the former case is when a person repents out of fear.

TEXT **18**

RABBI SHNE'UR ZALMAN OF LIADI, *TANYA*, CHAPTER 7

שֶׁהִיא תְּשׁוּבָה מֵאַהֲבָה, מֵעוּמְקָא דְלִבָּא, בְּאַהֲבָה רַבָּה וַחֲשִׁיקָה וְנֶפֶשׁ שׁוֹקֵקָה לְדָבְקָה בּוֹ יִתְבָּרֵךְ; וְצָמְאָה נַפְשׁוֹ לַה' כְּאֶרֶץ עֲיֵפָה וְצִיָּה. לִהְיוֹת כִּי עַד הֵנָּה הָיְתָה נַפְשׁוֹ בְּאֶרֶץ צִיָּה וְצַלְמָוֶת, הִיא הַסִּטְרָא אַחֲרָא, וּרְחוֹקָה מֵאוֹר פְּנֵי ה' בְּתַכְלִית, וּלְזֹאת צָמְאָה נַפְשׁוֹ בְּיֶתֶר עָז מִצִּמְאוֹן נַפְשׁוֹת הַצַּדִּיקִים. כְּמַאֲמָרָם זִכְרוֹנָם לִבְרָכָה, "בִּמְקוֹם שֶׁבַּעֲלֵי תְּשׁוּבָה עוֹמְדִים כוּלֵי'". וְעַל תְּשׁוּבָה מֵאַהֲבָה רַבָּה זוֹ אָמְרוּ שֶׁזְּדוֹנוֹת נַעֲשׂוּ לוֹ כִּזְכֻיּוֹת, הוֹאִיל וְעַל יְדֵי זֶה בָּא לְאַהֲבָה רַבָּה זוֹ.

This is "*teshuvah* out of love," coming from the depths of the heart, with great love and fervor, and from a soul passionately desiring to cleave to God, and thirsting for God like a parched desert soil. For inasmuch as his soul had been in a barren wilderness, and in the shadow of death, which is the "other side" [i.e., evil], and infinitely removed from the light of the divine countenance, his soul now thirsts [for God] even more than the souls of the righteous. As our sages say: "In the place where penitents stand, even the perfectly righteous cannot stand." It is concerning repentance out of such great love that they have said: "The penitent's deliberate sins become like virtues"—because it is through them that he has achieved this great love.

TEXT 19

MAIMONIDES, *MISHNEH TORAH*, LAWS OF *TESHUVAH*, 3:4 ⊕

צָרִיךְ כָּל אָדָם שֶׁיִּרְאֶה עַצְמוֹ . . . כְּאִילוּ חֶצְיוֹ זַכַּאי וְחֶצְיוֹ חַיָּב. וְכֵן כָּל
הָעוֹלָם, חֶצְיוֹ זַכַּאי וְחֶצְיוֹ חַיָּב. חָטָא חֵטְא אֶחָד, הֲרֵי הִכְרִיעַ אֶת עַצְמוֹ
וְאֶת כָּל הָעוֹלָם כֻּלּוֹ לְכַף חוֹבָה, וְגָרַם לוֹ הַשְׁחָתָה. עָשָׂה מִצְוָה אַחַת, הֲרֵי
הִכְרִיעַ אֶת עַצְמוֹ וְאֶת כָּל הָעוֹלָם כֻּלּוֹ לְכַף זְכוּת, וְגָרַם לוֹ וְלָהֶם תְּשׁוּעָה
וְהַצָּלָה.

A person should always see themselves as equally balanced between virtue and guilt, and the entire world as also equally balanced between virtue and guilt. So that if the person does one sin, they have tipped their balance, and that of the entire world, to the side of guilt, and have brought destruction upon themselves. And if the person does one mitzvah, they have tipped their balance, and that of the entire world, to the side of virtue, and have brought deliverance and salvation to themselves and to everyone else.

KEY POINTS

1 Time is a mystery, and most of us have a difficult relationship with it. We are frustrated by the way that time moves too fast or too slow for us, and by the fact that we cannot change the past or know the future.

2 Judaism teaches that time is a creation. God exists entirely outside of time, and the whole of time is accessible to Him as a "continual present."

3 The "Doctrine of Perpetual Creation" states that in each and every moment of time, God creates the entire universe out of absolute nothingness, exactly like in the very first moment of creation.

4 The implications of Perpetual Creation include: (a) The present moment is entirely free of the constraints of the past. (b) Everything in our lives, down to the most minute detail, is significant and purposeful. (c) Nothing in the world can be contrary to what God desires from us at this present moment. (d) Each moment has its own distinct purpose, and warrants our full investment of mind, heart, and soul.

5 It is not only the present moment that is a new creation. The whole of time—past, present, and future—is created anew each and every moment out of absolute nothingness. Thus, both the past and the future are shaped by our present actions. *Teshuvah* (repentance) can reach back in time to change a negative into a positive. A single positive action can "tip the balance" for global redemption.

Additional Readings

THE TIME BEFORE TIME

BY RABBI BENYOMIN WALTERS

Chassidus explains that G-d Himself completely transcends time. Time is a creation, just like the heavens and the earth. G-d creates time as we know it in three stages: (1) the spiritual "order" of time, (2) the essential flow of time, and (3) measurable time.

The order of time is the creation of a structure and laws that will govern creation: for example, the creation of the *sfiros*, the limitation to ten, the definition of each *sfirah*, the creation of opposites, such as *chesed* and *gevurah*, and the order of the *sfiros* (*chesed*, *gevurah*, *tiferes*, etc.). G-d's Wisdom decided that the expansion of *chesed* opposes the constriction of *gevurah*: they cannot occur simultaneously. Therefore, *chesed* has to come first, then stop and leave, before *gevurah* can begin to act. The analogy for this is breathing. The lungs expand and contract to breathe. Inhaling and exhaling are opposites that cannot occur simultaneously—therefore, it takes time to breathe. One must inhale and only *after* can one exhale and only *after* that can he inhale again. Thus the structure and rules that govern breathing necessitate a before and after—"Let there be time!" Similarly, the constraints, rules, or structure that G-d set up for the world necessitates time. Nevertheless, there is no actual time at this point; only a series of rules that, if a world were conducted by them, would necessitate time.

RABBI BENYOMIN WALTERS, 1982–

Chasidic educator and author. Rabbi Walters specializes in showing the relevance and practicality of kabbalistic concepts found in *Chasidus*. He is a member of the JLI curriculum development team, and has translated and adapted many Chasidic texts, including *Moshiach Day-by-Day*, and the *Seder Hishtalshelut* audio series.

Then, when the physical world is created there is the flow of time and measurable time. The flow of time is created by the "running and returning" of the creative energy. That is, since each moment has its own unique life force, and since the previous life force must leave before the next can enter, time is born.

However, the essential passing of time and flow of life force is imperceptible. This time only has meaning to us when it causes changes or motion in physical beings. The idea of cause and effect, before and after, only becomes apparent when we can observe change. Therefore, it is the effect of time on physical beings—their motion and changes—that allow us to measure time. For example, imagine an empty flipbook. There would be no real perception of how fast the pages were being flipped. On the other hand, when there are images on the flipbook, the speed of the figures' motion and change gives us a tangible feeling of time. If the book were flipped too fast or too slow, we would notice.[1]

The *order* of time existed before the world was created, as a higher spiritual creation (sometimes called the Supernal Torah, the blueprint for creation). The *flow* of time began immediately with the existence of the physical world, and the universe as we know it is inseparable from time. The *measurement* of time began (primarily) on the fourth day of creation with the setting of the sun, moon, and other heavenly bodies in orbit. The sun gives us the year, the moon the month, and entire universe gives day and night. We use these heavenly "clocks" as standards of time, subdividing their movements into smaller increments of time, like hours, minutes, and seconds.[2]

Of course, the orbits of the heavenly bodies are only signs of time: clocks that measure time, but not time itself. The length of time measured by a full day, from sunrise to sunrise, existed before the sun was set in orbit. After all, if G-d did not know how long this time was, how could He set the sun to orbit for precisely that long? Our Sages teach that for the first three days of creation, before the sun and moon were set in their orbits, each "day" of creation was equivalent to twenty-four hours. G-d already knew the order of time, which is the real source of measurable time.

Every happening in the universe can be broken down into tiny changes—the very ebb and flow of time. There is a maximum speed limit for these changes. According to current scientific knowledge, the fastest that any change can happen is the speed of light (about 300,000 km per second). We might think of a day as consisting of about 26 billion of these micro changes. The pattern of sunrises and sunsets is merely a clock set to tick 26 billion[3] times per cycle.[4]

Higher than Time in Time

In the process of creation, time began with the "first thought," which is the general concept of what the world will be like. It includes all of time at once. As time progresses down the process of creation, it becomes divided into smaller bits. Kabbalah explains that what to us on earth is a decade, century, or millennium is mere days in the higher spiritual worlds.

In order to understand how this can be—how much time can be fit into a short period—we have to understand some basic concepts of how time (and space) are created. We previously explained that the division of a flow (of energy or of something else) into parts that must come one after the other creates time. This is compared to the inhale-exhale of breathing. Likewise, the flame of a candle takes time to burn because it wants to go up and down at the same time. Its nature is to rise, but its fuel is below, thus it flickers, jumping and returning again and again. This dual process is what makes it take so long for a candle to burn. Were the burning a single process—only rising or only descending—the candle would burn instantly.

The division of time can be compared to a teacher explaining a concept to a student. The teacher understands the entire concept at once, as a single point. However, in order to explain it to a student on a lower level, the teacher divides the concept into parts and stages and explains each one separately. The lower the student, the more everything needs to be explained and laid out in detail, leaving no room for confusion. Therefore, teaching requires dividing an idea into many parts and many words. Yet, a greater student could grasp the same concept—*in its entirety*—in only a few words with only a few steps. Someone on the teacher's level will understand everything with the mention of a single word, such as the name of the concept. To such a colleague, the very definition of the word includes the entire explanation of the concept.

So, too, as time descends level by level through the spiritual worlds in the process of creation, the same original point (of the first thought) is divided into smaller and smaller pieces. For example, in *Malchus* of *Atzilus* it is divided into seven millennia. Each millennium is one division and is called one "day," for this stage can receive an entire millennium at once. From there it divides into each Jubilee cycle of fifty years, then to each *Shmitah* cycle of seven years, then to each Rosh Hashanah, then to each new moon (the Jewish month starts on the new moon), then to each Shabbos (week), then to each day, then to each hour. Each stage receives a portion of G-d's light, which includes a measure of time, but as the light descends it is subdivided into smaller portions, each with its own time.

We find that when a *tzaddik* is elevated to a higher spiritual plane, he can see many years in a moment. For example, our Sages teach that G-d showed Adam all of the generations that would come out from him, with all of history until the end of time.

Likewise, there is a story with the Baal Shem Tov, where he sent a letter to his brother-in-law in Israel, asking him to inform a certain Rabbi that he did such and such as sin and that it was decreed on high that he would die for it unless he returned, and the Baal Shem Tov prescribed a course of repentance. The Baal Shem Tov's brother-in-law wrote back with a question: the letter was received a few days after the sin was performed, which meant that it was sent much earlier. So how did the Baal Shem Tov know, and how could the Heavenly Court prosecute before the event? The Baal Shem Tov answered that he had ascended to the world of *Yetzirah* and that there one can see ten or fifteen years at once. Thus, at that stage it had already happened.

To understand the division of time further, let us use a physical analogy. Imagine ten points arranged in a line like this: [..........]. The points are all laid out in front of you, and you can see them all at once. Now imagine if these points had to pass in a line past a narrow crack in a wall, like this: (you are the "x").

$$\frac{[\,\cdots\cdots\cdots\,]}{X}$$

With this setup, you would only be able to see one dot at a time, and it would take ten units of time to view all ten dots.[5] Here we see how the passage of time is limited according to our ability to receive it.

The same is true with space. For example, when limiting space to one dimension (a line), only one point can correspond to any given point on the line (like this: _._._____._____). Once a point of the line is taken up, no other point can fit there. On the other hand, if another dimension is added, removing some of the limitations, *infinite* points can fit along *any* point of the line. In two dimensions, infinite points can be stacked over a single point of a line, like this: _:_:____:_____. If someone lived in one-dimensional space, it would be unfathomable to fit more than one thing on one point of a line. Similarly, a two-dimensional person could not fathom three-dimensional space. Our view and definition of space is limited only in our own perception and only by our own limitations. Yet, our limits in no way mean that there is any true essential limitation.

Along these lines, our Sages teach that the Ark took up no space in the Holy Temple's Holy of Holies. For even though it had definite dimensions—two and a half, by one and a half cubits—the room retained its full ten cubits of space—five on each side of the Ark. How can more than one object occupy the same space? Simple: just go even *one* dimension higher, and there is no difficulty at all—just like there is no difficulty to fit many things on a single point if they may be stacked. Thus the Ark was a tangible revelation of something beyond our limits of space, as viewed within our limits. These limits are created by G-d, but

G-d transcends them all. Were G-d to allow more of a revelation into the world, the limitations we know would cease.

The Bridge of Time

Time is really an intermediary between the physical dimensions of space and a higher, spiritual reality. Time allows the physical world to contain something beyond it, without bursting the world's limitations and nature. For example, two-dimensional space can be revealed in the world of one-dimensional space in two ways: The one-dimensional people can see a point that really is hovering over their line of space. This point will appear to take up space, but when measured, it won't, similar to the Ark, because it does not rest within the bounds of their line, but is above it. This is a revelation of beyond nature within nature, but this sort of breaks the rules, creating a paradox within one-dimensional space. The other way to reveal a two-dimensional figure in one-dimensional space is to run it through the line. A plane would be viewed line by line in sequence—in other words, it would be revealed in time.

A movie reel works in much the same way. The entire film is present *at once* on the movie reel. The entire movie could be laid out on the ground and viewed at once. However, the movie is *not* viewed this way. Rather it is passed over a narrow opening and viewed only *one frame at a time*. This creates the need for a long time to view the movie and creates the illusion of motion, as the frames change. (The movie reel is like a line, one-dimensional space, being viewed point by point, or in zero-dimensional space.)

This is the purpose of time—to allow something of a greater dimension to exist within a lower dimension, because it exists there bit by bit over time. In this manner, even a three-dimensional figure could be viewed even in zero-dimensional space, point by point, line by line, plane by plane. It would just take a lot of time.[6]

So, too, G-d's intent in creation is to reveal that which is higher than our three-dimensional world *within* the limits of our world. Time bridges this gap. *Chassidus* describes time as the channel between the soul's life and the physical world. When a higher level enters a lower level through the intermediary of time, the lower level becomes animated, moving and changing. Pictures become "animated" when the one-dimensional film enters the zero-dimension by way of the projector's shutter. So, too, when our higher-dimensional soul enters the body, it creates movement and change. This is why life and movement are synonymous. Everything in our world—even a rock—has a soul that enters it, changing it over time. Time bridges the physical and the spiritual.[7]

The ultimate intent for creation is to reveal G-d Himself in our world. Time as we know it reveals higher spiritual realities (the soul) within our limits. Yet, the difference between us and these spiritual realms is only relative. Ultimately, we will experience G-d Himself Who transcends all limitation.

Infinite Time

Now we come to the age-old questions about time, such as: Can it be infinite? Is it continuous or made of units?[8] And so on. In order to answer these questions, some things have to be clarified about number theory: the relationship of the finite to the infinite.

This can be understood in terms of the relationship between points and a line. In the world of points, each point is a single, finite unit. Points can be counted (one point, two points, three points), added, and subtracted. A line is defined by geometry as a series of points. However, this is not entirely true. For a point has *zero* dimensions. That means that it has no length *at all*. Relative to a line, a point is not a one, but rather a *zero*; it is nonexistent in the world of lines. In the world of lines, each line is a single, finite unit. Lines can be counted, added and subtracted, just as points can. These are two distinct dimensions. Points have no existence in the world of lines, because they are nothing in that realm. Likewise, lines have no existence in the world of points: there is no such thing as length in the realm of points, and so there is no possibility for a line's existence, or even the understanding of a line.

Can points be strung together to make a line? Not really, because no matter how many points are added, it is still zero relative to a line. An infinite series of

zeros does not make one. Points simply lack the possibility of entering the world of two dimensions. Even the infinite totality of the world of points does not reach even the smallest line segment. Rather there is a jump, a sort of qualitative leap, between the world of points and the world of lines. Were mathematics made of only zeros, nothing could happen. Placing the number one before a series of zeros is a leap, a new creation, a new number, something that did not exist before. However, once a line exists, every piece of it includes or encompasses *infinite* points. For example, the space between 0 and 1 can be subdivided into infinite parts. Yet, each point between zero and one is itself a zero.[9]

Infinity is infinitely bigger than one million. By the law of symmetry this means that one million is infinitely small relative to infinity. This makes one million dimensionless, like a point to a line. Thus, all finite numbers are like zero and irrelevant to infinite numbers. Finite numbers can only become infinite, such as having an infinite series of numbers or points, when an infinite number (such as a line) descends into the realm of finite numbers (such as points) and makes the finite infinite. For example, when a line descends into the realm of points and is viewed and defined by the limits of points, it creates an infinite series of points. On the other hand, from the point of view of finite numbers, infinity can never be reached. That is, were a person to have the power of adding ones, or even millions, and did so unceasingly, he would never even approach infinity, but remain zero in relation.

Points can never gain length by their own right, but when length—even the smallest length—is defined in terms of points, it creates infinite points. This is because the first dimension is an infinitely higher realm than the zero dimension. Even something finite in the realm of lines, such as a line segment, is completely infinite in the realm of points. So too, any plane or two-dimensional figure is infinite in the realm of lines, and any three-dimensional figure is infinite in the realm of planes. Any physical object that we encounter, no matter how small, includes infinite planes, lines, and points, just because it is in the third dimension.

This is how relative infinities are possible. Two lines are twice as great as one line, and a plane is infinitely greater than a line, yet in the realm of points, two lines, or even a plane, does not have more points than a single line. Once something is in a higher dimension, it encompasses an infinity of the lower dimension. Any addition to this is a function of finite numbers and only has meaning in that realm, such as adding lines. Two lines are twice as great in the realm of lines, but nothing can be added to the realm of points by this. One includes just as many zeros as two does.

So, too, time can be viewed on three levels or dimensions: as finite time, as infinite time, or as infinite time within finite time. If time is viewed as finite, it is a series of points, definite parts and not a continuum. When time and space are viewed this way, time and motion work in increments like the frames of a movie. Space may also be viewed this way (and to be consistent it must be), as existing in definite parts.

On the other hand, if time and space are viewed as infinite, they are a continuum and not a series of points. Rather, each movement and change is a single fluid unit. In this scheme, time and space are like line segments—they are finite in the realm of lines, but infinite to the realm of points, and points have no relevance to their world.

There is also a third way to think of time, when the infinite descends within the finite. This is like how a line encompasses infinite points and creates an infinite series of points when expressed in terms of points. Thus for every infinitely small point of space, there is an infinitely small point of time. This is indeed a paradox, for the mind cannot comprehend this. Here the points take on the quality of a line, which should be impossible, because the points are zeros, they lack any length, so how can length be made of them? The answer is that although points cannot make length of their own accord, and finite numbers can never reach infinity, yet when infinity descends into the finite, the finite is able to become infinite too.

Although such a leap is illogical, nay impossible, when viewed by the standards of the finite, there can still be recognition that this is so and that this is possible for a higher power, not bound by the same limits. In this way, time can be both points and a continuum. Such phenomena are the result of a higher realm interfacing and merging with a lower one. This is [the] purpose of time in general—to bridge a higher realm with a lower, as explained previously.

This is one of the ways that the Infinite Creator is revealed in our world. The fact that matter is infinitely divisible and that time is infinitely divisible and that the world is set in such a way that it can continue forever and that matter cannot be destroyed, all reveal something of G-d's infinity within our finite world. Particularly, the ability to merge the finite with the infinite points to G-d, for only G-d, Who is beyond the limits of both finite and infinite, can merge the two.

And so, very soon, we will experience infinite time, with the coming of Moshiach. That time is described as the "day that is all long," meaning completely infinite time. Furthermore, "all" long implies that its beginning is long like its end. This means that not only will we experience G-d for eternity in an infinite future, we will also retroactively experience Him in an infinite past, extending even before the world was created. For the world is made with an Author, a Book and a Story. And just like a story starts in the middle of a scene with a complete world, so too, our world started in mid-scene. But in the time of Moshiach, G-d will reveal everything to us, including His intent of the past history of the world.[10] And just as G-d is infinite, so too will the revelation of Him in our finite world be infinite, breaking all bounds in all directions and all dimensions.

Based on *Imrei Binah*, chapters 39 and 40; *Derech Mitzvotecha, Emanut Elokut*, chapters 11 and 12; *Derech Emunah (Sefer Hachakirah)*; *Likkutei Sichot*, vol. 10, *Hosofot*, pg. 176; and other sources.
Reprinted with permission of the author.

Endnotes

[1] The essential flow of time can be compared to a screen's frame-rate, or how many times a second it can renew a picture. We don't notice the screen changing, because it is imperceptibly fast. When we see an image moving across a video screen, we are really seeing each pixel change in sequence, which creates the sense of motion. Yet, the fundamental flow of time is really the speed at which the screen can write and re-write each pixel.

[2] Some measures of time have purely spiritual significance. The week matches no natural pattern. Instead, it reminds us of how G-d created the world in six days and rested on the seventh. Similarly, the division into hours corresponds to the permutations of the Divine names—the Tetragrammaton for day and *Adon-ai* for night.

3 Modern physics has an approximate value for what might be the actual smallest unit of time—Planck time. One second would be 1.8 x 10^{43} Planck units. That is a number with 43 zeros. So time seems to be divided into "frames" of length equal to the Planck time, and space divided into "pixels" with dimensions equal to the Planck length.

4 The Rebbe points out that Einstein's Theory of Relativity discusses only measurable time. Every person's "clock" is different, and any two "clocks" will not necessarily agree about when events happened, or even their order. Yet, the actual flow of time for each person remains the same (one second per second), and the speed of change from their reference frame remains the same (the speed of light). Therefore, some of the sensational popular "conclusions" of the Theory of Relativity, such as the idea that time slows down as one approaches the speed of light, are misrepresented. My ability to measure the time (or change) of someone traveling away from me near the speed of light will slow down, but the traveler will experience no slowing of time from his reference frame. It will just take a long time for me to see those changes. Indeed, from his perspective, he is stationary and it is I who speeds away from him, distorting his perception of my time. This is not so different from the Doppler effect, where the sound of a siren seems to slow (decrease in frequency) as a police car speeds away.

5 Nineteen, if you count the spaces in between.

6 Old TV screens worked like this—a beam of electrons was pulled across the screen. The beam was a single point, and it scanned pixel by pixel across the screen and then down row by row. This just happened so fast that to our eye it appeared as a single image.

7 These are the three levels of "*Olam, Shanah, Nefesh*"—World, Time, Soul. Time is the intermediary between World and Soul.

8 Such as Zeno's Paradoxes.

9 A famous question considers whether (the numeral) a decimal point followed by a never-ending sequence of nines (.999 . . .) equals the number 1 or not. The simple answer is that yes, they are equal. Yet, in a way, perhaps the question is flawed. When using whole numbers, it is like we are in the world of lines. Each whole number represents a line, and this can be divided into fractions and decimals. However, an infinite series such as .999 . . . seeks to define a single point, not a line. We have no common representation for an infinite series of zeros followed by a one (.000 . . . 1). Such a series would represent a point. However, this point is infinitely small, and thus has *no* existence or relevance to the world of whole numbers. Asking if .999 . . . equals 1 is like asking if infinity minus one equals infinity, or if a line minus one point is a line. The entire question is wrong, because finite numbers have no relevance to infinite numbers, and points have no relevance to lines. A point is a zero—as it is infinitely small—and adding or subtracting it from a line does nothing. When in the realm of points, there is relevance to points and they can be added or subtracted. However, in the realm of lines, points have no relevance. So too, in general, finite numbers are like zeros to infinite numbers.

10 These potential realities are also "real" because they are a thought of G-d, which is one with Him, and He is the ultimate reality.

Lesson

3

IS GOD REAL?

What are we talking about when we talk about God? Is "God" just a word we use when we can't explain something? If God cannot be explained or described, does this not render the concepts, "knowledge of God," "love of God," or even "belief in God," completely meaningless?

Illustration from the *Hijman Binger Haggadah*, copied and decorated by Hijman (Hayyim ben Mordecai) Binger, parchment, Amsterdam, 1796. (The Braginsky Collection)

QUESTION FOR DISCUSSION

When you say the word "God," what do you mean?

The Art of Weaving: Design and Motifs, jamdani weaving, Dr. Saifur Rashid, Rupganj, Bangladesh, 2017. (ICHCAP Collection, South Korea)

TEXT **1**

MIDRASH TEMURAH, END OF CHAPTER 3

וּמַעֲשֶׂה שֶׁבָּא מִין וְאָמַר לְרַבִּי עֲקִיבָא, הָעוֹלָם הַזֶּה מִי בְּרָאוֹ? אָמַר לֵיהּ, הַקָּדוֹשׁ בָּרוּךְ הוּא. אָמַר לֵיהּ, הַרְאֵינִי דָבָר בָּרוּר . . . אָמַר לֵיהּ מָה אַתָּה לוֹבֵשׁ? אָמַר לֵיהּ, בֶּגֶד. אָמַר לֵיהּ, מִי עֲשָׂאוֹ? אָמַר לֵיהּ, הָאוֹרֵג. אָמַר לֵיהּ, אֵינִי מַאֲמִינְךָ הַרְאֵינִי דָבָר בָּרוּר. אָמַר לֵיהּ, וּמָה אַרְאֶה לְךָ? וְאֵין אַתָּה יוֹדֵעַ שֶׁהָאוֹרֵג עֲשָׂאוֹ? אָמַר לֵיהּ, וְאַתָּה אֵינְךָ יוֹדֵעַ שֶׁהַקָּדוֹשׁ בָּרוּךְ הוּא בָּרָא אֶת עוֹלָמוֹ?

A heretic once came to Rabbi Akiva and asked: "Who created the world?"

Said Rabbi Akiva: "God."

Said the man: "Prove it to me." . . .

Said Rabbi Akiva to him: "What are you wearing?"

Said he: "A robe."

Said Rabbi Akiva: "Who made it?"

Said he: "The weaver."

Said Rabbi Akiva: "I do not believe you. Prove it to me."

Said he: "What is there to prove? Do you not see that it was made by a weaver?"

Said Rabbi Akiva: "Do you not see that the world was made by God?"

MIDRASH TEMURAH

Midrash Temurah is a small *midrash*, attributed to the Tannaim Rabbi Yishmael and Rabbi Akiva. It was first published by Rabbi Chaim Yosef David Azulai, who found it in manuscript form, and appended it to the second part of his *Shem Hagedolim.* This *midrash* is copied in its entirety in the *Sefer Hapardes* (attributed to Rashi's disciples) and also cited by Me'iri (as *"Midrash Temurot"*).

TEXT 2

NACHMANIDES, GLOSSES ON MAIMONIDES'S *SEFER HAMITZVOT,*
NEGATIVE COMMANDMENTS

שֶׁנִּצְטַוִּינוּ מִצְוָה רִאשׁוֹנָה בְּקַבָּלַת מַלְכוּת שָׁמַיִם. כְּלוֹמַר, שֶׁנַּאֲמִין שֶׁיֵּשׁ
אֱלוֹקָהּ פּוֹעֵל כָּל הַנִּמְצָאוֹת, מוֹצִיאָן מֵאַיִן מֻחְלָט אֶל הַיֵּשׁ שֶׁהֵם עָלָיו,
וְאֶל הַיֵּשׁ שֶׁיַּחְפּוֹץ בּוֹ בְּכָל זְמַן מִן הַזְּמַנִּים. וְהוּא שֶׁאָמַר יִתְבָּרֵךְ וְיִתְעַלֶּה:
"אָנֹכִי ה' אֱלֹקֶיךָ...".

**RABBI MOSHE BEN NACHMAN
(NACHMANIDES, RAMBAN) 1194–1270**

Scholar, philosopher, author, and
physician. Nachmanides was born
in Spain and served as leader of
Iberian Jewry. In 1263, he was
summoned by King James of
Aragon to a public disputation with
Pablo Cristiani, a Jewish apostate.
Though Nachmanides was the
clear victor of the debate, he had to
flee Spain because of the resulting
persecution. He moved to Israel and
helped reestablish communal life
in Jerusalem. He authored a classic
commentary on the Pentateuch and
a commentary on the Talmud.

The first mitzvah that we were commanded is to accept
the sovereignty of Heaven. Meaning: To believe that
there is a God who creates all existences, bringing them
forth out of absolute nothingness into whatever state of
being they are in, and into whatever state of being He
desires at any given time. God Himself said this to us [at
Mount Sinai]: "I am God your God. . . ."

TEXT 3

ZOHAR 2:25A

> "וְיַדַעְתֶּם כִּי אֲנִי ה' אֱלֹקֵיכֶם וְגוֹמֵר" (שְׁמוֹת ו,ז). פִּקּוּדָא דָא קַדְמָאָה דְכָל
> פִּקּוּדִין . . . לְמִנְדַּע דְּאִית שַׁלִּיטָא עִלָּאָה, דְּאִיהוּ רִבּוֹן עָלְמָא, וּבְרָא עָלְמִין
> כֻּלְהוּ, שְׁמַיָּא וְאַרְעָא וְכָל חֵילֵיהוֹן.

"You shall know that I am God your God" (EXODUS 6:7). This commandment is primary to all commandments . . . to know that there is a supernal ruler who is the master of the world, who created all worlds—the heavens and the earth and everything in them.

ZOHAR

The seminal work of kabbalah, Jewish mysticism. The *Zohar* is a mystical commentary on the Torah, written in Aramaic and Hebrew. According to the Arizal, the *Zohar* contains the teachings of Rabbi Shimon bar Yocha'i, who lived in the Land of Israel during the second century. The *Zohar* has become one of the indispensable texts of traditional Judaism, alongside and nearly equal in stature to the Mishnah and Talmud.

TEXT 4

RABBI SHNE'UR ZALMAN OF LIADI, *TORAH OHR,* MEGILAT ESTHER 99B

> לֹא זֶהוּ עִיקָר הָאֱלֹקוּת מַה שֶׁהָעוֹלָמוֹת מִתְהַוִּוים מִמֶּנּוּ וּמְקַבְּלִים חַיּוּתָם
> וְשִׁפְעָם מִמֶּנּוּ יִתְבָּרֵךְ. שֶׁהֲרֵי "אַתָּה הוּא עַד שֶׁלֹּא נִבְרָא הָעוֹלָם וּלְאַחַר
> שֶׁנִּבְרָא" בְּשָׁוֶה מַמָּשׁ. וְגַם אִילוּ לֹא הָיָה בּוֹרֵא הָעוֹלָמוֹת הָיָה הַכֹּל שָׁוֶה
> לְפָנָיו יִתְבָּרֵךְ.

The fact that all the worlds are brought into existence by God and receive their vitality and sustenance from Him—this is not the essence of what God is. For as we say, "You are who You are before the world was created, and [You are who You are] after the world was created" (SIDDUR, MORNING PRAYERS)—exactly the same. Also if God would not create the worlds, all would be the same regarding Him.

RABBI SHNE'UR ZALMAN OF LIADI (ALTER REBBE) 1745–1812

Chasidic rebbe, halachic authority, and founder of the Chabad movement. The Alter Rebbe was born in Liozna, Belarus, and was among the principal students of the Magid of Mezeritch. His numerous works include the *Tanya*, an early classic containing the fundamentals of Chabad Chasidism, and *Shulchan Aruch HaRav*, an expanded and reworked code of Jewish law.

TEXT **5**

MAIMONIDES, *COMMENTARY ON THE MISHNAH,*
INTRODUCTION TO CHAPTER *CHELEK*

הַיְסוֹד הָרִאשׁוֹן, לְהַאֲמִין מְצִיאוּת הַבּוֹרֵא יִתְבָּרֵךְ. וְהוּא שֶׁיֵּשׁ שָׁם נִמְצָא
שָׁלֵם בְּכָל דַּרְכֵי הַמְצִיאוּת . . . וְאֵין הָאַחְדוּת וְהָאֲדְנוּת אֶלָּא לוֹ לְבַד
הַשֵּׁם יִתְבָּרֵךְ שְׁמוֹ . . . וְדַי לוֹ בְּעַצְמוֹ, וְאֵין צָרִיךְ בִּמְצִיאוּת זוּלָתוֹ, וְכָל מַה
שֶׁזוּלָתוֹ . . . הַכֹּל צְרִיכִין בִּמְצִיאוּתָם אֵלָיו.

**RABBI MOSHE BEN MAIMON
(MAIMONIDES, RAMBAM) 1135–1204**

Halachist, philosopher, author, and
physician. Maimonides was born in
Córdoba, Spain. After the conquest
of Córdoba by the Almohads, he
fled Spain and eventually settled
in Cairo, Egypt. There, he became
the leader of the Jewish community
and served as court physician to the
vizier of Egypt. He is most noted
for authoring the *Mishneh Torah,* an
encyclopedic arrangement of Jewish
law, and for his philosophical work,
Guide for the Perplexed. His rulings
on Jewish law are integral to the
formation of halachic consensus.

The First Foundation is belief in the existence of the
Creator, blessed be He. Namely, that there is a being
who is perfect in every manner of existence. . . . Only
He possesses true unity and mastery. . . . He is utterly
self-sufficient and does not require the existence of any
other thing, whereas all other existences . . . require Him
in order to exist.

TEXT 6

RABBI YOSEF ALBO, *IKARIM* 1:15

מִן הָעִיקָר הָרִאשׁוֹן שֶׁהוּא בִּמְצִיאוּת הַשֵּׁם, יִסְתַּעֲפוּ מִמֶּנּוּ אַרְבָּעָה שָׁרָשִׁים, כּוֹלְלִים כָּל הַדְּבָרִים הַנִּתְלִים בִּמְצִיאוּת הַשֵּׁם שֶׁהוּא מְחוּיָּב הַמְּצִיאוּת. וְהֵם: הָאַחְדוּת עַל הַדֶּרֶךְ שֶׁכָּתַבְנוּ, וְשֶׁאֵינוֹ גוּף וְלֹא כֹּחַ בַּגּוּף, וְשֶׁאֵין לוֹ הִתְּלוֹת בַּזְּמַן, וְשֶׁהוּא יִתְבָּרֵךְ מְסוּלָּק מִן הַחֶסְרוֹנוֹת.

**RABBI YOSEF ALBO
CA. 1380–1444**

Spanish rabbi and philosopher. A student of Rabbi Chasdai Crescas, Albo is renowned for his philosophical work *Sefer Ha'ikarim* (*Book of Fundamentals*). The work stresses three fundamental aspects of Jewish belief: the existence of God, Torah from Sinai, and reward and punishment.

From the first principle, which is the existence of God, extend four "roots," which include all the truths that are derived from the fact that God's existence is an "absolute existence." These are: the divine unity, as we explained [in the previous chapter]; that God is neither a body nor a bodily force; that God is timeless; and that God has no deficiencies.

TEXT 7

MIDRASH, BEREISHIT RABAH 68:9

רַב הוּנָא בְּשֵׁם רַבִּי אַמִי אָמַר: מִפְּנֵי מָה מְכַנִּין שְׁמוֹ שֶׁל הַקָּדוֹשׁ בָּרוּךְ הוּא וְקוֹרְאִין אוֹתוֹ "מָקוֹם"? שֶׁהוּא מְקוֹמוֹ שֶׁל עוֹלָם, וְאֵין עוֹלָמוֹ מְקוֹמוֹ.

Rav Huna said in the name of Rabbi Ami: Why do we call God by the title *Makom* ("Place")? Because God is the place of the world, whereas the world is not the place of God.

BEREISHIT RABAH

An early rabbinic commentary on the Book of Genesis. This Midrash bears the name of Rabbi Oshiya Rabah (Rabbi Oshiya "the Great"), whose teaching opens this work. This Midrash provides textual exegeses and stories, expounds upon the biblical narrative, and develops and illustrates moral principles. Produced by the sages of the Talmud in the Land of Israel, its use of Aramaic closely resembles that of the Jerusalem Talmud. It was first printed in Constantinople in 1512 together with four other Midrashic works on the other four books of the Pentateuch.

TEXT 8

MAIMONIDES, *MISHNEH TORAH*, LAWS OF THE TORAH'S FOUNDATIONS 1:1–2

(א) יְסוֹד הַיְסוֹדוֹת וְעַמּוּד הַחָכְמוֹת לֵידַע שֶׁיֵּשׁ שָׁם מָצוּי רִאשׁוֹן, וְהוּא מַמְצִיא כָּל נִמְצָא. וְכָל הַנִּמְצָאִים מִשָּׁמַיִם וָאָרֶץ וּמַה שֶׁבֵּינֵיהֶם לֹא נִמְצְאוּ אֶלָּא מֵאֲמִתַּת הִמָּצְאוֹ.

(ב) וְאִם יַעֲלֶה עַל הַדַּעַת שֶׁהוּא אֵינוֹ מָצוּי, אֵין דָּבָר אַחֵר יָכוֹל לְהִמָּצְאוֹת.

(1) The foundation of all foundations and the pillar of all wisdom is to know that there is a primary existence, who brought all existences into being. All the beings of the heavens, the earth, and what is between them came into existence only from the truth of His existence.

(2) Should it arise in the mind that He is not in existence, no other thing could possibly exist.

TEXT 9

YEDAYAH BEN ABRAHAM HAPENINI *(CITED IN IKARIM, 2:30)*

אִלּוּ יְדַעְתִּיו הָיִיתִיו.

If I knew Him, I would be Him.

YEDAYAH BEN ABRAHAM HAPENINI
C. 1270–C. 1340

Poet, physician, philosopher. Yedayah ben Abraham HaPenini was born in Béziers. Among his numerous writings is an ethical work, *Bechinat Olam*, and a philosophical commentary on various *Midrashim*. During the controversy surrounding the study of philosophy, he wrote *Igeret Hitnatzelut* ("Apologetic Letter"), addressed to Rabbi Shlomo ibn Aderet, in defense of philosophical study, and entreating him to withdraw his ban against such study.

A *shiviti* plaque oftentimes hung in synagogues inscribed with verse from Psalm 16:8 "I have set God before me, always" (detail), Menahem Goldberger, Szatmár, Hungary, Ink and paint on paper, c. 1911. (The Jewish Museum, New York)

TEXT **10**

SEFER HACHINUCH, INTRODUCTION

לֵידַע וּלְהַאֲמִין שֶׁיֵּשׁ אֱלוֹקָה.

To know and to believe that there is a God.

SEFER HACHINUCH

13th century, Barcelona, Spain. *Sefer Hachinuch* ("Book of Education") is a compilation of the 613 *mitzvot* (divine commandments) of the Torah, each with a summary of its possible rationales and the basic laws applicable to it. The work was published anonymously; some scholars have identified the author as Rabbi Aharon Halevi of Barcelona (1235–1290), a disciple of Nachmanides, and the author *Bedek Habayit*, an important commentary on the Rashba's halachic code, *Torat Habayit*.

Le Sermon du Daian Cardozo; synagogue d'Amsterdam (Sermon of Dayan Cardozo; Amsterdam synagogue), Edouard Brandon, oil on canvas, 1867. (Walters Art Museum, Baltimore, Md.)

TEXT **11**

TALMUD, BERACHOT 6A

גַּנָּבָא אַפּוּם מַחְתַּרְתָּא רַחֲמָנָא קָרֵי.

The thief at the entrance of his tunnel calls out to God.

BABYLONIAN TALMUD

A literary work of monumental proportions that draws upon the legal, spiritual, intellectual, ethical, and historical traditions of Judaism. The 37 tractates of the Babylonian Talmud contain the teachings of the Jewish sages from the period after the destruction of the Second Temple through the fifth century CE. It has served as the primary vehicle for the transmission of the Oral Law and the education of Jews over the centuries; it is the entry point for all subsequent legal, ethical, and theological Jewish scholarship.

TEXT 12

RABBI YESHAYAH HOROWITZ, *SHENEI LUCHOT HABERIT,*
BE'ASARAH MAAMAROT, 40A

"וְיָדַעְתָּ הַיּוֹם וַהֲשֵׁבֹתָ אֶל לְבָבֶךָ כִּי ה' הוּא הָאֱלֹקִים" (דְּבָרִים ד לט). רְצֶה
לוֹמַר יְדִיעָה בַּלֵּב, בַּהֲשָׂגָה מוֹפְתִית, נוֹסָף עַל הַקַּבָּלָה מִצַּד אֲבוֹתָיו . . .
וְזֶהוּ מְרוּמָז בְּמַה שֶׁכָּתוּב (דִּבְרֵי הַיָּמִים א כח) "דַּע אֶת אֱלֹקֵי אָבִיךָ". רְצֶה
לוֹמַר נוֹסָף עַל מַה שֶׁהוּקְבְּעָה אֱמוּנַת הָאֱלֹקוּת בִּלְבָבְךָ מִצַּד אָבִיךָ, דְּהַיְינוּ
הַקַּבָּלָה אִישׁ מִפִּי אִישׁ, דַּע אַתָּה בְּעַצְמְךָ מִצַּד הַהֲשָׂגָה.

וְזֶהוּ רֶמֶז הַפָּסוּק (שְׁמוֹת טו ב) "זֶה אֵ-לִי וְאַנְוֵהוּ, אֱלֹקֵי אָבִי וַאֲרֹמְמֶנְהוּ."
רְצֶה לוֹמַר: כְּשֶׁזֶּה אֵלִי, שֶׁהוּא אֵ-לִי מִצַּד הַשָּׂגָתִי וִידִיעָתִי, אָז "וְאַנְוֵהוּ"
מִלְשׁוֹן אֲנִי וְהוּא (רַשִׁ"י שַׁבָּת קלג ב דִּיבּוּר הַמַּתְחִיל הֱוֵי דוֹמֶה לוֹ). רְצֶה
לוֹמַר, אֲנִי וְהוּא דְּבוּקִים בְּיַחַד כִּבְיָכוֹל, כִּי הַיְדִיעָה נִתְפֶּסֶת בַּלֵּב. אָמְנָם
כְּשֶׁאֵין לִי הַיְדִיעָה מִצַּד הַהֲשָׂגָה, רַק מִצַּד הַקַּבָּלָה שֶׁהוּא אֱלֹקֵי אָבִי,
אָז "וַאֲרֹמְמֶנְהוּ", כִּי הוּא רָם וְנִשְׂגָּב מִמֶּנִּי, וַאֲנִי מְרוּחָק מֵאִתּוֹ בְּמַצְפּוֹן
הַלֵּב . . .

**RABBI YESHAYAH HALEVI HOROWITZ
(*SHELAH*) 1565–1630**

Kabbalist and author. Rabbi
Horowitz was born in Prague
and served as rabbi in several
prominent Jewish communities,
including Frankfurt am Main and
his native Prague. After the passing
of his wife in 1620, he moved to
Israel. In Tiberias, he completed
his *Shenei Luchot Haberit,* an
encyclopedic compilation of
kabbalistic ideas. He is buried in
Tiberias, next to Maimonides.

"Know today, and bring unto your heart, that God is
the God" (DEUTERONOMY 4:39). That is to say, know
God with an in-depth knowledge, with logical proofs—
in addition to the tradition received from one's forefathers. . . . This is alluded to in the verse (I CHRONICLES
28:9), "Know the God of your fathers." Meaning to say,
in addition to the faith established in your heart by
your "fathers"—by the tradition handed down through
the generations—you should also know by yourself, by
means of your own understanding.

This is also the allusion in the verse (EXODUS 15:2),
"This is my God, and I shall beautify Him; the God of

my fathers, and I shall exalt Him." That is to say: When He is *my* God, due to my knowledge and understanding, then *ve'anvei* ["I shall beautify Him," which can also be read as a combination of the words] *ani vahu*, "I and He," meaning, I and He are bonded together, so to speak, because my knowledge of God is internalized in my heart. However, when I do not possess a knowledge of God that is the product of my understanding, and have only the tradition that He is "the God of my fathers," then "I shall exalt Him"—God remains aloof and elevated from me, and I am distant from Him in the inner recesses of my heart. . . .

TEXT 13

RABBI DOV BER OF MEZERITCH, *MAGID DEVARAV LEYAAKOV,* ADDENDA 26 AND 28

וְזֶהוּ שֶׁבֵּיאֵר הָרַב הַמַּגִיד מִמֶעזְרִיטְשׁ נִשְׁמָתוֹ עֵדֶן מַה שֶׁכָּתוּב וְאָהַבְתָּ אֶת
ה' אֱלֹקֶיךָ וְגוֹמֵר הֲלֹא אַהֲבָה הִיא מִדָּה שֶׁבַּלֵּב, וְאֵיךְ שַׁיָּךְ עִנְיַן הַצִיוּוּי?
דְּמִי שֶׁיֵּשׁ לוֹ אַהֲבָה, הוּא אוֹהֵב. וּמַה יַּעֲשֶׂה מִי אֲשֶׁר חַס וְשָׁלוֹם אֵין
הָאַהֲבָה תְּקוּעַ בְּלִבּוֹ? וְאֵיךְ אוֹמֵר "וְאָהַבְתָּ" לָשׁוֹן צִיוּוּי, כְּאִלּוּ הוּא בַּעַל
בְּחִירָה בָּזֶה?

אֶלָּא שֶׁהַצִיוּוּי הוּא עַל הַהִתְבּוֹנְנוּת הַקָּדוֹם לָהּ בְּפָסוּק "שְׁמַע יִשְׂרָאֵל."
דִּשְׁמַע עִנְיָנוֹ הֲבָנָה, כְּמוֹ "כִּי שׁוֹמֵעַ עַבְדֶּךָ". וְזֶהוּ "וְאָהַבְתָּ" לָשׁוֹן צִיוּוּי,
דְּהַצִיוּוּי הוּא עַל הִתְבּוֹנְנוּת ...

שֶׁפֵּירוּשׁ וְאָהַבְתָּ שֶׁהוּא מִלְּשׁוֹן הַבְטָחָה דְּסוֹפָךְ לָבוֹא לִידֵי אַהֲבָה וְהוּא
עַל יְדֵי הַקְדָּמַת שְׁמַע יִשְׂרָאֵל וְכוּלֵי.

RABBI DOV BER "THE MAGID" OF MEZERITCH
D. 1772

Was the primary disciple and eventual successor of the Baal Shem Tov. Amongst his disciples were the founders of various Chasidic dynasties, including Rabbi Nachum of Chernobyl, Rabbi Levi Yitschak of Berditchev, and Rabbi Shne'ur Zalman of Liadi. His teachings, recorded by his students, appear in various volumes including the *Magid Devarav LeYaakov.*

The Magid of Mezeritch explained the verse (DEUTERONOMY 6:5), "You shall love God your God." Love is a feeling in the heart; so how can it be commanded? One who loves God, loves; but what shall one do if this love is not embedded in his heart, God forbid? How can the Torah say, in the manner of a command, "You shall love," as if the person has a choice in the matter?

But the commandment is regarding the contemplation described in the preceding verse (DEUTERONOMY 6:4), "Hear O Israel, [God is our God, God is one]." The Hebrew word *shema* ("hear") means "understand." . . . This is why it says, "You shall love," as an imperative, and the commandment is to contemplate and understand. . . .

The meaning of "You shall love" can [also] be understood as a promise: You *will* come to love God, when you preface it with [the understanding and contemplation of] "Hear O Israel . . ."

having a relationship with god.

TEXT 14

I CHRONICLES 28:9 ⚏

דַּע אֶת אֱלֹקֵי אָבִיךָ וְעָבְדֵהוּ בְּלֵב שָׁלֵם וּבְנֶפֶשׁ חֲפֵצָה.

Know the God of your fathers, and serve Him with a whole heart and a desirous soul. — *requires knowledge*

Religion is about belief
Judiasm is that + relationships

TEXT 15

RABBI MEIR IBN GABAI, *AVODAT HAKODESH*, 1:8 (AS CITED BY RABBI SHALOM DOVBER
SCHNEERSOHN IN *SEFER HAMAAMARIM* 5657, P. 48)

כְּשֵׁם שֶׁיֵּשׁ לוֹ כֹּחַ בְּבִלְתִּי בַּעַל גְּבוּל, כַּךְ יֵשׁ לוֹ כֹּחַ בְּגְבוּל. שֶׁאִם תֹּאמַר
שֶׁיֵּשׁ לוֹ כֹּחַ בְּבִלְתִּי בַּעַל גְּבוּל וְאֵין לוֹ כֹּחַ בְּגְבוּל, אַתָּה מְחַסֵּר שְׁלֵימוּתוֹ.

Just as God has the power of infinity, so does He have
the power of finiteness. For should you say that He has
the power of infinity but does not have the power of
finiteness, you would be detracting from His perfection.

RABBI MEIR IBN GABAI
1480–AFTER 1540

Kabbalist and author. Ibn Gabai
was born in Spain, from where he
left during the 1492 Expulsion.
Eventually he settled in Egypt.
He authored three books, in
which he elucidates many basic
mystical concepts, and which
have become kabbalistic classics:
Tola'at Yaakov (which he authored
at the age of 26), *Derech Emunah*,
and *Avodat Hakodesh*.

TEXT 16

RABBI YEHUDAH LOEW, *GEVUROT HASHEM, HAKDAMAH* 2

אֲבָל הוּא יִתְבָּרֵךְ שֶׁקְּרָאוּהוּ רַבּוֹתֵינוּ זִכְרוֹנָם לִבְרָכָה בְּשֵׁם הַקָּדוֹשׁ בָּרוּךְ
הוּא . . . שֶׁעִנְיָן "קָדוֹשׁ" נֶאֱמַר עַל מִי שֶׁהוּא נִבְדָּל, כִּי הוּא יִתְבָּרֵךְ פָּשׁוּט
בְּתַכְלִית הַפְּשִׁיטוּת. וּמִזֶּה בְּעַצְמוֹ שֶׁהוּא בְּתַכְלִית הַפְּשִׁיטוּת אֵין דָּבָר
נִבְדָּל מִמֶּנּוּ.

כִּי הַדָּבָר שֶׁיֵּשׁ לוֹ גֶדֶר וּמְיוּחָד בְּדָבָר מַה, בִּשְׁבִיל אוֹתוֹ גֶדֶר, נִבְדָּל מִמֶּנּוּ
דָּבָר שֶׁאֵינוֹ בִּגְדָרוֹ. אֲבָל מִפְּנֵי כִּי הוּא יִתְבָּרֵךְ פָּשׁוּט וְאֵין לוֹ גֶדֶר כְּלָל, אֵין
דָּבָר נִבְדָּל מִמֶּנּוּ. וְאִם כֵּן הוּא יוֹדֵעַ הַכֹּל וְהוּא יָכוֹל הַכֹּל. וְכָל זֶה מִפְּנֵי שֶׁאֵין
לוֹ גֶדֶר יִגְדַּר בְּדָבָר מְיוּחָד. וּבִשְׁבִיל זֶה הַכֹּל נִמְצָא מֵאִתּוֹ גַּם כֵּן.

Be Holy means
✶ Seperate
Yourself from
the mundane!

Our sages, of blessed memory, refer to God as "The Holy
One, Blessed Be He." . . . The term "holy" denotes an
entity that is apart and removed. [It therefore describes
God,] because God is abstract in the most ultimate sense
of abstraction. But precisely because God is the ultimate
abstraction, there is nothing that is excluded from Him.

When something has a definition, and is distinguished by certain characteristics, that same definition will exclude from it things that are outside of that definition. But because God has no definition at all, nothing is excluded from Him. Therefore, He knows everything and can do anything. All this is because God is not defined by any specific definitions; therefore, everything comes from Him.

RABBI YEHUDAH LOEW (MAHARAL OF PRAGUE) 1525–1609
Talmudist and philosopher. Maharal rose to prominence as leader of the famed Jewish community of Prague. He is the author of more than a dozen works of original philosophic thought, including *Tiferet Yisrael* and *Netsach Yisrael*. He also authored *Gur Aryeh*, a supercommentary to Rashi's biblical commentary, and a commentary on the non-legal passages of the Talmud. He is buried in the Old Jewish Cemetery of Prague.

TEXT **17**

GENESIS 1:26

וַיֹּאמֶר אֱלֹקִים נַעֲשֶׂה אָדָם בְּצַלְמֵנוּ כִּדְמוּתֵנוּ.

God said: "Let us make man in our image, after our likeness."

TEXT 18

MIDRASH TEHILIM, 103:3

מַה הַנֶּפֶשׁ מְמַלְאָה אֶת הַגּוּף, כָּךְ הַקָּדוֹשׁ בָּרוּךְ הוּא מְמַלֵּא אֶת עוֹלָמוֹ.

As the soul fills the body, so does God fill His world.

MIDRASH TEHILIM
A rabbinic commentary on the Book of Psalms. Midrash is the designation of a particular genre of rabbinic literature usually forming a running commentary on specific books of the Bible. This particular Midrash provides textual exegeses and develops and illustrates the principles of the Book of Psalms.

TEXT 19

TALMUD, SHABBAT 105A

"אָנֹכִי" נוֹטְרִיקוֹן "אֲנָא נַפְשִׁי כְּתָבִית יְהָבִית".

The word *Anochi* ["I am"—the first word of the Ten Commandments] is an acronym for "I have written and given Myself."

Figure 3.1

White Space: Infinite Potential Forms

Limit + define his
infinate potential

All the finiteness that we see is coming from G-ds infinity.

why → G̲o̲d̲ Choosing to express his infinite self in a specific way. (potential)

Figure 3.2

Did the Word "things" Exist Within the White Space of Figure 3.1?

Not something outside of G-d

The most godly thing We do is creating something from nothing. (pro-creation)

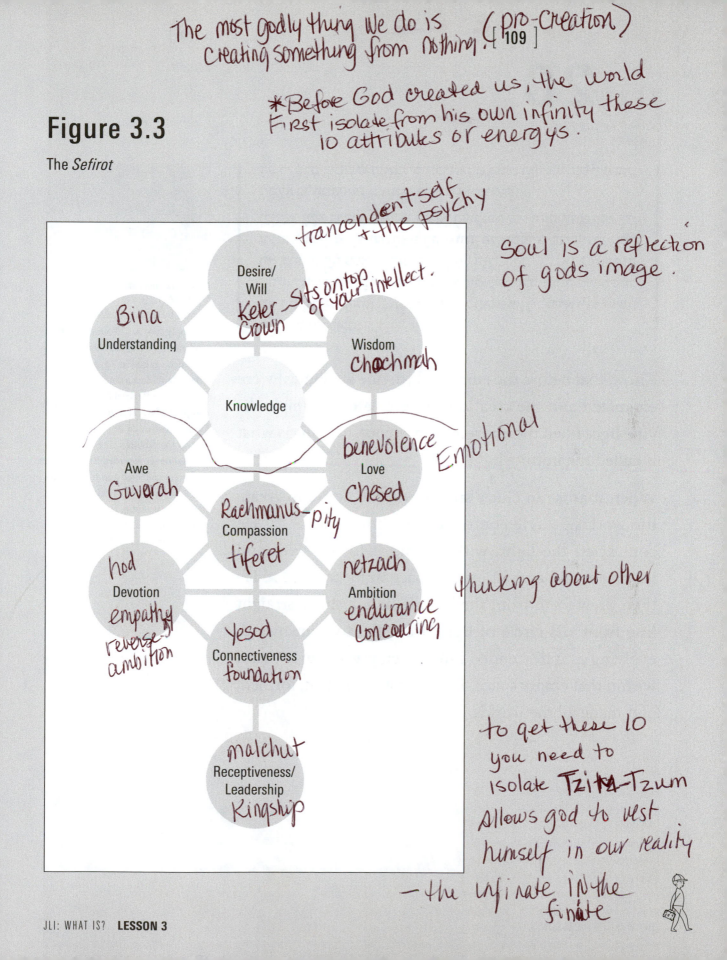

Figure 3.3

The *Sefirot*

*Before God created us, the world First isolate from his own infinity these 10 attribules or energys.

trancendent self + the psychy

Soul is a reflection of gods image.

Bina
Understanding

Desire/Will
Keter - Sits on top of your intellect.
Crown

Wisdom
Chochmah

Knowledge

Awe
Guvarah

benevolence
Love
Chesed
Emotional

Rachmanus - pity
Compassion
tiferet

hod
Devotion
empathy
reverse ambition

netzach
Ambition
endurance
conqueuring
thinking about other

Yesod
Connectiveness
foundation

malchut
Receptiveness/
Leadership
Kingship

to get these 10 you need to isolate Tzita-Tzum Allows god to vest himself in our reality

— the infinate in the finate

[109]

TEXT **20**

RABBI YITSCHAK LURIA, *ETZ CHAYIM* 1:2

דַּע כִּי טֶרֶם שֶׁנֶּאֱצְלוּ הַנֶּאֱצָלִים וְנִבְרְאוּ הַנִּבְרָאִים הָיָה אוֹר עֶלְיוֹן פָּשׁוּט מְמַלֵּא כָּל הַמְּצִיאוּת . . . וְהוּא הַנִּקְרָא אוֹר אֵין סוֹף.

וְכַאֲשֶׁר עָלָה בִּרְצוֹנוֹ הַפָּשׁוּט לִבְרוֹא הָעוֹלָמוֹת . . . וְהִנֵּה אָז צִמְצֵם אֶת עַצְמוֹ אֵין סוֹף . . . וְצִמְצֵם הָאוֹר הַהוּא וְנִתְרַחֵק אֶל צְדָדֵי סְבִיבוֹת הַנְּקוּדָה הָאֶמְצָעִית, וְאָז נִשְׁאַר מָקוֹם פָּנוּי וַאֲוִיר וְחָלָל רֵקָנִי . . . וְאָז הִמְשִׁיךְ מִן אוֹר אֵין סוֹף קַו א' יָשָׁר מִן הָאוֹר הָעָגוּל שֶׁלּוֹ מִלְמַעְלָה לְמַטָּה וּמִשְׁתַּלְשֵׁל וְיוֹרֵד תּוֹךְ הֶחָלָל הַהוּא . . . וּבִמְקוֹם הֶחָלָל הַהוּא הֶאֱצִיל וּבָרָא וְיָצַר וְעָשָׂה כָּל הָעוֹלָמוֹת כֻּלָּם.

RABBI YITSCHAK LURIA
1534–1572

Known by the acronym "Arizal," or simply "the Ari." Founder of the Lurianic school of kabbalah. Born in Jerusalem; raised in Egypt; died in Safed. Rabbi Luria studied Talmud under Rabbi Betsalel Ashkenazi, compiler of the *Shitah Mekubetset*. Despite his youth, he was accepted among the rabbinic elite of Safed. The Ari never recorded his teachings; they were collected and transcribed by his disciples. His leading disciple, Rabbi Chaim Vital, is generally considered the most authoritative recorder of the Arizal's teachings.

Know, that before the emanated [divine attributes] were emanated and the creations were created, a simple divine light filled the entirety of existence. . . . This is what is called the infinite light.

When it arose in God's simple will the desire to create the worlds . . . He contracted His infinite self. . . . He contracted the light, withdrawing it to the sides and leaving a void and an empty space in its center. . . . He then drew forth from the infinite light a single straight line from His circle of light, from the top downward, evolving as it descended into the empty space. . . . And within that empty space, He emanated, created, formed, and made all the worlds.

TEXT **21**

JOB 19:26

גִּמִבְּשָׂרִי אֶחֱזֶה אֱלוֹקַה.

From my flesh I perceive God.

TEXT **22**

PROVERBS 3:6

בְּכָל דְּרָכֶיךָ דָעֵהוּ.

Know Him in all your ways.

TEXT 23

SIDDUR, BEGINNING OF MORNING PRAYERS

אֲדוֹן עוֹלָם אֲשֶׁר מָלַךְ, בְּטֶרֶם כָּל יְצוּר נִבְרָא:
לְעֵת נַעֲשָׂה בְחֶפְצוֹ כֹּל, אֲזַי מֶלֶךְ שְׁמוֹ נִקְרָא:
וְאַחֲרֵי כִּכְלוֹת הַכֹּל, לְבַדּוֹ יִמְלֹךְ נוֹרָא:
וְהוּא הָיָה, וְהוּא הֹוֶה, וְהוּא יִהְיֶה בְּתִפְאָרָה:
וְהוּא אֶחָד וְאֵין שֵׁנִי, לְהַמְשִׁיל לוֹ לְהַחְבִּירָה:
בְּלִי רֵאשִׁית בְּלִי תַכְלִית, וְלוֹ הָעֹז וְהַמִּשְׂרָה:
וְהוּא אֵ-לִי וְחַי גּוֹאֲלִי, וְצוּר חֶבְלִי בְּעֵת צָרָה:
וְהוּא נִסִּי וּמָנוֹס לִי, מְנָת כּוֹסִי בְּיוֹם אֶקְרָא:
בְּיָדוֹ אַפְקִיד רוּחִי, בְּעֵת אִישַׁן וְאָעִירָה:
וְעִם רוּחִי גְוִיָּתִי, ה' לִי וְלֹא אִירָא:

SIDDUR

The siddur is the Jewish prayer book. It was originally developed by the sages of the Great Assembly, and later reconstructed by Rabban Gamliel after the destruction of the Second Temple. Various authorities continued to add prayers, from then until contemporary times. It includes praise of G-d, requests for personal and national needs, selections of the Bible, and much else. Various Jewish communities have slightly different versions of the siddur.

Master of the world
who reigned before any creature was created.

When by His will all things were made
then was His name called King

After all shall cease to be
the Awesome One shall reign alone.

He was, He is
and He shall be; in glory

He is one; there is no second
to compare with Him, or to be joined.

Without beginning, without end
might and dominion are His.

He is my God, my living redeemer
my rock and lot in times of distress.

He is my banner and my refuge
my portion, my cup, on the day I call.

In His hand I entrust my soul
when I sleep and when I awake.

With my soul and body
God is for me, I shall not fear.

QUESTIONS FOR DISCUSSION

1 Where does the first part end, and the second part begin?

2 What is the essential message of the first part?

3 What is the essential message of the second part?

KEY POINTS

1 The Torah instructs us to not only believe in God, but also to know and love God. This indicates that God is real in a way that is comprehensible to us, and challenges us to seek ways to understand God's reality.

2 Our understanding of who and what God is begins with the knowledge that God is the creator and master of our existence. Yet "Creator" is only a role that God chooses to assume, not what God is in essence.

3 God is described as the most absolute and perfect existence. Yet the very notions of "existence" and "reality" were created by God. "Absolute Existence" is also a role that God chooses to assume, rather than what God is in essence.

4 This presents the following paradox: If the term "God" has logical meaning, that's not God. But if there is nothing logical or intelligible that we can say or even contemplate about God, in what sense are we enjoined to "know God"?

5 The key to resolving this paradox lies in the understanding that true infinity excludes nothing—not even finiteness. If God is truly infinite and undefinable, He also possesses "the power of of finiteness"—the capacity to express Himself in any form or formula He desires.

6   God could have created a world that has nothing of Himself in it. But then God would be beyond our reality, precluding us from having any knowledge of God or any relationship with Him. So God chose to create our world as an act of *tsimtsum* ("constriction"). This means that God isolated the primary definitions of our reality from within His own infinite self-expression, and constructed the underlying truths of our existence out of these *sefirot*, or "divine attributes."

7   This is why we are able to describe God as "good," "compassionate," "wise," "creator," "all-powerful," and similar terms that have meaning to us. In doing so, we are not projecting truths from our own existence unto God. Rather, we are recognizing that our own reality contains certain divine self-expressions, which God chose to extract from His own undefinable reality and invest in our existence.

Additional Readings

ANTHROPOMORPHISM AND METAPHORS

BY RABBI JACOB IMMANUEL SCHOCHET

1. Anthropomorphism

The terminology of Kabbalah and Chassidism, and thus in the expositions following, is highly anthropomorphic. The terms are borrowed from human concepts and the empirical world. The reason is because these are the only type of words that man can use in any meaningful way. The forms of spatial-temporal concepts are imposed upon the mind of man who lives in a spatial-temporal world.

It is for this very reason that the Torah, the Prophets, and our Sages use anthropomorphic language, as it is stated, "'The Torah speaks in the language of man.'"[1] For

> "Had they limited themselves to abstract terms and concepts appropriate to G-d, we would have understood neither the terms nor the concepts. The words and ideas used have accordingly to be such as are adapted to the hearer's mental capacity so that the subject would first sink into his mind in the corporeal sense in which the concrete terms are understood. Then we can proceed to an understanding that the presentation is only approximate and metaphorical, and that the reality is too subtle, too exalted and remote for us to comprehend its subtlety.

RABBI JACOB IMMANUEL SCHOCHET, PHD, 1935–2013

Torah scholar and philosopher. Rabbi Schochet was born in Switzerland. Rabbi Schochet was a renowned authority on kabbalah and Jewish law and authored more than 30 books on Jewish philosophy and mysticism. He also served as professor of philosophy at Humber College in Toronto, Canada. Rabbi Schochet was a member of the executive committee of the Rabbinical Alliance of America and of the Central Committee of Chabad-Lubavitch Rabbis and served as the halachic guide for the Rohr Jewish Learning Institute.

> "The wise thinker will endeavor to strip the husk of the terms (i.e., their materialistic meaning) from the kernel, and will raise his conception step-by-step until he will at last attain to as much knowledge of the truth as his intellect is capable of apprehending."[2]

Thus it is to be kept it mind at all times that the terms and concepts need to be stripped of all and any temporal, spatial and corporeal connotations. All and any anthropomorphic notions and concepts, strictly speaking, are non-ascribable to the Divinity, as Scripture states explicitly: "To whom then will you liken G-d? Or what likeness will you compare to Him? . . . To whom will you liken Me that I should be equal, says the Holy One" (Isaiah 40:18, 25).

This cardinal premise was adopted by Maimonides as the third in his compilation of the "Thirteen Fundamental Principles of Faith."[3]

At the same time, however, it should also be noted that the anthropomorphic terminology used in Scripture, by the mystics and by others, is not arbitrary just because it is under the protection of the above qualification. Rather, these terms are carefully chosen and possess a profound meaning.

The Rabbinic-Midrashic and mystical writings abound with references to the idea that the world below in general, and man in particular, are created in the "image" of the "world above."[4] All the categories to be found in the world below and in man are homonymous representations of, and allusions to, certain supernal concepts and notions *to which they correspond.*

To be sure, there is no likeness whatever between G-d and the creation, and on the supernal levels of the strictly spiritual realm there are no such things as eyes, ears, hands, and so on, nor such activities and affections as hearing, seeing, walking, talking and so on. However, all these spatial-temporal activities and concepts do symbolize, and, indeed, for *that reason come into being in correspondence to* the original supernal, strictly and purely spiritual, categories.

In a widely-quoted passage, R. Joseph Gikatilla aptly explains this correspondence-relationship by means of the following analogy. When writing the name of a person on a piece of paper, there *is* surely no likeness, link or relationship between the written letters or words on paper and the physio-mental entity of the person whose name has been recorded. Even so, that writing is a symbol or sign relating to, calling to mind and denoting the full concrete entity of that person.

Thus it is with the anthropomorphic and anthropopathic concepts and terms: There is no concrete or direct link or likeness between them and the meanings they seek to express, but nonetheless, they are corresponding signs and symbols relating to, and denoting, specific categories, notions and concepts that are of a strictly spiritual nature, non-spatial and non-temporal."[5]

This, then, is the way the anthropomorphic terminology is to be understood.[6]

2. The Man-Metaphor

In discussing Divinity relative to the Universe, the favourite metaphor of the mystics (as of many philosophers) is the analogy to man. Theological concepts and the G-d-world relationship are often explained in terms of the soul-body relationship, and in particular in terms of the various soul-powers, their faculties, functions and manifestations.

The "proof-texts" for this usage are the verse "From my flesh I envisage G-d" (Job 19:26) and the Rabbinic analogy "Just as the soul permeates the whole body . . . sees but is not seen . . . sustains the whole body . . . is pure . . . abides in the innermost precincts . . . is unique in the body . . . does not eat and does not drink . . . no man knows where its place is . . . so the Holy One, Blessed is He."[7] This, too, in a sense, follows on the above-mentioned principle of a "terrestrial-supernal correspondence."[8]

But even while an understanding of the soul is helpful in understanding matters relating to the Divinity, this is but an anthropomorphic approximation which cannot be carried too far and needs to be qualified. It must be remembered, as R. Schneur Zalman points out, that in some respects the analogy breaks down, and is completely inadequate:

"This parallel is only to appease the ear. In truth, however, the analogy has no similarity whatever to the object of comparison. For the human soul . . . is affected by the accidents of the body and its pain . . . while the Holy One, blessed is He, *is* not, Heaven forbid, affected by the accidents of the world and its changes, nor by the world itself; they do not effect any change in Him. . . ."[9]

Also, "The soul and the body are actually distinct, one from the other, in their very sources, for the source of the body and its essence does not come into being from the soul. . . ."[10] Thus while the body may be fully subordinate to the soul, they are nevertheless two distinct entities. In contrast, "in relation to The Holy One, blessed is He, who brings everything into existence *ex nihilo,* everything is absolutely nullified, just as the light of the sun is nullified in the sun itself."[11]

3. The Light-Metaphor

Just as the soul provides a favourite metaphor, so we find that the term "light" is favoured by the mystics to describe the various emanations and manifestations of the Divinity.[12] This term is carefully chosen for a number of reasons. R. Joseph Albo sees in it the following advantages that may analogously be related to G-d:

a. The existence of light cannot be denied.
b. Light is not a corporeal thing.
c. Light causes the faculty of sight and the visible colours to pass from potentiality to actuality.
d. Light delights the soul.
e. One who has never seen a luminous body in his life cannot conceive colours nor the agreeableness and delightfulness of light.
f. And even he who has seen luminous objects cannot endure to gaze upon an intense light, and if

he insists upon gazing beyond his power of endurance his eyes become dim so that he cannot see thereafter even that which is normally visible.

By possessing all these qualities, light bears a greater similarity to the things which are free from matter than anything else to which such things may be compared, and hence they are compared to light so as to make the matter intelligible.[13]

Likewise, R. Joseph Ergas lists the following advantages:[14] (a) Light is the most subtle and tenuous of all sense-perceptions.[15] (b) Light has numerous qualities characteristic of the Divine emanations, as, for example:

a. Light is emitted from the luminary without ever becoming separated from it. Even when its source is concealed or removed, thus no longer emitting perceptible light, the previous rays do not remain entities separate from the luminary but are withdrawn with it. This is a unique quality of light which is not shared with any other substance.

b. Light spreads itself instantaneously.

c. Light irradiates all physical objects and is able to penetrate unhindered all transparent objects.

d. Light does not mix and mingle with another substance.

e. Light per se never changes. The perception of more or less intense light, or of differently coloured lights, is not due to any change in the light per se but is due to external factors.

f. Light is essential to life in general.

g. Light is received and absorbed relative to the capacities of the recipient; and so on.[16]

But here again, this term is only an homonymous approximation, used by way of metaphor and analogy. It is not to be taken in its full, literal sense. R. Joseph Albo already cautions that "No error should be made to the effect that intellectual light is something emanating from a corporeal object like sensible light"[17] R. Moses Cordovero is still more emphatic in warning that this metaphor must not be carried too far "For there is no image whatever that can be imagined that is not corporeal."[18]

Indeed, R. Menachem Mendel of Lubavitch shows how, in some respects, this analogy, too, evidently breaks down and is inadequate. For example, the emittance of perceptible light from its source is automatic and intrinsically necessary: the luminary cannot withhold the light. Needless to say that this restrictive quality cannot be ascribed to the emanations of the Omnipotent.[19]

In conclusion, then, as the mystics never tire to say, it cannot be mentioned too often or stressed too much that all terms and concepts related to the Divinity must be stripped of all and any temporal, spatial and corporeal connotations and must be understood in a strictly spiritual sense.

From Jacob Immanuel Schochet, *Mystical Concepts in Chabad Chassidism: An Introduction to Kabbalistic Concepts and Doctrines* (Brooklyn, NY: Kehot Publication Society, 1988), reprinted with permission from the publisher.

Endnotes

[1] *Berachot* 31b; *Mechilta*, and *Tanchuma*, on *Exodus* 15:7 and 19:18; *Sifra* on *Levit.* 20:2.

[2] R. Bachya ibn Pakuda, *Chovot Halevovot, Sha'ar Hayichud:* ch. 10. Cf. *Otzar Hageonim, Berachot,* Responsa no. 357 (I: p. 131), and Comment, no. 271 (II: p. 92); R. Judah Halevi, *Kuzari* IV:5; Maimonides, *Hilchot Yesodei Hatorah* I:7–12, and *Moreh Nevuchim* I:26, 33, *35f.* and 46; *Tanya* II:10.

[3] *Commentary on Mishnah, Sanhedrin,* Intr. to ch. 10. Cf. *Hilchot Teshuvah* III:7; *Moreh Nevuchim* I:36 (and the references to Maimonides, *supra,* note 2).

[4] *Midrash Tanchuma,* Pekudei: 3; *Avot de R. Nathan,* ch. 31; *Eccles. Rabba* I:4; *Zohar* I:38a, 140a, 205b; *ibid.* II:20a, 48b, 75bf.; *ibid.* III:65b, 117a; *et passim.* See also *Chovot Halevovot,* l: ch. 10, and II: ch. 2, 3 and 5. (Most of these sources are quoted in the discussion of the "correspondence-theory" in J. l. Schochet, "*The Psychological System of R. Schneur Zalman of Liadi*" parts I and II, *Di Yiddishe Heim,* vol. XI (New York 1970), nos. 3–4.)

[5] *Sha'arei Orah,* Sha'ar I (ed. Warsaw 1883, p. 2b). Cf. R. Solomon ibn Aderet, *Chidushei Harashba al Agadot Hashass,* on *Bava Batra* 74b (Jerusalem 1966, p. 90). For a fuller discussion of the mystics' view of anthropomorphisms see R. Meir ibn Gabbai, *Avodat Hakodesh,* part III, esp. ch. 26ff. and ch. 65; R. Moses Cordovero, *Pardes Rimonim,* sect. XXII (*Sha'ar Hakinuyim*), esp. ch. 2; R. Isaiah Horowitz, *Shenei Luchot Habrit, Toldot Adam: Bayit Neeman;* (all of which quote R. Joseph Gikatilla). In addition, the whole of R. Moses Cordovero's *Shi'ur Komah* is devoted to this topic. See also R. Joseph Ergas, *Shomer Emunim* 1:24f.

R. Isaiah Horowitz (*ad loc. cit.,* p. 10d) makes the interesting point that strictly speaking it is not that "the Torah speaks in the language of man," but—in accordance with the aforesaid—exactly the other way around, because all terrestrial concepts are allusions to supernal ones! *Cf. Peri Etz Chayim, Sha'ar Hakorbanot*, ch. 6, *s.v. Berayta de R. Yishmael; Likutei Sichot*, vol. II, p. 363f.

6 This should be remembered with particular regard to the so-called "erotic" concepts and symbolisms, like the frequent occurrence of terms as "masculine" and "feminine," and "conjunctio," and so on. In general these denote the aspects of the active, emanating (influencing) category and the passive, receiving qualities and categories, the mode or form of emanation-reception, and so forth (see *Igeret Hakodesh*, sect. XV, note 9). "The whole universe functions according to the principium of masculine and feminine" (R. Chayim Vital, *Etz Chayim* 11:6). "There are four principles: masculine and feminine (זו"ן); Judgment (*Din*) and compassion (*Rachamim);* upper and lower; influencer or emanator (*Mashpia*) and influenced (*Mushpa';* also called *Mekabel*—recipient). As a rule, the masculine corresponds to compassion, upper and emanator; and the feminine corresponds to judgment, lower and recipient; idem" *Peri Etz Chayim, Hakdamah* II: end of *Derush* 2 (ed. Tel Aviv 1966, p. 13a), and *"Olat Tamid,"* beg. of *Sha'ar Hatefillah (ed.* Tel Aviv 1963, p. 2a).

Actually, such terminology is not uniquely Kabbalistic. It may be found in the Talmudic writings—

[*Bava Batra* 74b: "All that the Holy One, blessed is He, created in His world, He created male and female"; see the commentaries *ad loc.*, and esp. *Chidushei Harashba al Agadot Hashass, op. cit.*, pp. 91*ff.*, quoted at length by R. Jacob ibn Chabib in his *Hakotev* on *Ayin Ya'akov* as well as in the philosophical literature [e.g., *Moreh Nevuchim*, Introduction, and *ibid.*, l: ch. 6 and 17, and III: ch. 8 and 12].

R. Schneur Zalman explains at length why the mystics purposely chose such delicate and seemingly peculiar terminology; see *Likutei Torah* V:9a, and *Biurei Hazohar*, ed. R. Dov Ber of Lubavitch (New York, 1955), Noach: pp. 6a*ff.* The earlier mystics, too, elaborate on the usage of these particular concepts; see *Pardes Rimonim* XXII:1; *Shi'ur Komah*, ch. 18; *Shenei Luchot Habrit, ad loc. cit.* (p. 8d*f.);* *Shomer Emunim* I:26f.

7 *Berachot* 10a; *Midrash Tehillim (ed.* Buber) 103:4, 5 (see notes *ad loc.*); *Tikunei Zohar* 13:28a. See *Shomer Emunim* II:9; *Igeret Hakodesh*, beg. of sect. XV, and sect. XXV and XXIX.

8 See references *supra*, note 4.

9 *Tanya*, I, ch. 42.

10 *Ibid.*, ll:6.

11 *Ibid.* See at length R. Menachem Mendel of Lubavitch, *Sefer Hachakirah* 1:8 (New York 1955, pp. 7b–8b and 26a-b). *Cf. infra*, ch. 2, note 18, and ch. 3, end of section 4.

12 This metaphor, too, like the previous one, abounds in the Talmudic-Midrashic and mediaeval-philosophic writings; see, e.g., *Berachot* 17a, 64a and so forth (the concept of *Ziv Hashechinah;* the radiation of the *Shechinah); Sifre*, and *Midrashim*, on *Numbers* 6:25; *Pirkei de R. Eliezer*, ch. 3; *Levit. Rabba*, ch. 31 (esp. par. 6); *Numbers Rabba* 15:5; etc. See further R. Sa'adiah Gaon, *Emunot Vede'ot* III:10; *Kuzari* II:7--8 and III:17, and especially IV:3; *Moreh Nevuchim* I, ends of ch. 5, 19 and 25, and *ibid.*, ch. 76; also, R. Moses Narboni, *Commentary on Moreh Nevuchim* I:35; and so on. In general, though, the philosophical works use mostly the term *shefa'* (effluence; emanation} rather than *or;* see more on that in R. Menachem Mendel of Lubavitch, *Derech Mitzvotecha, Haamanat Elokut:* ch. 5 (New York, 1956, p. 50b*f.).*

The mystics have a special affinity for the term *Or* because its numerical value (*gimatriya*) is equivalent to that of *raz* (mystery): "'Let there be light' (Gen. 1:3)—i.e., let there be *Raz* (Mystery; Concealment); for *Raz* and *Or* are one thing"; *Zohar* I:140a and *Zohar Chadash*, Bereishit: 8d; see *Tikunei Zohar* 21:53b, and *cf.* R. Moses Cordovero, *Or Ne'erav* (Fuerth, 1701), III: ch. 4.

13 *Ikkarim* II:29.

14 *Shomer Emunim* II:11.

15 *Cf. Kuzari* IV:3: "The noblest and finest of all material things. . . ."

16 *Cf. Tanya* I, ch. 52, and *ibid.*, II:10. See also R. Schneur Zalman, *Torah Or*, Vayakhel: 87a–b, and *Siddur 'im Perush Hamilot*, pp. 48a*ff.* and 164c*ff.*

Obviously this "descriptive analysis" of light is based on the general human perception—the sense-perception—of it, while an exact "scientific analysis" is not really relevant to our purposes. Apart from the fact that this metaphor is qualified in any case (as we shall see), they are the *empirical perceptions* that make the use of this analogy so attractive and helpful in our context.

17 *Ikkarim, ad loc. cit.;* see there at length.

18 R. Moses Cordovero, *Elima Rabbati*, l:i:9 (p. 4h). See also *Emunot Vede'ot* I:3 and II:2 with regard to light being an accident (as opposed to substance) and having a limit and boundary.

19 *Derech Mitzvotecha, ad loc. cit. (supra*, note 12). See also *Shi'ur Komah*, ch. 3–4.

WHAT IS G-D?
THE NOT-THING

BY RABBI TZVI FREEMAN

Question

Somewhere along the way, I misplaced G-d. The other day I realized that I hadn't seen G-d in quite a while—probably not since childhood. And it's not just that I can't find G-d—I also seem to have lost my sense of *what* G-d is. . . . Why did this happen? If I had Him when I was a child, why shouldn't I have Him now?

Answer

You've got one clue, but you missed the other. It has to do with your language. Call it "thing-fixation."

That's probably the main disaster of your childhood—not being weaned, not leaving behind Pampers for underpants, not sitting in a desk in first grade—but when you learned about *things*.

I don't mean, "you learned about things of the world." I mean, you learned the idea of things. You learned that the world is made of stuff, objects, material goomp that's just "out there." Later in life, you started running after those things, accumulating them, amassing more and more mounds of things to fill your home, your backyard, and your driveway. By now, the entire world has been reduced in your mind to nothing but a mass junkyard of thingy stuff. So even G-d gets defined as a thing—and you're trying to find the place where He fits. Because, after all, all *things* fit in places.

When you woke up to life as a small child, it wasn't like that. There were no things. There was just the experience of being. Of sensing, of living, of breathing

RABBI TZVI FREEMAN, 1955–

Rabbi, computer scientist, and writer. A published expert, consultant, and lecturer in the field of educational technology, Rabbi Freeman held posts at the University of British Columbia and the Digipen School of Computer Gaming. Rabbi Freeman is the author of *Bringing Heaven Down to Earth* and *Men, Women & Kabbalah*. He is a senior editor at Chabad.org.

and doing. Screaming, nursing, burping. Those were all real. Those are life. Things are not real. Things are fiction. They don't exist. We made them up.

The Birth of Thinginess

How did things come to be? Here's my take on it.

In the beginning, there were no things. All of humankind knew life as does a small child, even as they grew older and wiser. But then someone got it into his head to draw pictures of all the stuff he had. Eventually, pictures became glyphs, a nifty device for esoteric communication. Glyph-lovers—such as the cult-priests of ancient Egypt—created thousands of glyphs to represent all the stuff Pharaoh was accumulating. Soon the idea seeped into the spoken language, as well: the idea of a "thing"—a static snapshot of a distinct whateveritis in a frozen moment of time. Stuff was born. And the world was never again the same.

Evidence? Because in ancient, biblical Hebrew, there is no word for stuff. Or thing. Or object, or anything similar. In raw, primal Hebrew, you don't say, "Hey, where's that thing I put over here?" You say, "Where is the *desired* (*chefetz*) that I put here?" You don't say, "What's that thing?"—you say, "What's that *word*?" That's the closest you can get to the idea of thing: a word. All of reality is made of words. Look in the creation story: The whole of heaven and earth is nothing but words.

In languages like English, nouns are the masters and verbs are their slaves, with adjectives and associated forms dancing about to serve them. In Hebrew, verbs rule. *Big, little, wise, foolish, king, priest, eye, ear*—all of these sound like things, but in Hebrew they are forms of verbs. In fact, according to Rabbi Yeshayahu Horowitz (1560?–1630), author of the classic *Shnei Luchot HaBrit*, everything in Hebrew is really a verb. Everything is an event, a happening, a process—flowing, moving, never static. Just like when you were a small child.[1]

In Hebrew, there is not even a present-tense. There are participles, but the idea of a present tense only arose later. In real Hebrew, nothing ever *is*—all is movement.

That fits, because Hebrew was not written in glyphs. Hebrew was the first language we know of to be written with symbols that represent sounds, not things. With the Hebrew alphabet—the mother of all alphabets—you don't see *things*, you see sounds. Even the process of reading is different: when you read glyphs, the order doesn't matter so much. You just sort of look and everything is there. Even modern Chinese glyphs can be written in any direction. With an alphabet, sequence is everything. Nothing has meaning standing on its own. Everything is in the flow.

Get the Flow

The flow is real. Things are not real. Ask a physicist: the more we examine stuff—what they call *matter*—we see that it's not there. All that's really there is events: waves, vibrations, fields of energy. Life is a concert, not a museum.

Think of writing music, as opposed to painting a portrait. The portrait artist stands back and beholds his art, his still rendition of a frozen moment—and he beholds it all at once. Then he politely asks his model to please return to the pose of that which has now become the prime reality, the portrait. A portrait of that which is but never was.

A composer of music cannot do this. You can't freeze a moment of music—it vanishes as soon as you attempt to do so. Like the fictional stuff they call matter: Frozen to absolute zero, without energy, without movement, it no longer exists. Because, in truth, all that exists is the flow of being.

The Name

The flow of being: now you have found G-d. In fact, in Hebrew, that's His name. G-d's name is a series of four letters that express all forms of the verb of all verbs, the verb *to be*: is, was, being, will be, about to be, causing to be, should be—all of these are in those four letters of G-d's name. As G-d told Moses when he asked for His name, "I will be that which I will be."

In our modern languages that doesn't work. We quickly slip into the trap of thingness again. Who is G-d? We answer, "He is One who was, is, and will be."

There we go with the "thing that is" business again. No, G-d is not a *thing* that is or was or will be. G-d is *isness* itself. Oy! The frustration of the language. We need new words: Ising. Isness. Isingness. Isifying. Isifier. In Hebrew you can conjugate the verb *to be* in all these ways and more. Perhaps in English one day we will do the same. Until then, we are like artists using pastels to imitate Rembrandt; like musicians trying to play middle-eastern strains in tempered C Major.

And the proof: We ask questions that make sense only in English, but in Hebrew are plainly absurd. Such as, "Does G-d exist?" In Hebrew, that's a tautology, somewhat the equivalent of "Does existence exist?"

There is no need to "believe" in this G-d—if you know what we are talking about, you just know. You will know, also, that there is nothing else but this G-d—what is there that stands outside isness?

As for faith and belief, those are reserved for greater things. Like believing that this great Isness that isifies all that ises cares, knows, has compassion, can be related to. In other words, saying that reality is a caring experience. Which reduces to saying that compassion is real, purpose is real, life is real. That's something you have to believe. But G-d's existence—like most ideas that men argue about—that's just a matter of semantics.

Think simple: You wake up in the morning and, even before coffee, *there is*. Reality. Existence. Not "the things that exist," but existence itself. The flow. The infinite flow of light and energy. Of being, of existence. Of *is*. Think of all that flow of isingness all in a single, perfectly simple point. Get into it, commune with it, speak to it, become one with it—that is G-d.

Reprinted with permission from Chabad.org.

Endnote
1 *Shnei Luchot HaBrit, Toldot Adam, Bayit Acharon* 12.

Lesson

4

IS EVIL REAL?

Why do bad things happen to good people? The question has been asked—and answered—for thousands of years. But even if we understood the purpose of evil, would this make it more palatable and acceptable? Would it aid us in our efforts to defeat evil?

Darkness (detail), Thomas Danaher, lithograph, c. 1939.
(The National Gallery of Art, Washington, D.C.)

Figure 4.1

The Problem of "Theodicy"

THREE TRUTHS ABOUT GOD

God is good.
God is all-knowing.
God is all-powerful.

TEXT 1

NACHMANIDES, *COMMENTARY ON THE TORAH*, GENESIS 1:1

וְאָמַר "אֱלֹקִים", בַּעַל הַכֹּחוֹת כֻּלָם. כִּי הַמִּלָה עִיקָרָה "אֵל", שֶׁהוּא כֹּחַ . . . כְּלוֹמַר כֹּחַ הַכֹּחוֹת כּוּלָם.

The Torah's word for "God," *Elokim*, means "the possessor of all powers." The root of the word is *el*, meaning "power". . . . Thus [*Elokim*] means: the power of all powers.

RABBI MOSHE BEN NACHMAN (NACHMANIDES, RAMBAN) 1194–1270

Scholar, philosopher, author, and physician. Nachmanides was born in Spain and served as leader of Iberian Jewry. In 1263, he was summoned by King James of Aragon to a public disputation with Pablo Cristiani, a Jewish apostate. Though Nachmanides was the clear victor of the debate, he had to flee Spain because of the resulting persecution. He moved to Israel and helped reestablish communal life in Jerusalem. He authored a classic commentary on the Pentateuch and a commentary on the Talmud.

TEXT 2

PROVERBS 15:3

בְּכָל מָקוֹם עֵינֵי ה' צֹפוֹת רָעִים וְטוֹבִים

The eyes of God are everywhere, observing the bad and the good.

Aggression III (detail), Mikalojus Povilas Vilutis, silkscreen, Lithuania, 1979. (Modern Art Center, Vilnius, Lithuania)

TEXT 3

MAIMONIDES, *COMMENTARY ON THE MISHNAH,*
INTRODUCTION TO CHAPTER *CHELEK*

הַיְסוֹד הָעֲשִׂירִי, כִּי הוּא הַשֵּׁם יִתְבָּרֵךְ יוֹדֵעַ מַעֲשֵׂיהֶם שֶׁל בְּנֵי אָדָם, וְאֵינוּ
מַעֲלִים עֵינוֹ מֵהֶם, לֹא כְּדַעַת מִי שֶׁאָמַר "עָזַב ה' אֶת הָאָרֶץ". אֶלָּא כְּמוֹ
שֶׁנֶּאֱמַר (יִרְמְיָהוּ לב, יט): "גְּדֹל הָעֵצָה וְרַב הָעֲלִילִיָ-ה אֲשֶׁר עֵינֶיךָ פְקֻחוֹת
עַל כָּל דַּרְכֵי בְּנֵי אָדָם וְגו'"

**RABBI MOSHE BEN MAIMON
(MAIMONIDES, RAMBAM) 1135–1204**

The Tenth Foundation is that God knows the deeds of man and pays attention to them, in contrast to those who say, "God has forsaken the world." Rather, as it is written (JEREMIAH 32:19), "[You, God,] who is great in counsel and mighty in work; for Your eyes are open to all the ways of mankind [to give each one according to their ways, and according to the fruit of their doings]."

Halachist, philosopher, author, and physician. Maimonides was born in Córdoba, Spain. After the conquest of Córdoba by the Almohads, he fled Spain and eventually settled in Cairo, Egypt. There, he became the leader of the Jewish community and served as court physician to the vizier of Egypt. He is most noted for authoring the *Mishneh Torah,* an encyclopedic arrangement of Jewish law, and for his philosophical work, *Guide for the Perplexed.* His rulings on Jewish law are integral to the formation of halachic consensus.

TEXT **4**

PSALMS 145:9, 17

טוֹב ה' לַכֹּל, וְרַחֲמָיו עַל כָּל מַעֲשָׂיו . . .
צַדִּיק ה' בְּכָל דְּרָכָיו, וְחָסִיד בְּכָל מַעֲשָׂיו.

God is good to all, and His compassion is upon all His creations. . . . God is just in all His ways, and benevolent in all His deeds.

Cornucopia of Fruit, Mabel S. Kelton, watercolor, 1939.
(National Gallery of Art, Washington D.C.)

TEXT 5

RABBI NAFTALI HERTS BACHARACH, *EMEK HAMELECH*, 1:1

> קוֹדֶם כָּל דָּבָר עָלָה בִּרְצוֹנוֹ הַפָּשׁוּט לִבְרוֹא הָעוֹלָמוֹת. כִּי . . . טֶבַע הַטּוֹב
> לְהֵיטִיב, וְאִם שֶׁאֵין עוֹלָם, לְמִי יֵיטַב?

Before everything, it arose in His simple will the desire to create the worlds. For . . . it is the nature of good to do good; and if there is no world, to whom would He do good?

**RABBI NAFTALI HERTS BACHARACH
17TH CENTURY**

Born in Frankfurt am Main, Germany, he was a rabbi and kabbalist and the author of *Emek Hamelech*, which he described as an explanation of passages and teachings from Lurianic kabbalah. The book had a major impact on later kabbalah, and is often quoted in Chabad Chasidic thought.

TEXT 6

GENESIS 1:31

> וַיַּרְא אֱלֹקִים אֶת כָּל אֲשֶׁר עָשָׂה, וְהִנֵּה טוֹב מְאֹד.

God saw all that He had made, and behold: it is exceedingly good.

QUESTIONS FOR DISCUSSION

1 Who is more likely to ask the question, "Why is there evil in the world?"—believers, or nonbelievers?

2 Why would a *believer* be more bothered by the problem of evil? Why would a believer be less bothered by the problem?

3 Why would a *nonbeliever* be more bothered by the problem of evil? Why would a nonbeliever be less bothered by the problem?

Anxiety, Edvard Munch, 1894. (The Munch Museum, Oslo, Norway)

TEXT 7

TALMUD, BERACHOT 9:2, 5

עַל הַבְּשׂוֹרוֹת הַטּוֹבוֹת אוֹמֵר "בָּרוּךְ הַטּוֹב וְהַמֵּטִיב". וְעַל שְׁמוּעוֹת רָעוֹת אוֹמֵר "בָּרוּךְ דַּיַּן הָאֱמֶת". . .

חַיָּב אָדָם לְבָרֵךְ עַל הָרָעָה כְּשֵׁם שֶׁהוּא מְבָרֵךְ עַל הַטּוֹבָה. שֶׁנֶּאֱמַר (דברים ו, ה) "וְאָהַבְתָּ אֵת ה' אֱלֹקֶיךָ בְּכָל לְבָבְךָ וּבְכָל נַפְשְׁךָ וּבְכָל מְאֹדֶךָ" . . . דָּבָר אַחֵר "בְּכָל מְאֹדֶךָ": בְּכָל מִדָּה וּמִדָּה שֶׁהוּא מוֹדֵד לְךָ, הֱוֵי מוֹדֶה לוֹ בִּמְאֹד מְאֹד.

BABYLONIAN TALMUD

A literary work of monumental proportions that draws upon the legal, spiritual, intellectual, ethical, and historical traditions of Judaism. The 37 tractates of the Babylonian Talmud contain the teachings of the Jewish sages from the period after the destruction of the Second Temple through the fifth century CE. It has served as the primary vehicle for the transmission of the Oral Law and the education of Jews over the centuries; it is the entry point for all subsequent legal, ethical, and theological Jewish scholarship.

Upon hearing good tidings, one says, "Blessed is the One who is good and does good." Upon hearing bad news, one says, "Blessed is the True Judge."

A person is obligated to bless God for the bad, just as one blesses God for the good. As it is written (DEUTERONOMY 6:5), "You shall love God your God with all your heart, and with all your soul, and with all your might". . . . Another meaning of the phrase *bechol me'odecha* ("with all your might") is: "Whatever measure He metes out to you, be exceedingly, exceedingly grateful to Him."

TEXT 8

GENESIS 18:23–25

וַיִּגַּשׁ אַבְרָהָם וַיֹּאמַר הַאַף תִּסְפֶּה צַדִּיק עִם רָשָׁע . . . חָלִלָה לְךָ מֵעֲשֹׂת
כַּדָּבָר הַזֶּה, לְהָמִית צַדִּיק עִם רָשָׁע, וְהָיָה כַצַּדִּיק כָּרָשָׁע. חָלִלָה לָךְ, הֲשֹׁפֵט
כָּל הָאָרֶץ לֹא יַעֲשֶׂה מִשְׁפָּט?

Abraham approached [God] and said: "Would You also perish the righteous with the wicked? . . . It is a sacrilege for You to do such a thing, to kill the righteous with the wicked, so that the righteous would be as the wicked! It is a sacrilege for You: Would the Judge of the entire world not do justice?"

Treblinka/Genocide (detail), Judy Chicago and Donal Woodman, sprayed acrylic, oil, and photography on photolinen, 1988. (Spertus Museum, Chicago)

TEXT 9

EXODUS 5:22–23

וַיָּשָׁב מֹשֶׁה אֶל ה׳ וַיֹּאמַר: אֲדֹנָ-י, לָמָה הֲרֵעֹתָה לָעָם הַזֶּה? לָמָּה זֶּה שְׁלַחְתָּנִי? וּמֵאָז בָּאתִי אֶל פַּרְעֹה לְדַבֵּר בִּשְׁמֶךָ, הֵרַע לָעָם הַזֶּה, וְהַצֵּל לֹא הִצַּלְתָּ אֶת עַמֶּךָ!

Moses returned to God, and he said: "My Lord! Why have You done bad to this people? Why have You sent me? From the time that I came to Pharaoh to speak in Your name, he has made it worse for this people, and You have not saved Your people!"

TEXT 10

JEREMIAH 12:1

צַדִּיק אַתָּה ה׳, כִּי אָרִיב אֵלֶיךָ, אַךְ מִשְׁפָּטִים אֲדַבֵּר אוֹתָךְ: מַדּוּעַ דֶּרֶךְ רְשָׁעִים צָלֵחָה?

You are righteous, O God, when I contend with You; yet I will argue justice with You: Why does the path of the wicked prosper?

TEXT 11

SIDDUR, FESTIVAL *MUSAF* PRAYER

וּמִפְּנֵי חֲטָאֵינוּ גָּלִינוּ מֵאַרְצֵנוּ

Because of our sins we were exiled from our land.

SIDDUR

The siddur is the Jewish prayer book. It was originally developed by the sages of the Great Assembly, and later reconstructed by Rabban Gamliel after the destruction of the Second Temple. Various authorities continued to add prayers, from then until contemporary times. It includes praise of G-d, requests for personal and national needs, selections of the Bible, and much else. Various Jewish communities have slightly different versions of the siddur.

After the Pogrom, Maurycy Minkowski, (detail), oil on canvas, c. 1910. (The Jewish Museum, New York)

TEXT 12

MAIMONIDES, *MISHNEH TORAH,* LAWS OF FASTS, 1:1–3

מִצְוַת עֲשֵׂה מִן הַתּוֹרָה לִזְעוֹק וּלְהָרִיעַ בַּחֲצוֹצְרוֹת עַל כָּל צָרָה שֶׁתָּבֹא עַל הַצִּבּוּר . . . כְּגוֹן בַּצֹּרֶת וְדֶבֶר וְאַרְבֶּה וְכַיּוֹצֵא בָּהֶן . . .

וְדָבָר זֶה מִדַּרְכֵי הַתְּשׁוּבָה הוּא. שֶׁבִּזְמַן שֶׁתָּבוֹא צָרָה, וְיִזְעֲקוּ עָלֶיהָ וְיָרִיעוּ, יֵדְעוּ הַכֹּל שֶׁבִּגְלַל מַעֲשֵׂיהֶם הָרָעִים הוּרַע לָהֶן, כַּכָּתוּב "עֲוֹנוֹתֵיכֶם הִטּוּ וְגוֹמֵר." וְזֶה הוּא שֶׁיִּגְרֹם לָהֶם לְהָסִיר הַצָּרָה מֵעֲלֵיהֶם. אֲבָל אִם לֹא יִזְעֲקוּ וְלֹא יָרִיעוּ, אֶלָּא יֹאמְרוּ: דָּבָר זֶה מִמִּנְהַג הָעוֹלָם אֵירַע לָנוּ וְצָרָה זוֹ נִקְרָה נִקְרֵית, הֲרֵי זוֹ דֶּרֶךְ אַכְזָרִיּוּת, וְגוֹרֶמֶת לָהֶם לְהִדָּבֵק בְּמַעֲשֵׂיהֶם הָרָעִים, וְתוֹסִיף הַצָּרָה צָרוֹת אֲחֵרוֹת.

It is a positive Torah commandment to cry out to God and to sound trumpets in the event of any trouble that befalls the community . . . such as famine, plague, locusts, or the like. . . .

This practice is one of the paths of repentance. For when a trouble comes, and they cry out to God and sound the trumpets, all will realize that the calamity occurred because of their bad deeds, as it is written (JEREMIAH 5:25), "Your sins have turned [the rains] away. . . ." This itself will cause the removal of the trouble. But if they do not cry out to God and sound the trumpets, and instead say, "This thing that happened to us is merely a natural phenomenon, and this trouble is just a happenstance that happened"—this is a path of cruelty, which causes them to remain attached to their bad deeds, and causes this trouble to spawn further troubles.

TEXT 13

RABBI CHAIM OF CZERNOWITZ, *BE'ER MAYIM CHAYIM,* EXODUS 10:1

כִּי הִנֵּה כַּאֲשֶׁר הַקָּדוֹשׁ בָּרוּךְ הוּא שׁוֹלֵחַ יִסּוּרִין וְצַעַר עַל הָאָדָם, וְהָאָדָם נוֹתֵן דַּעְתּוֹ וְלִבּוֹ לְהַשְׁגִּיחַ עַל מָה אֵירַע לוֹ כָּךְ. וַהֲלֹא אֵין דָּבָר בָּעוֹלָם שֶׁיַּעֲשֶׂה מֵעַצְמוֹ, וְהַכֹּל נִגְזָר מִן הַשָּׁמַיִם . . . וְאִם כֵּן עַל מָה עָשָׂה ה' כָּכָה לִשְׁלוֹחַ עָלַי יִסּוּרִין הָאֵלֶּה לְצַעֲרֵנִי? וַהֲלֹא טוֹב ה' לַכֹּל וְרַחֲמָיו עַל כָּל מַעֲשָׂיו! אִם לֹא שֶׁרְצוֹנוֹ אֲשֶׁר עַל יְדֵי יִסּוּרִין הָאֵלֶּה אֶזְכּוֹר בְּבוֹרְאִי יוֹצְרִי, שֶׁאָשׁוּב לְפָנָיו בִּתְשׁוּבָה שְׁלֵמָה וְלַחֲזוֹר לְתוֹרָתוֹ וּמִצְוֹתָיו לְעוֹבְדוֹ בְּלֵבָב שָׁלֵם.

וְנִמְצָא כַּאֲשֶׁר שָׂם הָאָדָם זֹאת עַל לִבּוֹ . . . וְשָׂשׂ וְשָׂמֵחַ בִּרְאוֹתוֹ הַטּוֹבָה הַגְּדוֹלָה שֶׁעָשָׂה לוֹ אֱלֹקִים, לְהַשְׁגִּיחַ עָלָיו וּלְפַקֵּחַ עַל עִנְיָנָיו . . . וּלְקָרְבוֹ אֶצְלוֹ כְּחִיבַּת אָב עַל בְּנוֹ. וּכְמַאֲמַר הַכָּתוּב (מִשְׁלֵי ג, יב) "כִּי אֶת אֲשֶׁר יֶאֱהַב ה' יוֹכִיחַ" וְאוֹמֵר "אַשְׁרֵי הַגֶּבֶר אֲשֶׁר תְּיַסְּרֶנּוּ יָ-הּ". הִנֵּה וַדַּאי אֲשֶׁר זֶה הַמַּכָּה הִיא לוֹ רְפוּאָה שְׁלֵמָה וְטוֹבָה גְדוֹלָה וְחֶסֶד גָּדוֹל מֵאֵת ה' לִרְפוּאָתוֹ רְפוּאַת הַנֶּפֶשׁ לְהֵטִיבוֹ בְּאַחֲרִיתוֹ.

RABBI CHAIM OF CZERNOWITZ 1760–C. 1816

Rabbi Chaim of Czernowitz was born in Galicia. He was known as one of the early trailblazers of *Chasidus,* spreading its teachings throughout Moldavia. He served as rabbi in several communities, including Mohilev, Batishan, Kishinev, and Czernowitz. He immigrated to Israel toward the end of his life, and passed away in Safed. He published a few works, including *Be'er Mayim Chayim,* a commentary on Torah; *Siduro shel Shabbat;* and *Shaar Hatefilah.*

When God sends pain and suffering to a person, and the person pays heed to why this has happened to them, recognizing that nothing in the world happens by itself and that all is decreed from Heaven . . . [That person will ask:] Why, then, did God do this to me, sending these afflictions to cause me suffering? Is God not "good to all, and His compassion is upon all His creations"? Certainly, then, His will is that through these sufferings I will remember my Creator, and repent before Him with a full *teshuvah* and return to His Torah and His *mitzvot,* and serve Him wholeheartedly.

When a person takes this to heart, they will rejoice in recognizing the great good that God has done for them, to watch over them and concern Himself with their affairs . . . bringing them close to Him with the love of a parent for a child. As is written (PROVERBS 3:12), "For the one whom God loves, He reproves"; and as it also says (PSALMS 94:12), "Fortunate is the person whom God afflicts." Certainly, then, this "blow" is in fact a great kindness from God . . . healing the person's soul and assuring their ultimate good.

TEXT **14**

RABBI NISSIM GERONDI, *COMMENTARY ON TORAH,* GENESIS 22:1

וְעִנְיַן הַנִּסָּיוֹן מְסֻפָּק מְאֹד . . . וְהָרַמְבַּ"ן זִכְרוֹנוֹ לִבְרָכָה אָמַר . . . כִּי עִם
הֱיוֹת הַשֵּׁם יִתְבָּרֵךְ יֵידַע לְבָבוֹ, צִוָּה בּוֹ לְהוֹצִיא הַדָּבָר מִן הַכֹּחַ אֶל הַפֹּעַל,
לִהְיוֹת לוֹ שְׂכַר מַעֲשֶׂה טוֹב לֹא שְׂכַר לֵב טוֹב לְבַד.

וַאֲנִי מוֹסִיף בּוֹ דְבָרִים, וְהוּא כְּדֵי שֶׁיִּתְחַזֵּק אֱמוּנָה בְּנֶפֶשׁ הַמְנוּסָה . . .
כִּי אֵין סָפֵק שֶׁכָּל מַעֲנֶה חָזָק יוֹלִיד תְּכוּנָה בַּנֶּפֶשׁ מִתְיַחֶסֶת אֵלָיו. כִּי כְּמוֹ
שֶׁפֹּעַל הַגְּבוּרָה יוֹלִיד בְּנֶפֶשׁ הַגִּבּוֹר תְּכוּנַת גְּבוּרָה . . . וְכָל שֶׁכֵּן כְּשֶׁיַּכְנִיס
עַצְמוֹ בְּעִנְיָן גָּדוֹל הַחָכְמָה. כֵּן תְּכוּנַת עֲבוֹדַת הַשֵּׁם יִתְבָּרֵךְ תּוֹלֵד בְּנֶפֶשׁ
כְּשֶׁיַּכְנִיס עַצְמוֹ לְדָבָר הַקָּשֶׁה מִצַּד עֲבוֹדָתוֹ.

RABBI NISSIM GERONDI
1320–1376

Talmudist, halachic authority, and philosopher. Rabbi Nissim was born in Barcelona and lived in Girona. He was one of the last of the great Spanish medieval Talmudic scholars. He did not hold any rabbinic post, but served as a physician in the royal palace. His works include commentaries on Rabbi Yitschak Alfasi's code, responsa literature, and a collection of sermons that elucidate fundamentals of Judaism.

The idea of a "test" is a difficult one. . . . The Ramban [Nachmanides] says . . . that while God knows a person's heart [i.e., God doesn't need to test a person in order to know how strong their faith is], God initiates the test in order bring forth the person's potential into actuality, so that the person should merit the reward of a good deed—not just the reward of a good character.

I would add to this, that a test actually intensifies the quality of faith in the soul of the one being tested. . . . For it is certain that any strong response will create a corresponding quality in the soul. For example, exercising one's physical strength makes one stronger. . . . and the same is true, to an even greater extent, when a person applies themselves to growing their wisdom. In the same way, the quality of one's service of God is developed in proportion to the difficulties it encounters.

TEXT 15

TALMUD, BERACHOT 60B

לְעוֹלָם יְהֵא אָדָם רָגִיל לוֹמַר: "כָּל דְּעָבִיד רַחֲמָנָא, לְטַב עָבִיד."

כִּי הָא דְּרַבִּי עֲקִיבָא, דַּהֲוָה קָאָזִיל בְּאוֹרְחָא. מָטָא לְהַהִיא מָתָא. בָּעָא אוּשְׁפִּיזָא, לֹא יָהֲבֵי לֵיהּ. אָמַר: "כָּל דְּעָבִיד רַחֲמָנָא לְטַב." אֲזַל וּבָת בְּדַבְרָא. וַהֲוָה בַּהֲדֵיהּ תַּרְנְגוֹלָא וַחֲמָרָא וּשְׁרָגָא. אָתָא זִיקָא כַּבְיֵיהּ לִשְׁרָגָא, אָתָא שׁוּנָרָא אַכְלֵיהּ לְתַרְנְגוֹלָא, אָתָא אַרְיֵה אַכְלֵיהּ לַחֲמָרָא. אָמַר: "כָּל דְּעָבִיד רַחֲמָנָא לְטַב." בֵּיהּ בְּלֵילְיָא, אָתָא גְּיָיסָא שַׁבְיֵיהּ לְמָתָא. אָמַר לְהוּ: "לָאו אַמְרִי לְכוּ, כָּל מַה שֶׁעוֹשֶׂה הַקָּדוֹשׁ בָּרוּךְ הוּא הַכֹּל לְטוֹבָה"?

A person should always accustom themselves to say, "Everything that the All-Merciful does, He does for the good."

As [demonstrated by the following incident]: Rabbi Akiva was traveling on the road, and he came to a certain town and sought lodgings, but they refused him. He said, "Everything the All-Merciful does is for good," and he went and spent the night in the open field. He had with him a rooster, a donkey, and a lamp. A gust of wind came and blew out the lamp, a cat came and ate the rooster, and a lion came and ate the donkey. He said: "Everything the All-Merciful does is for good." That night, brigands came and carried off the inhabitants of the town into captivity. Said Rabbi Akiva: "Did I not tell you that whatever God does, it is all for the good"?

TEXT

ECCLESIASTES 7:14

זֶה לְעֻמַּת זֶה עָשָׂה הָאֱלֹקִים.

This opposite the other, God made.

Day and Night, M.C. Escher, woodcut, 1938.

TEXT **17**

ZOHAR, 2:163A

בְּבֵיתָא דְמַלְכָּא, לְבַר, הֲוַת חֲדָא זוֹנָה, יָאָה בְּחֵיזוּ וּשְׁפִּירָא בְּרֵיוָא. לְיוֹמִין אָמַר מַלְכָּא: בְּעֵינָא לְמֶחֱמֵי רְעוּתֵיהּ דִּבְרִי לְגַבָּאי. קָרָא לָהּ לְהַהִיא זוֹנָה, וְאָמַר לָהּ: זִילִי וּתְפַתִּי לִבְרִי, לְמֶחֱמֵי רְעוּתֵיהּ דִּבְרִי לְגַבָּאי.

הַהִיא זוֹנָה מַאי עַבְדַת? אַזְלַת אֲבַתְרֵיהּ דִּבְרֵיהּ דְּמַלְכָּא, שָׁרָאת לְחַבְּקָא לֵיהּ וּלְנַשְׁקָא לֵיהּ, וּלְפַתֵּי לֵיהּ בְּכַמָּה פִתּוּיִין. אִי הַהוּא בְּרָא יֵאוֹת, וְאָצִית לְפִקּוּדָא דַּאֲבוֹי, גָּעַר בָּהּ, וְלָא אָצִית לָהּ, וְדָחֵי לָהּ מִנֵּיהּ. כְּדֵין אֲבוֹי חַדֵּי בִּבְרֵיהּ, וְאָעִיל לֵיהּ לְגוֹ פַּרְגּוֹדָא דְהֵיכָלֵיהּ, וְיָהִיב לֵיהּ מַתְּנָן וּנְבִזְבְּזָא וִיקָר סַגִּיא.

מַאן גָּרִים כָּל הַאי יְקָר לְהַאי בְּרָא? הֱוֵי אֵימָא הַהִיא זוֹנָה.

ZOHAR

The seminal work of kabbalah, Jewish mysticism. The *Zohar* is a mystical commentary on the Torah, written in Aramaic and Hebrew. According to the Arizal, the *Zohar* contains the teachings of Rabbi Shimon bar Yocha'i, who lived in the Land of Israel during the second century. The *Zohar* has become one of the indispensable texts of traditional Judaism, alongside and nearly equal in stature to the Mishnah and Talmud.

At the king's palace, outside, was a harlot, beautiful of visage and form. One day, the king said, "I wish to see my son's love for me." So he summoned that harlot, and said to her, "Go and attempt to seduce my son, for I wish to see my son's love for me."

What does this harlot do? She pursues the prince, and begins to embrace him and kiss him and to entice him with all sorts of enticements. If the king's son is virtuous and obeys the commandments of his father, he will reject her, and not listen to her, and drive her away. Then the father rejoices in his son, and invites him into his royal chambers, and bestows precious gifts and great honors on him.

Now, who is the cause of the great reward of the prince? I would say: the harlot.

TEXT **18**

MAIMONIDES, *GUIDE FOR THE PERPLEXED*, 3:10 ⊕

אָמְנָם הֵם רָעוֹת בְּעֶרֶךְ אֶל דָּבָר אֶחָד. וְכָל מַה שֶׁהוּא רַע בְּחוֹק נִמְצָא מִן הַנִּמְצָאוֹת, הָרַע הַהוּא הוּא הֶעְדֵּר הַדָּבָר הַהוּא אוֹ הֶעְדֵּר עִנְיָן טוֹב מֵעִנְיָנָיו. וּמִפְּנֵי זֶה אָמְרוּ גְּזֵרָה מֻחְלֶטֶת שֶׁהָרָעוֹת כֻּלָּם הֶעְדֵּרִים. וְהַמָּשָׁל בּוֹ בָּאָדָם, שֶׁמּוֹתוֹ רַע וְהוּא הֶעְדֵּרוֹ, וְכֵן חָלְיוֹ אוֹ עָנְיוֹ אוֹ סִכְלוּתוֹ הֵם רָעוֹת בְּחוּקּוֹ, וְכֻלָּם הֶעְדֵּרֵי קִנְיָנִים ...

וְאַחַר אֵלֶּה הַהַקְדָּמוֹת יֻדַע בֶּאֱמֶת שֶׁהָאֱלוֹקָה יִתְבָּרֵךְ לֹא יֵאָמֵר עָלָיו סְתָם שֶׁהוּא עוֹשֶׂה רַע בְּעַצְמוֹ כְּלָל. רְצוֹנִי לוֹמַר שֶׁיְּכַוֵּן כַּוָּנָה רִאשׁוֹנָה לַעֲשׂוֹת רַע - זֶה לֹא יִתָּכֵן! אֲבָל פְּעֻלּוֹתָיו כֻּלָּם טוֹב גָּמוּר. שֶׁהוּא אֵינוֹ עוֹשֶׂה רַק מְצִיאוּת, וְכָל מְצִיאוּת טוֹב. וְהָרָעוֹת כֻּלָּם הֶעְדֵּרִים, לֹא תִּתְלֶה בָּהֶם פְּעֻלָּה, רַק בְּצַד אֲשֶׁר בֵּאַרְנוּ, בְּהַמְצִיאוֹ אֶת הַחוֹמֶר עַל הַטֶּבַע הַזֶּה אֲשֶׁר הוּא עָלָיו, וְהוּא, הֱיוֹתוֹ מְחֻבָּר בּוֹ הַהֶעְדֵּר לְעוֹלָם ... וְלָזֶה סִיפֵּר הַסֵּפֶר אֲשֶׁר הֵאִיר מַחֲשַׁכֵּי הָעוֹלָם וְאָמַר (בְּרֵאשִׁית א, לא): "וַיַּרְא אֱלֹקִים אֶת כָּל אֲשֶׁר עָשָׂה וְהִנֵּה טוֹב מְאֹד" ...

וּזְכֹר מַה שֶׁאָמַרְתִּיו לְךָ בְּזֶה הַפֶּרֶק, וַהֲבִינֵהוּ, וְיִתְבָּאֵר לְךָ כָּל מַה שֶׁאָמְרוּהוּ הַנְּבִיאִים וְהַחֲכָמִים, שֶׁהַטּוֹב כֻּלּוֹ מִפְּעֻלַּת הָאֱלוֹקָה בְּעַצְם. וְלָשׁוֹן בְּרֵאשִׁית רַבָּה (נא, ג): "אֵין דָּבָר רַע יוֹרֵד מִלְמַעְלָה".

All bad is only bad in relation to some other state. Indeed, when we say that something is bad, we really mean that something is absent, or that one of its positive properties is partially absent. . . . For example, death is an absence of life; similarly, illness, poverty, or stupidity derive from the fact that a certain property [health, wealth, or wisdom] is partially absent. . . .

Therefore, it cannot be said of God that He does bad. . . . For all that God actively does is completely good. God creates existence, and all existence is good; the bad are simply absences, for God has made the nature of the material state that good will always be partially absent from it. . . . The book which enlightened the darkness of the world therefore says (GENESIS 1:31), "God saw all that He had made, and, behold, it is exceedingly good". . . .

Remember what I said in this chapter, understand it, and it will be clear to you everything that the prophets and sages said about the essential goodness of all that God does. In the words of the Midrash (BEREISHIT RA-BAH 51:3), "Nothing bad descends from Above."

TEXT 19

RABBI SHNE'UR ZALMAN OF LIADI, *TANYA, IGERET HAKODESH* 11

רַק אֱמוּנָה אֲמִתִּית בְּיוֹצֵר בְּרֵאשִׁית, דְּהַיְינוּ שֶׁהַבְּרִיאָה יֵשׁ מֵאַיִן . . . הִיא בְּכָל עֵת וְרֶגַע שֶׁמִתְהַוִּים כָּל הַבְּרוּאִים יֵשׁ מֵאַיִן מֵחָכְמָתוֹ יִתְבָּרֵךְ הַמְחַיָּה אֶת הַכֹּל, וּכְשֶׁיִּתְבּוֹנֵן הָאָדָם בְּעוֹמֶק הַבָּנָתוֹ וִיצַיֵּיר בְּדַעְתּוֹ הַוָּיָיתוֹ מֵאַיִן בְּכָל רֶגַע וְרֶגַע מַמָּשׁ, הֵאיךְ יַעֲלֶה עַל דַּעְתּוֹ כִּי רַע לוֹ, אוֹ שׁוּם יִסּוּרִים מִבְּנֵי חַיֵּי וּמְזוֹנֵי, אוֹ שְׁאָרֵי יִסּוּרִין בָּעוֹלָם?

הֲרֵי הָאַיִן, שֶׁהִיא חָכְמָתוֹ יִתְבָּרֵךְ, הוּא מָקוֹר הַחַיִּים וְהַטּוֹב וְהָעוֹנֶג, וְהוּא הָעֵדֶן שֶׁלְּמַעְלָה מֵעוֹלָם הַבָּא. רַק מִפְּנֵי שֶׁאֵינוֹ מוּשָּׂג, לָכֵן נִדְמָה לוֹ רַע אוֹ יִסּוּרִים. אֲבָל בֶּאֱמֶת "אֵין רַע יוֹרֵד מִלְמַעְלָה" וְהַכֹּל טוֹב. רַק שֶׁאֵינוֹ מוּשָּׂג לְגוֹדְלוֹ וְרָב טוּבוֹ.

וְזֶהוּ עִיקַר הָאֱמוּנָה . . . דְּלֵית אַתַר פָּנוּי מִינֵיהּ, וּבְאוֹר פְּנֵי מֶלֶךְ חַיִּים . . . אֲבָל הַמַּאֲמִין לֹא יָחוּשׁ מִשּׁוּם יִסּוּרִין בָּעוֹלָם, וּבְכָל עִנְיְנֵי הָעוֹלָם הֵן וְלָאו שָׁוִין אֶצְלוֹ בְּהַשְׁוָוָאָה אֲמִתִּית.

RABBI SHNE'UR ZALMAN OF LIADI (ALTER REBBE) 1745–1812

Chasidic rebbe, halachic authority, and founder of the Chabad movement. The Alter Rebbe was born in Liozna, Belarus, and was among the principal students of the Magid of Mezeritch. His numerous works include the *Tanya*, an early classic containing the fundamentals of Chabad Chasidism, and *Shulchan Aruch HaRav*, an expanded and reworked code of Jewish law.

God is the creator of all existence. . . . Meaning, in every moment of time, all creations are brought into existence out of absolute nothingness from the divine wisdom that gives life to everything. . . . When a person truly believes this, and contemplates this truth with the full depth of his understanding, and pictures this in his mind, how would it be possible for him to imagine that anything bad has befallen him, or that he is experiencing any type of suffering in matters pertaining to children, health, or sustenance, or any other suffering in the world?

For [the source of what he is experiencing is] the *ayin* (divine "nothingness"), the divine wisdom, which is the ultimate source of life, good, and delight. It is the Eden that is loftier than the World to Come. It is only that it cannot be grasped, which is why it seems bad or painful. But in truth, "nothing bad descends from Above." It is all good; it is only that it cannot be experienced as such, due to the greatness and magnitude of its goodness.

This is the mainstay of our belief in God . . . that no place is devoid of Him, and that all life derives from the light of His countenance. . . . One who so believes is not disturbed by any suffering whatsoever, and with respect to all worldly matters, "yes" and "no" are truly the same for him.

Blurred Waterscape (Two Suns), (detail), Joseph Jachna, gelatin silver print, 1970. (Center for Creative Photography, University of Arizona, Tucson, Ariz.)

? QUESTION FOR DISCUSSION

Were you satisfied by any of these explanations?

TEXT 20

ISAIAH 45:5–7

אֲנִי ה' וְאֵין עוֹד
זוּלָתִי אֵין אֱלֹקִים . . .
יוֹצֵר אוֹר וּבוֹרֵא חֹשֶׁךְ
עֹשֶׂה שָׁלוֹם וּבוֹרֵא רָע
אֲנִי ה' עֹשֶׂה כָל אֵלֶּה.

I am God, and there is none else
Besides Me there is no God . . .
Who forms light and creates darkness
Who makes peace and creates evil
I am God, who makes all these.

(Peace) good = light
evil = darkness

TEXT 21

RABBI SAADIA GA'ON, *EMUNOT VEDEI'OT* 1:3

הַחֹשֶׁךְ אֵינוֹ הֵפֶךְ הָאוֹר, אֲבָל הוּא הֶעְדֵּר הָאוֹר . . . כִּי לֹא רָאִיתִי שְׁנֵי גּוּפִים זֶה הֵפֶךְ זֶה שֶׁיֵּהָפֵךְ אֶחָד מֵהֶם וְיָשׁוּב הָאַחֵר עַל הַשְּׁלֵמוּת . . . וְכַאֲשֶׁר רָאִיתִי הָאֲוִיר הֶחָשׁוּךְ יָשׁוּב מֵאִיר, יָדַעְתִּי כִּי הַחֹשֶׁךְ אֵינֶנּוּ הֵפֶךְ הָאוֹר, אֲבָל הוּא הֶעְדֵּרוֹ.

Darkness is not the opposite of light, it is only the absence of light. . . . For I have never observed two opposite entities, of which one is transformed to become the other perfectly. . . . So when I see a dark space become illuminated, I know that darkness is not the opposite of light, only its absence.

RABBI SAADIA GA'ON (RASAG) 882–942 CE

Rabbinic scholar, philosopher, and exegete. Rabbi Saadia Ga'on was born in Egypt and came to the forefront of the rabbinic scene through his active opposition to Karaism, a divergent sect that denied the divinity of the Oral Law. In 928, the exilarch David ben Zakai invited him to head the illustrious yeshiva in Sura, Babylonia, thereby bestowing upon him the honorific title "Ga'on." He is renowned for his works on the Torah, Hebrew linguistics, Jewish philosophy, and his redaction of a *siddur*.

[Handwritten notes:]

Projection is G-d being finite

*everything I experience is a devine intervention

the power (of evil) lies NOT in what it is, but what it is NOT!
it is NOT G-d being revealed.

TEXT **22**

FROM THE DIARY OF RABBI MICHOEL SELIGSON

רוֹפֵא אֶחָד נִכְנַס לְקַבֵּל דָּמוֹ לִבְדִיקָה, וְשָׁאֲלוֹ הָרַבִּי: אֵיזֶה דָּבָר גּוֹרֵם שֶׁהַדָּם
יוֹצֵא אִם הַמַּחַט אוֹ הָרֵיקוּת שֶׁבּוֹ ("וואקיּם") שֶׁמּוֹשֵׁךְ הַדָּם מֵהַגִּידִים?
וְעָנָה הָרוֹפֵא: הָרֵיקוּת. וְהִמְשִׁיךְ הָרַבִּי: שֶׁפַּעַם הִתְעַנְיֵן בָּזֶה, שֶׁבָּא אֵלָיו
אָדָם אֶחָד וְטָעַן שֶׁהוּא רֵיק וְאֵינוֹ שַׁיָּךְ לִכְלוּם, וְאָמְרוּ לוֹ: אַדְּרַבָּה, דָּבָר
שֶׁל רֵיקוּת מוֹשֵׁךְ לְתוֹכוֹ כֹּחַ חָזָק יוֹתֵר, בִּמֵּילָא הוּא כְּלִי לְכָל הָעִנְיָנִים שֶׁל
טוֹב וּקְדוּשָׁה. וְסִיֵּם: הֲרֵי שְׁמִינִי עֲצֶרֶת הָרַבָּנִים אוֹמְרִים "סֶערְמָאנְס",
וּמִכֵּיוָן שֶׁאֲנִי אֵינִי מוּרְשֶׁה לְדַבֵּר בִּמֵּילָא אֲנִי אוֹמֵר מַה שֶׁאָמַרְתִּי וְאַתָּה
תִּמְסוֹר לְהַשְּׁאָר.

RABBI MICHOEL SELIGSON

Rabbi Seligson is an author of a
number of works relating to Chasidic
thought and practice. His works
include *Sefer Hamaftechot Lesichot
Kodesh*, an encyclopedic work of
the spoken words of the Rebbe,
spanning 63 years. Rabbi Seligson
has served as a scholar-in-residence
for Chabad institutions in the
United States and worldwide. He is
a teacher and mentor to hundreds
of young men and women.

One of the doctors entered the Rebbe's room to draw a
blood sample for testing. The Rebbe asked him: What
draws the blood out from the vein—the prick of the
needle, or the vacuum in the tube? The doctor replied:
The vacuum.

The Rebbe went on to explain: This matter interests me,
because a person once came to me and claimed that he
is empty and incapable of anything. I said to him that,
on the contrary, a vacuum draws into itself even more
powerfully, making him a ready receptacle to everything
good and holy.

The Rebbe concluded: On Shemini Atzeret, rabbis de-
liver sermons. But the doctors aren't permitting me to
speak publicly. So I'm saying this idea to you, and you
give it over to everyone else.

* Creates a nothing by concealing his self expression.

TEXT 23

ECCLESIASTES 2:13

וְרָאִיתִי אָנִי שֶׁיֵּשׁ יִתְרוֹן לַחָכְמָה מִן הַסִּכְלוּת כִּיתְרוֹן הָאוֹר מִן הַחֹשֶׁךְ.

I found that that there is an advantage to wisdom over folly, as the advantage of light over darkness.

TEXT 24

TANYA, CHAPTER 12

פֵּירוּשׁ כְּמוֹ שֶׁהָאוֹר יֵשׁ לוֹ יִתְרוֹן וּשְׁלִיטָה וּמֶמְשָׁלָה עַל הַחוֹשֶׁךְ, שֶׁמְעַט אוֹר גַּשְׁמִי דּוֹחֶה הַרְבֵּה מִן הַחֹשֶׁךְ, שֶׁנִּדְחֶה מִמֶּנּוּ מֵאֵלָיו וּמִמֵּילָא, כַּךְ נִדְחֶה מִמֵּילָא סִכְלוּת הַרְבֵּה שֶׁל הַקְּלִיפָּה וְסִטְרָא אַחֲרָא שֶׁבֶּחָלָל הַשְּׂמָאלִי . . . מִפְּנֵי הַחָכְמָה שֶׁבַּנֶּפֶשׁ הָאֱלֹהִית.

Meaning: Just as light has an advantage, power, and dominion over darkness, in that a small amount of physical light will banish a great deal of darkness, because darkness is spontaneously and automatically dispelled by light, so, too, is the great folly of the evil inclination in a person's heart automatically dispelled by the wisdom of the Godly soul.

TEXT 25

RABBI SHNE'UR ZALMAN OF LIADI, CITED IN *RAMACH OTIOT*
(KFAR CHABAD, 1966)

Darkness is not banished with a stick.

TEXT 26

ISAIAH 25:8

בִּלַּע הַמָּוֶת לָנֶצַח וּמָחָה ה' אֱלֹקִים דִּמְעָה מֵעַל כָּל פָּנִים

Death shall be annihilated forever, and the Lord God
will wipe away the tear from every face.

TEXT 27

MAIMONIDES, *MISHNEH TORAH*, LAWS OF KINGS, 12:5

וּבְאוֹתוֹ הַזְּמַן, לֹא יִהְיֶה שָׁם לֹא רָעָב וְלֹא מִלְחָמָה, וְלֹא קִנְאָה וְתַחֲרוּת. שֶׁהַטּוֹבָה תִּהְיֶה מוּשְׁפַּעַת הַרְבֵּה, וְכָל הַמַּעֲדַנִּים מְצוּיִּין כֶּעָפָר. וְלֹא יִהְיֶה עֵסֶק כָּל הָעוֹלָם אֶלָּא לָדַעַת אֶת ה' בִּלְבַד . . . שֶׁנֶּאֱמַר, "כִּי מָלְאָה הָאָרֶץ דֵּעָה אֶת ה' כַּמַּיִם לַיָּם מְכַסִּים".

In that time, there will be no famine and no war, and no jealousy and rivalry. For good will be plentiful, and all delicacies available as dust. The occupation of the entire world will be solely to know God. . . . As it is written (ISAIAH 11:9), "For the world shall be filled with the knowledge of God as the waters cover the sea."

KEY POINTS

1 The question, "Why is there evil in the world?" has been asked for thousands of years. But a no less important question is, "What is evil?" Because, when we understand what evil is, we are better equipped to deal with it and overcome it.

2 "Theodicy" is the philosophical problem of how to reconcile the belief that God is all-knowing, all-powerful, and good, with the existence of evil in the world. Judaism affirms that we accept the righteousness and goodness of the "True Judge." At the same time, however, the greatest believers of Jewish history challenged God over the pain and suffering in His world.

3 Jewish sources contain a number of different explanations for the problem of evil, including: the negative things in life atone for our wrongdoings and rouse us to repentance; they contribute to our spiritual growth; they are blessings in disguise; they are a necessary component of the gift of free choice; they are a function of the finite nature of our existence; they constitute a gift from God that is too sublime to be experienced as revealed good. But notwithstanding all the explanations, the human soul refuses to accept the reality of evil.

4 The problem of evil runs deeper than the contradiction of a good God allowing bad things to happen. The very existence of evil contradicts the principle that nothing exists that is not some form of God's self-expression. Hence the conclusion that evil is a nonexistence rather than an existence, in the same way that darkness is not an existence, only the absence or concealment of light.

5 The "nonexistence" of evil may not make it any less challenging or painful. It does, however, reveal to us that "a little bit of light will banish a great deal of darkness"—that increasing our own Godly light is the most impactful way to vanquish evil. It also reinforces our conviction that it is within our power to eliminate evil from the world, and that this goal will inevitably be realized.

Appendix

TEXT 28

ELIEZER BERKOVITS, *FAITH AFTER THE HOLOCAUST*
(JERSEY CITY, N.J.: KTAV PUBLISHING HOUSE, 1973), P. 68

The "reasoning" with God is a need of faith; it issues from the very heart of faith. When, in Elie Wiesel's *Night*, at the hanging of the little boy, someone asks: "Where is God now?" it is the right question to be asked. Not to ask it would have been blasphemy. Faith cannot pass by such horror in silence. Faith, because it is trust in God, demands justice of God. It cannot countenance God's involvement in injustice and cruelty. And yet, for faith, God is involved in everything under the sun. What faith is searching for is, if not to understand fully, at least to gain a hint of the nature of God's involvement.

This questioning of God with the very power of faith stands out as a guidepost at the earliest beginnings of the Jewish way in history. Abraham wrestled with God over the fate of Sodom and Gomorrah. We note how the man who, in his piety, sees himself as mere "dust and ashes," nonetheless has the audacity to challenge God with the words: "Shall the Judge of all the earth not do justice?" There is no contradiction here. The man of faith questions God because of his faith. It is the faith of Abraham in God that cannot tolerate injustice on the part of God.

**ELIEZER BERKOVITS, PHD
1908–1992**
Rabbi, theologian, and educator. Born in Romania, he served in the rabbinate in Berlin before World War II. In 1958 he became chairman of the Department of Jewish Philosophy at the Hebrew Theological College in Chicago. Author of *Faith after the Holocaust* and *With God in Hell*.

This is also the essence of Job's dilemma. The sustained fire of his plaint is derived not from his personal plight, but from the passion of his faith. There is no weakening of faith here. On the contrary. It is the very power of faith that lends force to the accusation. What has happened to Job is wrong; it is terribly wrong because it is judged by the ideal of justice that Job formed for himself on the strength of his faith in God. That Job will not accept the arguments of his friends in defense of divine providence is not a matter of stubborn self-righteousness, nor is it due to a sense of exaggerated self-importance. What the friends attempt to do is to defend a wrong as justice. By doing so, they—without being aware of it—degrade Job's idea of God.

TEXT 29

HAROLD S. KUSHNER, *WHEN BAD THINGS HAPPEN TO GOOD PEOPLE*
(NEW YORK, N.Y.: ANCHOR BOOKS, 2004), P. 156

Life is not fair. The wrong people get sick and the wrong people get robbed and the wrong people get killed in wars and in accidents. Some people see life's unfairness and decide, "There is no God; the world is nothing but chaos." Others see the same unfairness and ask themselves, "Where do I get my sense of what is fair and what is unfair? Where do I get my sense of outrage and indignation, my instinctive response of sympathy when I read in the paper about a total stranger who has been hurt by life? Don't I get these things from God? Doesn't He plant in me a little bit of His own divine outrage at injustice and oppression . . . ? Isn't my feeling of compassion for the afflicted just a reflection of the compassion He feels when He sees the suffering of His creatures?" Our responding to life's unfairness with sympathy and with righteous indignation, God's compassion and God's anger working through us, may be the surest proof of all of God's reality.

Religion alone can affirm the afflicted person's sense of self-worth. Science can describe what has happened to a person; only religion can call it a tragedy. . . .

HAROLD S. KUSHNER, PHD
1935–

Kushner was ordained at the Jewish Theological Seminary in 1960. In 1966, Kushner accepted a rabbinical position for Temple Israel in Natick, Massachusetts; he remained at Temple Israel for twenty-four years. In 1972, he earned his PhD from the Jewish Theological Seminary. Some of his works include *When Bad Things Happen to Good People* and *When Children Ask about God*.

TEXT 30

EXCERPT FROM A LETTER FROM THE REBBE, RABBI MENACHEM MENDEL
SCHNEERSON, TO ELIE WIESEL, APRIL 26, 1965. PUBLISHED IN *IGROT KODESH*,
VOL. 23, PP. 369–375 🎙️

RABBI MENACHEM MENDEL SCHNEERSON
1902–1994

The towering Jewish leader of
the 20th century, known as "the
Lubavitcher Rebbe," or simply as "the
Rebbe." Born in southern Ukraine,
the Rebbe escaped Nazi-occupied
Europe, arriving in the U.S. in June
1941. The Rebbe inspired and guided
the revival of traditional Judaism
after the European devastation,
impacting virtually every Jewish
community the world over. The
Rebbe often emphasized that the
performance of just one additional
good deed could usher in the era
of Mashiach. The Rebbe's scholarly
talks and writings have been printed
in more than 200 volumes.

אִיךְ בִּין, זֶעלְבְּסטְפַארשְׁטֶענדְלִיךְ, מַסְכִּים מִיט אַייךְ, אַז דִי טַעֲנָה
פוּן "הַשׁוֹפֵט כָּל הָאָרֶץ לֹא יַעֲשֶׂה מִשְׁפָּט!" קֶען זַיין אוֹיטֶענטִיש אוּן
הָאבְּן דִי גֶעהֶעריקֶע שְׁטַארקַייט - נָאר װֶען זִי רַייסְט זִיךְ אַרוֹיס פוּן
אַן אָנגֶעװֵייטִיקְטֶער הַארץ פוּן אַ טִיפְן מַאֲמִין. דֶעריבֶּער גֶעפִינֶען מִיר
טַאקֶע, אַז דֶער עֶרשְׁטֶער װֶעלְכֶער הָאט זִיךְ אוֹיסְגֶעדרִיקְט דִי טַעֲנָה אִיז
גֶעװֶען אַבְרָהָם אָבִינוּ, דֶער גְּרוֹיסֶער מַאֲמִין אוּן פָאטֶער פוּן דִי מַאֲמִינִים
בְּנֵי מַאֲמִינִים.

אוֹיךְ דֶערצֵיילְן אוּנזֶערֶע חֲכָמִים זִכְרוֹנָם לִבְרָכָה, אַז דֶער עֶרשְׁטֶער
װֶעלְכֶער הָאט אוֹיפגֶעהוֹיבְּן דִי פְרַאגֶע פוּן "צַדִּיק וְרַע לוֹ, רָשָׁע וְטוֹב
לוֹ" אִיז גֶעװֶען נִיט קֵיין אַנדֶערֶער װִי מֹשֶׁה רַבֵּנוּ, דֶער װֶעלְכֶער הָאט
עֶרקְלֶערט צוּ דִי אִידְן, אוּן צוּ דֶער גַאנצֶער װֶעלְט, דִי אַיידֶע פוּן "אָנֹכִי
ה' אֱלֹקֶיךָ" אוּן "לֹא יִהְיֶה לְךָ אֱלֹקִים אֲחֵרִים", װָאס "אֱלֹקִים אֲחֵרִים" אִיז
כּוֹלֵל אוֹיךְ דֶעם מֶענטשְׁלֶעכְן שֵׂכֶל אוּן פַארשְׁטַאנד װֶען מֶען מַאכְט זֵיי
אַן אָפגָאט אוּן פּוֹסֵק אַחֲרוֹן ...

אוּן דִי אֵיינצִיקֶע דֶערקְלֶערוּנג אִיז גֶעװֶען – "כָּךְ עָלָה בְּמַחֲשָׁבָה
(הָעֶלְיוֹנָה)", װָאס אִיז אֵייגֶענטְלֶעךְ גָאר נִיט קֵיין עֶרקְלֶערוּנג.
פוּנדֶעסטװֶעגְן הָאט עֶס נִיט אָפּגֶעשׁװַאכְט דִי אֱמוּנָה בַּא מֹשֶׁה רַבֵּנוּ
אוּן בַּא אַלֶע אַנדֶערֶע אוֹיטֶענטִישֶׁע פְרֶעגֶער אוּן מָאנֶער. אַדְרַבָּה, דָאס
הָאט נָאךְ פַארשְׁטַארקְט זֵייֶער אֱמוּנָה, װִי מִיר גֶעפִינֶען דָאס בְּפֵירוּשׁ בַּיי
אִיּוֹב'ן; אַזוֹי אוֹיךְ בַּיי אַבְרָהָם אָבִינוּ, װָאס אִיז נִיט נָאר גֶעבְּלִיבְּן פֶעסְט
בַּא זַיין אֱמוּנָה, נָאר הָאט אוֹיךְ גֶעקֶענט אוֹיסשְׁטֵיין אַלֶע נִסְיוֹנוֹת; אוּן
אַזוֹי אוֹיךְ אַנדֶערֶע "רֶעבֶּעלְן" זַיינֶען גֶעבְּלִיבְּן טִיפֶע מַאֲמִינִים בִּיז צוּם
לֶעצְטְן טָאג פוּן זֵייֶער לֶעבְּן.

אִיךְ גְלוֹיב, אַז אִיר װֶעט מִיט מִיר מַסְכִּים זַיין אַז עֶס [אִיז] נִיט גֶעװֶען
סְתַּם אַ צוּפַאל דָאס װָאס דִי אַלֶע אוֹיטֶענטִישֶׁע פְרֶעגֶער זַיינֶען
גֶעבְּלִיבְּן בַּא זֵייֶער אֱמוּנָה; נָאר אַז עֶס הָאט גָאר אַנדֶערשׁ נִיט גֶעקֶענט
זַיין. װָארוּם, אוֹיבּ נָאר מ'מֵיינְט דִי קַשְׁיָא' מִיט אַן אֱמֶת. ... אוּן זִי אִיז
דָאךְ פַארשְׁטֶענדְלֶעךְ, אַז אַזַא טִיפֶער גֶעפִיל קֶען קוּמֶען נָאר פוּן דֶער
אִיבֶּערצַיִיגוּנג, אַז דֶער אֱמֶת'ער אִיז דֶער צֶדֶק װָאס שְׁטַאמְט פוּן

אָן אִיבֶּער מֶענְטְשְׁלֶעכְן מָקוֹר, דָאס הֵייסְט, וָואס אִיז הֶעכֶער סַיי פֿון דֶעם מֶענְטְשְׁלֶעכְן שֵׂכֶל אוּן סַיי פֿוּנֶעם מֶענְטְשְׁלֶעכְן גֶעפִיל. דֶערְפַֿאר רֵידְט דִי קַשְׁיָא אָן נִיט נָאר רֶגֶשׁ אוּן שֵׂכֶל, נָאר אוֹיךְ זַיין פְּנִימִיּוּת אוּן עֶצֶם מְצִיאוּת.

אָבֶּער נָאךְ דֶעם עֶרְשְׁטְן שְׁטוּרְמִישְׁן אַרוֹיסְטְרִיט, מוּז עֶר זִיךְ כַאפְּן אַז דֶער גַאנְצֶער צוּגַאנְג פֿון שְׁטֶעלְן דִי קַשְׁיָא אוּן פֿון וֶועלְן פַֿארְשְׁטֵיין מִיטְן שֵׂכֶל דָאס וָואס אִיז הֶעכֶער פֿון שֵׂכֶל, הָאט קֵיין אָרְט נִיט. דֶערִיבֶּער מוּז עֶר - נָאךְ אַ דֶערְשִׁיטֶערְנְדֶען אַמְפֶּערְן זִיךְ אוּן דוּרְכְוֵוייטִיקְן - סוֹף כָּל סוֹף קוּמֶען צוּם אוֹיסְפִּיר - עִם כָּל זֶה אֲנִי מַאֲמִין!" אַדְרַבָּא - נָאךְ שְׁטַארְקֶער."

I obviously agree with you that the argument, "Would the Judge of the entire world not do justice?" can be authentic and truly forceful only when it issues from the aching heart of a true believer. Indeed, we find that the first one to express this argument was our father Abraham, the great believer and the father of the "believers who are the children of believers."

Our sages also tell us that the first one who raised the question of "the righteous who suffer and the wicked who prosper" was none other than our teacher Moses—the one who elucidated to the Jewish people, and to the whole world, the concept of "I am G-d your G-d," and of "You shall have no other gods before Me"—"other gods" including also the human intellect, when a person makes of it an idol and a final arbiter. . . .

The only answer [to Moses's question] was "so it arose in G-d's mind," which is essentially no answer at all.

Nevertheless, this did not weaken Moses's faith, or the faith of all the other authentic questioners and demanders. To the contrary, it strengthened their faith, as we find it explicitly recounted in the case of Job. Abraham, too, did not just remain steadfast in his faith; he was also able to withstand all his subsequent "tests." Similarly, the other "rebels" remained strong believers to the very last day of their lives.

I believe that you will agree with me that it is no coincidence that all the authentic questioners remained in their faith; indeed, it could not have been otherwise. For when the question is asked truly and sincerely, it is self-understood that such a deep feeling can only come from the conviction that true justice flows from a suprahuman source—i.e., a source that is higher than both human understanding and human feeling. Indeed, for this reason the question agitates not only the emotions and the intellect, but also one's inner self and the very essence of one's being.

But after the initial storm abates, the [believing questioner] will inevitably realize that the entire premise—that one can seek to understand that which is higher than the intellect by using the intellect—has no place. Therefore, after a tumultuous and painful inner debate, he must in the end conclude that, "Despite all that, I believe!"—and, furthermore, more strongly than before.

TEXT 31

EXCERPT FROM A PUBLIC ADDRESS BY THE REBBE, RABBI MENACHEM MENDEL SCHNEERSON, DELIVERED ON HOSHANA RABAH, 5744 (SEPTEMBER 28, 1983) 📖

לְאַחֲרֵי כָּל הַבֵּיאוּרִים דִּירִידָה צוֹרֶךְ עַלִּי' – הֲרֵי כְּלָלוּת עִנְיַן הַגָּלוּת... אֵין לוֹ מָקוֹם וְהַסְבָּרָה בְּשֵׂכֶל (אֲפִילוּ שֵׂכֶל דִּקְדוּשָׁה) כְּלָל וּכְלָל. דְּמִכֵּיוָן שֶׁהַקָּדוֹשׁ בָּרוּךְ הוּא "כֹּל יָכוֹל", הֲרֵי בְּוַדַאי שֶׁבִּיכָלְתּוֹ לְהָבִיא אֶת כָּל הַ"שְׁטוּרְעַם" שֶׁל הָעַלִּי' לְמַעְלָה מַעְלָה בְּיוֹתֵר לְלֹא צוֹרֶךְ בְּעִנְיַן שֶׁל גְּבוּרוֹת!...

וְעַל פִּי זֶה – הָעִנְיַן דְּ"אוֹדְךָ הַוַי' כִּי אָנַפְתָּ בִּי", שֶׁלְּעָתִיד לָבוֹא יֹאדוּ בְּנֵי יִשְׂרָאֵל לְהַקָּדוֹשׁ בָּרוּךְ הוּא עַל עִנְיַן הַגָּלוּת, אֵינוֹ שַׁיָּךְ לְהַבָנָה וְהַשָּׂגָה בְּשִׂכְלוֹ שֶׁל הָאָדָם, אֶלָּא עִנְיַן זֶה הוּא בְּאוֹפֶן שֶׁל אֱמוּנָה בִּלְבָד.

וְכַאֲמוּר – מִצַּד הַשֵּׂכֶל אֵין מָקוֹם כְּלָל לְעִנְיַן הַגָּלוּת: לְשֵׁם מַה צְּרִיכִים אֶת כָּל הַ"מַאטֶערְנִישׁ"... דִּשְׁכִינְתָּא בְּגָלוּתָא, מָשִׁיחַ בְּגָלוּתָא, וְכָל אֶחָד וְאֶחָד מִיִּשְׂרָאֵל בְּגָלוּתָא,... וּבְאוֹפֶן דְּהוֹלֵךְ וּמוֹסִיף – שֶׁלֹּא לְמַעֲלִיּוּתָא, "בְּכָל יוֹם וָיוֹם... מְרוּבָּה כו' מִשֶּׁל חֲבֵירוֹ"?!...

לֶעָתִיד לָבוֹא תִּתְגַּלֶּה מַעֲלַת הַגָּלוּת, אֲבָל בִּזְמַן הַזֶּה – אֵין זֶה בְּגִילוּי. דְּהִנֵּה, אַף שֶׁכָּל עִנְיְנֵי הַתּוֹרָה, "תּוֹרָה אוֹר", הֵם בְּאוֹפֶן שֶׁל גִּילוּי, וְעַד שֶׁכַּמָּה וְכַמָּה עִנְיָנִים בָּאִים בַּהֲבָנָה וְהַשָּׂגָה בְּשִׂכְלוֹ שֶׁל הָאָדָם, אֲפִילוּ בְּשֵׂכֶל הָאֱנוֹשִׁי, וְעַל אַחַת כַּמָּה וְכַמָּה בְּשֵׂכֶל דְּנֶפֶשׁ הָאֱלֹקִית – הֲרֵי עִנְיָן זֶה (בֵּיאוּר מַעֲלַת הַגָּלוּת) אֵינוֹ בְּגִילוּי, וְעַד שֶׁאֵינוֹ יָכוֹל לָבוֹא לִידֵי גִילוּי, מִכֵּיוָן שֶׁעִנְיַן הַגָּלוּת בִּכְלָלוּתוֹ, וּבִפְרָט הַגָּלוּת דְּעִקְבְתָא דִמְשִׁיחָא, לְאַחֲרֵי שֶׁכְּבָר עָבְרוּ יוֹתֵר מִי-1900 שָׁנָה... וַעֲדַיִן לֹא נוֹשַׁעְנוּ,... – אֵין לוֹ מָקוֹם כְּלָל... בְּכָל סֵדֶר הַהִשְׁתַּלְשְׁלוּת... וּבִלְשׁוֹן הַיָּדוּעַ: "לָבָא לְפוּמָא לֹא גַלְיָא" – אֲפִילוּ לְפוּמָא שֶׁל הַקָּדוֹשׁ בָּרוּךְ הוּא כִּבְיָכוֹל!...

וְטַעַם הַדָּבָר (שֶׁהַקָּדוֹשׁ בָּרוּךְ הוּא הֶעֱלִים עִנְיָן זֶה) – מִכֵּיוָן שֶׁרְצוֹנוֹ שֶׁל הַקָּדוֹשׁ בָּרוּךְ הוּא שֶׁיְּהוּדִי יְבַקֵּשׁ וְיִצְעַק בַּאֲמִתִּיּוּת... "אֶת צֶמַח דָּוִד עַבְדְּךָ מְהֵרָה תַצְמִיחַ.. כִּי לִישׁוּעָתְךָ קִוִּינוּ כָּל הַיּוֹם"... וְאִם תִּהְיֶה אֵיזוֹ נְקוּדָה בְּשֵׂכֶל דְּנֶפֶשׁ הָאֱלֹקִית (אֲפִילוּ בִּנְקוּדַת הַשֵּׂכֶל בִּלְבָד)... שֶׁשָּׁם מוּבָן שֶׁיֵּשׁ עִנְיַן טוֹב בְּגָלוּת... שׁוּב לֹא יוּכַל לִצְעוֹק... בַּאֲמִתִּיּוּת וּבְכָל הַ"שְׁטוּרְעַם".

הַקָּדוֹשׁ בָּרוּךְ הוּא רוֹצֶה אָמְנָם שֶׁיְּהוּדִי יַאֲמִין בֶּאֱמוּנָה פְּשׁוּטָה... שֶׁ"טוֹב וְיָשָׁר הַוַי'"...וְיַאֲמִין שֶׁלְּעָתִיד לָבוֹא יֹאמְרוּ "אוֹדְךָ הַוַי' כִּי אָנַפְתָּ

בִּי". אֲבָל חַס וְשָׁלוֹם שֶׁעִנְיָן זֶה יוּבָן בְּשֵׂכֶל . . . שֶׁהֲרֵי אָז לֹא יוּכַל לְקַיֵּים
אֶת רְצוֹנוֹ שֶׁל הַקָּדוֹשׁ בָּרוּךְ הוּא לִצְעוֹק בַּאֲמִיתִּיּוּת "כִּי לִישׁוּעָתְךָ קִוִּינוּ
כָּל הַיּוֹם", כָּל רֶגַע וְרֶגַע שֶׁבַּיּוֹם!

וְנִמְצָא, שֶׁתּוֹבְעִים מִיְהוּדִי דָבָר וְהֵיפּוּכוֹ: מִצַּד אֶחָד עָלָיו לְהַאֲמִין
שֶׁלֶּעָתִיד לָבוֹא יֹאמְרוּ "אוֹדְךָ הוי' כִּי אָנַפְתָּ בִּי", וּבְיַחַד עִם זֶה – עָלָיו
לִצְעוֹק בְּכָל כֹּחוֹת נַפְשׁוֹ הָאֱלֹקִית שֶׁרְצוֹנוֹ לָצֵאת מֵהַגָּלוּת! . . .

After all the explanations of "a descent that is for the purpose of ascent," the whole idea of *galut* . . . defies any logical explanation whatsoever, even an explanation of the G-dly intellect. For since G-d is all-powerful, it must certainly be within His ability to bring about all the tremendous achievements of the "ascent," to the highest level, without the need of any harsh conditions at all! . . .

Accordingly, the idea that "I will thank You, G-d, for having rebuked me"—that in the future messianic era we will thank G-d for the *galut*—is incomprehensible by the human mind, and can be accepted only by faith alone.

For as we said, logically there is no place for the idea of *galut*. What possible need is there for the suffering of the *Shechinah* (Divine Presence) in exile, Mashiach in exile, every single Jew in exile, in a way that keeps getting worse all the time, so that "each and every day, the troubles are more severe than the previous day"?

In the future messianic era, the greatness of the *galut* will be revealed; but at present, it is not manifest. Everything about the Torah, "the Torah of light," is in a mode of revelation, to the extent that many things can be grasped by the human mind, even by its mundane intellect, and how much the more so by the intellect of the G-dly soul. Yet the idea of the advantage of *galut* remains hidden, and impossible to reveal. The very idea of *galut* in general, and in particular these closing stages of *galut* as Mashiach approaches, after more than 1900 years have already gone by and we have still not been redeemed, has no place at all in the entire *seder hishtalshelut* (chain of creation). As our sages expressed it, "the divine heart does not reveal it to the divine mouth"—even G-d Himself cannot articulate [the purpose of *galut*], if we dare say such a thing!

The reason that G-d has hidden this matter is that He desires that a Jew should sincerely request and cry out, "Speedily cause the scion of David Your servant to flourish . . . for we hope for Your salvation all day." Were there some point in the G-dly intellect where some aspect of good in the *galut* would be justified, we could no longer sincerely cry out [for the Redemption] as truly and as passionately.

Yes, G-d desires that a Jew should believe with simple faith that "G-d is good and righteous," and believe that in the messianic era it will be said, "Thank you, G-d, for having rebuked me"; but G-d forbid that this should be logically acceptable! For then we could not fulfill G-d's will to truly cry, ". . . we hope for Your salvation all day," each and every moment of the day.

This means that two contradictory things are demanded of us. On the one hand, we must believe that in the future we will say, "Thank You, G-d, for having rebuked me"; and at the same time, we must cry out, with all the power of our G-dly soul, that we want to get out of this *galut!*

Additional Readings

EXCERPT FROM *PARDES RIMONIM*, 25:3

BY RABBI MOSHE CORDOVERO

Now we must explain the benefit of this *kelipah*[1] and what it is about in the world, for it is not enough to say that it is just for the sake of punishment. That would raise the question about punishment itself, for is punishment not caused by the evil inclination and *kelipah*? Why then should there just not be *kelipah* or the evil inclination, in which case punishment would be unnecessary?

We will say: The reason that evil was willfully created by the Creator is that the world and the creations need to receive their nourishment and sustenance from the force of justice, righteousness, and uprightness. Had the creatures all been angels, without the power of choosing their actions, the world would not receive any reward for its actions, for they would have been the result of necessity, as the actions of angels are. For that reason, human beings had to have choice, which results from their being composed of both an evil and a good inclination, so that if a person desires by nature to incline towards the good, the evil inclination will be at their left side to oppose them and to turn them towards evil; and when the person wants to turn after evil, the good inclination will be at their right side to admonish them and to remind them of the words of their Creator. In this way, the person will receive a recompense for inclining towards one of the two poles, whether good or bad.

In order for G-d to give each person according to their ways and according to the fruit of their deeds,

RABBI MOSHE CORDOVERO (RAMAK), 1522–1570

Prominent kabbalist. Ramak belonged to the circle of Jewish mystical thinkers who flourished in 16th-century Safed. The name Cordovero indicates that his family originated in Córdoba, Spain. His most famous kabbalistic work is *Pardes Rimonim*.

there needed to be an impure side, the servant who rebels against his master. This will afflict the wicked precisely according to their wickedness. Evil will seek out its wickedness and cling to that side that matches itself and there find its punishment.

This matter is explained well in the Zohar, *Parashat Terumah* (161a):

> Everything the God made, both above and below, is all in order to reveal His glory, and all is for the sake of His service. For has one ever seen a servant who opposes the master who created him, opposing all that fulfills the will of his master? Is it not God's desire that the children of man should be constantly in His service and follow the path of truth, in order that they should merit much good? Seeing that this is God's desire, why is it that this evil servant [i.e., the evil inclination] comes and opposes the will of his master, and turns people to an evil path, diverting away them from the path of good, and causing them not to do the will of their master. . . ? Certainly, then, this servant is doing the will of his master.
>
> A king had an only son whom he loved very much, and in his love, he commanded his son that he should not bring himself close to a bad woman, for any person who approaches her is not worthy to enter into the king's palace. The king's son affirmed that he would do the will of his father with love.
>
> At the king's palace, outside, was a harlot, beautiful of visage and form. One day, the king said, "I wish to see my son's love for me." So he summoned that harlot, and said to her, "Go and attempt to seduce my son, for I wish to see my son's love for me." What does this harlot do? She pursues the prince, and begins to embrace him and kiss him and to entice him with all sorts of enticements. If the king's

son is virtuous and obeys the commandments of his father, he will reject her, and not listen to her, and drive her away. Then the father rejoices in his son, and invites him into his royal chambers, and bestows precious gifts and great honors on him.

Now, who is the cause of the great reward of the prince? I would say: the harlot. Is this harlot praiseworthy or not? Certainly she is worthy of praise on every account. First, that she carried out the command of the king. Second, that she is the cause of the king's son receiving all the honor, all the good, and all the love that the king gives to him.

Thus it is written (Genesis 1:31): ["God saw all that He had made, and behold: it is exceedingly good."] "Behold it is good" is the angel of life; "exceedingly good," this is the angel of death, as [the evil inclination] is indeed exceedingly good for those who obey the command of their Master.

See now: Were it not for this opposition, the righteous would not inherit the supernal treasures that are prepared for them in the World to Come. Meritorious are those who encountered the opposer, and meritorious are those who did not encounter the opposer. Meritorious are those who encountered the opposer and were saved from his clutches, that because of him they inherit all the good, and all the pleasures, and all the desirable things, regarding which it is said (Isaiah 64:3), "No eye has seen it save Yours, O God." And meritorious are those who did not encounter [the evil inclination], as they would have inherited hell on his account and have been banished from the Land of the Living—those who would not have obeyed their master and would have been drawn after him.

Therefore the righteous ought to be grateful to the [evil inclination], seeing that because of him they will inherit all the goodness and pleasure and desirable things in the World to Come. . . .

The Zohar's words are as clear and refined as sterling silver. This is the clear reason, for the *kelipah* serves the divine necessity and is something beneficial for the world and for the righteous.

We have another good reason for there being an evil inclination. It is well known that the workings of the supernal roots[2] are given into the hands of man. This is what was meant by the Torah's saying (Deuteronomy 32:18), "You have enfeebled the Rock who bore you." This is also the meaning of the verse (Deuteronomy 33:26), "He who rides the heavens is in your aid."[3]

So it is in this matter: The deeds of man transform the supernal quality of judgment to compassion, and compassion to judgment. . . . Given this, it follows that it is necessary that the human being should be a composite of both judgment and compassion, so that by means of these two branches they will have an effect on high on their hidden roots. Now, the evil inclination comes from the side of *gevurah* (severity) and the good inclination from the side of *chesed* (lovingkindness), being that the evil inclination emerges from the mystic principle of *kelipah* and the good inclination from that of holiness.

Accordingly, when the righteous person's inclination seeks to overpower them and turn them from the righteous path to a path that is not good, this causes the overpowering *kelipah* to act in accordance with that power of *gevurah* that flows to it and from which it derives its sustenance, and then the force of judgment overpowers the force of compassion. Then, when the righteous person mindfully empowers the good inclination over the evil inclination, this causes the power of *kelipah* to be subdued; judgment is tempered, the quality of compassion prevails, and the quality of judgment is transformed into the quality of compassion. This is the mystery of the branches which are in the hand of the righteous person to determine and to incline to one of the two sides.

But when, God forbid, the wicked person empowers the evil inclination over the good, this causes the force of *gevurah* to rule over the force of compassion; judgment results and the *kelipah* has the upper hand. That is the meaning of the teaching of the Sages: "Cursed are the wicked who transform the divine force of compassion into the force of judgment." For through the mystery of the branches, the actions of the lower beings affect their supernal roots.

That is the reason why God created the evil inclination: so that it should be subdued under the hand of the good inclination, whereupon the quality of judgment is transformed into compassion and the supernal roots are nourished from the brilliance of the supernal light and are united in in a perfect unity. This is the entire reason for the matter of the evil inclination.

There is another and more beautiful reason that finds its support in the words of Rabbi Shimon bar Yochai in the Zohar. This is the idea that the *kelipah* was caused by the outward scattering [of holiness]. . . . That outward scattering was itself caused by [the sin of Adam,] the first human. . . . Consequently, the human is the one who made things crooked and caused ruination; therefore the human must repair what was ruined. How does man subdue the power of *kelipah*? Through empowering the good inclination to prevail over the evil inclination, causing the *kelipah* to be subjugated and crushed, thereby repairing that which was ruined. Moreover, this purifies that which was impure, for by subduing evil through performing the mitzvah, a person restores it to holiness; it is purified and brought back into holiness as it had been at first.

The *kelipah* is re-included within holiness and all is pure. . . . Certainly, then, the evil inclination is purified and made into an inclination for good.

Translated by Rabbi Shmuel Klatzkin and Rabbi Yanki Tauber

Endnotes

1 The teachings of Kabbalah, evil is referred to as *kelipah* ("husk"; or *kelipot*, "husks," in the plural), indicating that they are extraneous to Godly and desirable elements of creation (the "kernel" or "fruit" in this analogy). As the husk encases and conceals the kernel, so do the *kelipot* conceal the Godly essence of creation. As the husk needs to be separated from the kernel before the kernel can be gainfully utilized, so are we tasked with separating the evil from the good so that the "sparks of holiness" embedded in creation can be redeemed and elevated. And as the husk is discarded after it has served its purpose of protecting the kernel, so is evil destined to be obliterated after its ultimate purpose is fulfilled.

2 The *sefirot* or "divine attributes" that define God's relationship with creation.

3 Meaning, that all that happens in the supernal realms, including the weakening or strengthening of the flow of divine vitality into creation, is influenced by our actions in this world.

Portrait de Dora Maar (Portrait of Dora Maar), Pablo Picasso, oil on canvas, Paris, 1937. (Musée Picasso, Paris, France)

Lesson

5

IS THE SELF REAL?

All injustice and strife, and even personal unhappiness, can be traced to selfishness. Yet self-esteem is essential for a healthy psyche and a productive life. To navigate this paradox, we first need to unravel the mystery of self-awareness: Where does our sense of self come from?

TEXT

MICHIO KAKU, FROM AN INTERVIEW BY ARUN RATH,
NATIONAL PUBLIC RADIO, FEBRUARY 22, 2014

There are about 20,000 papers on consciousness with no consensus. Nowhere in history have so many people devoted so much time to produce so little.

MICHIO KAKU, PHD
1947–

Physicist. Cofounder of string field theory (SFT), Kaku studied at Harvard University and later at the Berkeley Radiation Laboratory at the University of California, Berkeley, where he received his PhD. He held a lectureship at Princeton University before starting to teach at the City College of New York. Kaku is an author of several books, including *Physics of the Impossible.* He has also appeared on numerous television and radio programs.

Ego Center (detail), Alison Mason Kingsbury, oil painting, 1950. (Division of Rare and Manuscript Collections, Cornell University, Ithaca, N.Y.)

TEXT 2

RABBI ELI RUBIN AND MAX ARIEL ABUGOV, "DO CHABAD TEACHINGS SAY ANYTHING ABOUT THE MIND-BODY PROBLEM?" CHABAD.ORG

On the one hand we have physical bodies, complete with arms, legs, a heart and a brain. On the other hand we have mental states: we think, we become emotional, we desire things, we understand things, we enjoy sunsets and the scent of flowers. This led the 17th-century [philosopher] René Descartes to a conclusion that schisms the mind from the body. He postulated that there is a mental substance, *res cogitans*, and a physical substance, *res extensa*. . . .

From a philosophical point of view, Descartes' position, known as *dualism*, is deeply problematic. If mind and body exist independently of each other, if the mental and the physical are in fact two completely different substances, how do they interact with one another? How does the brain, a physical lump of grey meat, apprehend ethereal mental concepts? . . .

Descartes' dualism has often been rejected, usually in favor of *monistic* theories positing that mental and physical phenomena actually consist of the same substance. There is *physicalism*, claiming that all is matter. There is *idealism*, claiming all is mind. There is *neutral monism*, which suggests that all is neither one nor the other, but a third, unified substance that is the combination of both.

RABBI ELI RUBIN

Researcher, writer. Rubin studied Chasidic literature and Jewish Law at the Rabbinical College of America and at *yeshivot* in the U.K., the U.S., and Australia. He has been a research writer and editor at Chabad.org since 2011, focusing on the social and intellectual history of Chabad Chasidism. His work has also appeared in *Hakirah* and *Mosaic Magazine*.

MAX ARIEL ABUGOV

Abugov graduated with a B.A. in psychology from the University of Pennsylvania, where he worked at the Boundaries of Anxiety and Depression Lab. He also attended Yeshivas Kol Yakov Yehudah Hadar HaTorah in Crown Heights, where he developed an appreciation of *Chasidus*. He is passionate about the interdisciplinary study of psychology, philosophy, and religion.

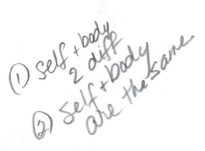

(1) self + body 2 diff
(2) self + body are the same

TEXT 3

FRANCIS CRICK, *THE ASTONISHING HYPOTHESIS* (LONDON, U.K.: REED BUSINESS INFORMATION, INC., 1994), P. 1

The Astonishing Hypothesis is that "You," your joys and your sorrows, your memories and your ambitions, your sense of identity and free will, are in fact no more than the behaviour of a vast assembly of nerve cells and their associated molecules. As Lewis Carroll's Alice might have phrased it: "You're nothing but a pack of neurons."

FRANCIS CRICK, PHD
1916–2004

Biophysicist, neuroscientist, biologist, physiologist. Crick helped develop radar and magnetic mines during World War II. He is the co-discoverer of the structure of the DNA molecule. He, James Watson, and Maurice Wilkins were jointly awarded the 1962 Nobel Prize for Physiology or Medicine. Crick later held the post of Research Professor at the Salk Institute for Biological Studies in La Jolla, California.

QUESTION FOR DISCUSSION

Do you think that the *self* and the *body* are two distinct entities, or are they one and the same?

Self-Portrait with Seven Fingers, Marc Chagall, oil on canvas, Paris, 1913. (Stedelijk Museum, Amsterdam, Netherlands)

TEXT **4**

GENESIS 1:26, 2:7, AND 5:2

וַיֹּאמֶר אֱלֹקִים: "נַעֲשֶׂה אָדָם בְּצַלְמֵנוּ כִּדְמוּתֵנוּ . . . "

וַיִּיצֶר ה' אֱלֹקִים אֶת הָאָדָם עָפָר מִן הָאֲדָמָה, וַיִּפַּח בְּאַפָּיו נִשְׁמַת חַיִּים.
וַיְהִי הָאָדָם לְנֶפֶשׁ חַיָּה. . . .

זָכָר וּנְקֵבָה בְּרָאָם. וַיְבָרֶךְ אֹתָם, וַיִּקְרָא אֶת שְׁמָם אָדָם בְּיוֹם הִבָּרְאָם.

God said: "Let us make a human in our image, after our likeness. . . ."

And God Almighty formed the human of the soil of the earth, and He blew into his nostrils the breath of life; and the human became a living soul. . . .

Male and female He created them. And He blessed them, and He called their name *Adam* ("human") on the day He created them.

(humanity)

The ten sefirot *as the Divine Countenance* (detail). From *Merapeh le-Nefesh*, written and illustrated by Sasson ben Mordechai Moshe, Baghdad, c. 1792. (Gross Family Collection, Tel Aviv)

TEXT 5

RABBI YESHAYAH HOROWITZ, *SHENEI LUCHOT HABERIT, TOLDOT ADAM*, 3A

"וַיִּקְרָא אֶת שְׁמָם אָדָם", זֶהוּ פֵּירוּשׁ עַל תּוֹלְדוֹת אָדָם וְסוֹפוֹ. אִם דָּבוּק
הוּא לְמַעְלָה, וּמִתְדַּמֶּה לוֹ יִתְבָּרֵךְ לֵילֵךְ בִּדְרָכָיו, נִקְרָא שְׁמוֹ בְּעֶצֶם "אָדָם"
מִלְּשׁוֹן "אֲדַמֶּה לְעֶלְיוֹן", "וְעַל . . . כִּסֵּא . . . דְּמוּת . . . אָדָם". וְאִם הוּא
מַפְרִיד אֶת עַצְמוֹ מֵהַדְּבֵיקוּת, אָז נִקְרָא אָדָם עַל שֵׁם הָאֲדָמָה אֲשֶׁר לוּקַּח
מִמֶּנָּה, וְעָפָר הוּא וְלֶעָפָר יָשׁוּב.

RABBI YESHAYAH HALEVI HOROWITZ (SHELAH) 1565–1630

Kabbalist and author. Rabbi Horowitz was born in Prague and served as rabbi in several prominent Jewish communities, including Frankfurt am Main and his native Prague. After the passing of his wife in 1620, he moved to Israel. In Tiberias, he completed his *Shenei Luchot Haberit*, an encyclopedic compilation of kabbalistic ideas. He is buried in Tiberias, next to Maimonides.

"He called their name Adam," as this [name] is the explanation of the story of the human being and his ultimate purpose.

If a person connects himself Above, and emulates God and goes in His ways, then he is called by the name "Adam" in the sense of *Edameh le'Elyon* ("I resemble the Supernal One," ISAIAH 14:14), and *V'al kisei demut adam* ("Upon the throne is the likeness of a man," EZEKIEL 1:26).

But if a person separates himself from this divine attachment, then he is called "Adam" in the sense of the *adamah* ("soil") from which he was taken, as the human is dust, and to dust does the human return (GENESIS 3:19).

Figure 5.1

The Meanings of the Name "Adam"

HEBREW	TRANSLITERATION	MEANING
אֶדְמֶה	edameh	I resemble
אֲדָמָה	adamah	soil
אָדָם	adam	human

the human being is a combination of loftiest + the lowest

we are a walking dichotomy

soil - lowest
soul - portion of Godliness - only creature that has this infinite soul of Godliness

Godly soul -
Animal soul -

I am me -

we have the ability to be better than I am me.

TEXT 6

SIDDUR, DAILY MORNING BLESSINGS

אֱלֹקַי, נְשָׁמָה שֶׁנָּתַתָּ בִּי, טְהוֹרָה הִיא. אַתָּה בְרָאתָהּ, אַתָּה יְצַרְתָּהּ, אַתָּה
נְפַחְתָּהּ בִּי, וְאַתָּה מְשַׁמְּרָהּ בְּקִרְבִּי.

My God, the soul You have given in me, it is pure. You created it, You formed it, You blew it into me, and You keep it within me.

SIDDUR

The siddur is the Jewish prayer book. It was originally developed by the sages of the Great Assembly in the 4th century BCE, and later reconstructed by Rabban Gamliel after the destruction of the Second Temple. Various authorities continued to add prayers, from then until contemporary times. It includes praise of God, requests for personal and national needs, selections of the Bible, and much else. Various Jewish communities have slightly different versions of the siddur.

Belonging-Together-Within, Bo Young Jeong, oil on canvas, South Korea, 2009. (Korean Art Museum Association, South Korea)

TEXT 7

RABBI SHNE'UR ZALMAN OF LIADI, *TANYA*, CHAPTERS 1–2

לְכָל אִישׁ יִשְׂרָאֵל . . . יֵשׁ שְׁתֵּי נְשָׁמוֹת, דִכְתִיב "וּנְשָׁמוֹת אֲנִי עָשִׂיתִי",
שֶׁהֵן שְׁתֵּי נְפָשׁוֹת.

נֶפֶשׁ אַחַת מִצַּד הַקְּלִיפָּה וְסִטְרָא אַחֲרָא, וְהִיא הַמִּתְלַבֶּשֶׁת בְּדַם הָאָדָם
לְהַחֲיוֹת הַגּוּף. וּכְדִכְתִיב, "כִּי נֶפֶשׁ הַבָּשָׂר בַּדָּם הִיא". . .

וְנֶפֶשׁ הַשֵּׁנִית בְּיִשְׂרָאֵל הִיא חֵלֶק אֱלוֹקַהּ מִמַּעַל מַמָּשׁ. כְּמוֹ שֶׁכָּתוּב,
"וַיִּפַּח בְּאַפָּיו נִשְׁמַת חַיִּים", "וְאַתָּה נָפַחְתָּ בִּי."

**RABBI SHNE'UR ZALMAN OF LIADI
(ALTER REBBE) 1745–1812**

Chasidic rebbe, halachic authority, and founder of the Chabad movement. The Alter Rebbe was born in Liozna, Belarus, and was among the principal students of the Magid of Mezeritch. His numerous works include the *Tanya*, an early classic containing the fundamentals of Chabad Chasidism, and *Shulchan Aruch HaRav*, an expanded and reworked code of Jewish law.

Every Jew . . . possesses two souls, as it is written (ISAIAH 57:16), "*Neshamot* (souls) I have made," referring to the two souls [in every individual].

One soul originates in non-holiness. This is the soul that is clothed in the blood of the person to animate the body; as it is written (LEVITICUS 17:11), "For the soul of the flesh is in the blood". . .

The second soul in the Jew is literally a part of God above. As it is written (GENESIS 2:7), "He blew into his nostrils a breath of life (*nishmat chayim*)," and [as we say in the morning blessings], "You blew it into me."

TEXT 8

TALMUD, SANHEDRIN 4:5

בִּשְׁבִילִי נִבְרָא הָעוֹלָם.

The world was created for my sake.

BABYLONIAN TALMUD

A literary work of monumental proportions that draws upon the legal, spiritual, intellectual, ethical, and historical traditions of Judaism. The 37 tractates of the Babylonian Talmud contain the teachings of the Jewish sages from the period after the destruction of the Second Temple through the fifth century CE. It has served as the primary vehicle for the transmission of the Oral Law and the education of Jews over the centuries; it is the entry point for all subsequent legal, ethical, and theological Jewish scholarship.

TEXT 9

TALMUD, KIDUSHIN 82B

אֲנִי נִבְרֵאתִי לְשַׁמֵּשׁ אֶת קוֹנִי.

I was created to serve my Creator.

TEXT 10

RABBI SHNE'UR ZALMAN OF LIADI, *TANYA*, CHAPTER 19

> "נֵר ה' נִשְׁמַת אָדָם" (מִשְׁלֵי כ, כז). פֵּירוּשׁ . . . נִשְׁמָתָם הִיא, לְמָשָׁל,
> כְּאוֹר הַנֵּר, שֶׁמִּתְנַעְנֵעַ תָּמִיד לְמַעְלָה בְּטִבְעוֹ. מִפְּנֵי שֶׁאוֹר הָאֵשׁ חָפֵץ
> בְּטֶבַע לִיפָּרֵד מֵהַפְּתִילָה וְלִידָּבֵק בְּשָׁרְשׁוֹ לְמַעְלָה . . . וְאַף שֶׁעַל יְדֵי זֶה
> יִכְבֶּה וְלֹא יָאִיר כְּלוּם לְמַטָּה, וְגַם לְמַעְלָה בְּשָׁרְשׁוֹ יִתְבַּטֵּל אוֹרוֹ בִּמְצִיאוּת
> בְּשָׁרְשׁוֹ, אַף עַל פִּי כֵן, בְּכָךְ הוּא חָפֵץ בְּטִבְעוֹ. כַּךְ נִשְׁמַת הָאָדָם . . . חֶפְצָהּ
> וְחֶשְׁקָהּ בְּטִבְעָהּ לִיפָּרֵד וְלָצֵאת מִן הַגּוּף וְלִידָּבֵק בְּשָׁרְשָׁהּ וּמְקוֹרָהּ בַּה' . . .
> הֲגַם שֶׁתִּהְיֶה אַיִן וָאֶפֶס וְתִתְבַּטֵּל שָׁם בִּמְצִיאוּת לְגַמְרֵי, וְלֹא יִשָּׁאֵר מִמֶּנָּה
> מְאוּמָה מִמַּהוּתָהּ וְעַצְמוּתָהּ הָרִאשׁוֹן, אַף עַל פִּי כֵן, זֶה רְצוֹנָהּ וְחֶפְצָהּ
> בְּטִבְעָהּ.

It is written, "==The soul of man is a lamp of God==" (PROV-ERBS 20:27). The meaning of this verse is that the [God-ly] soul is analogous to the flame of a lamp, which by nature constantly vacillates upward. This is because it is the nature of a flame to strive to tear free of the wick and attach itself to its source above . . . [If the flame were to achieve this goal,] it would be extinguished and would no longer illuminate here below; also above, its light would be utterly nullified within its source; nevertheless, this is the striving of the flame, by its very nature. So, too, the [Godly] soul in man naturally desires and yearns to tear free of the body and attach itself to its root and source in God. Although this would render it naught and nothingness, and its existence would be utterly nullified there, leaving nothing of its original substance and essence, nevertheless, <u>this is the soul's striving and desire, by its very nature.</u>

Striving to be NOT ME!

TEXT 11

RABBI SHNE'UR ZALMAN OF LIADI, *TANYA*, CHAPTER 1

וּמִמֶּנָּה בָּאוֹת כָּל הַמִּדּוֹת רָעוֹת . . . דְּהַיְינוּ כַּעַס וְגַאֲוָה . . . וְתַאֲוַת
הַתַּעֲנוּגִים . . . וְהוֹלֵלוּת וְלֵיצָנוּת וְהִתְפָּאֲרוּת וּדְבָרִים בְּטֵלִים . . . וְעַצְלוּת
וְעַצְבוּת . . .

[From the animal soul] stem all the negative characteristics . . . namely: anger and arrogance . . . the lust for pleasures . . . frivolity and cynicism, boasting and idle talk . . . and laziness and melancholy.

Pretty Harsh!

I am me is more prone to these 4 modes.

Aggression I, Mikalojus Povilas Vilutis, silkscreen, Lithuania, 1979. (Modern Art Center, Vilnius, Lithuania)

Learning Exercise 5.1

Using the rating scale provided below, give a rating to each of these traits in both columns. For example, if you get angry very often when you're in an "I am me" mode of consciousness, but rarely get angry when in an "I'm not me" mode, then assign a rating of "4" to "Anger" in the first column, and a rating of "2" in the second column.

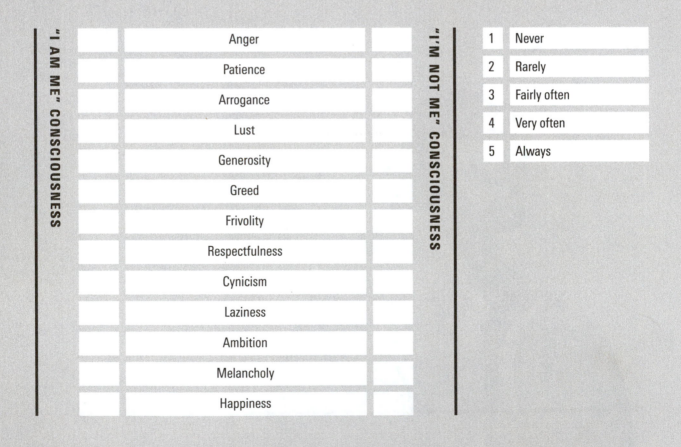

"I AM ME" CONSCIOUSNESS	Trait	"I'M NOT ME" CONSCIOUSNESS
	Anger	
	Patience	
	Arrogance	
	Lust	
	Generosity	
	Greed	
	Frivolity	
	Respectfulness	
	Cynicism	
	Laziness	
	Ambition	
	Melancholy	
	Happiness	

1	Never
2	Rarely
3	Fairly often
4	Very often
5	Always

TEXT 12

RABBI SHALOM DOVBER SCHNEERSOHN, *MAAMAR HEICHALTSU* 5659, SECTION 4

עִנְיַן הַמָּדוֹן וְהָרִיב וְהַשִּׂנְאָה . . . אֵינוֹ מִצַּד אֵיזֶה פְּרָט, כִּי אִם מִפְּנֵי שֶׁאֵינוֹ יָכוֹל לִסְבּוֹל אֶת זוּלָתוֹ . . . וְאִי אֶפְשָׁר לְהִתְאַחֵד עִמּוֹ כוּ'. וְזֶהוּ הַנִּקְרָא "שִׂנְאַת חִנָּם", שֶׁהוּא שׂוֹנֵא אוֹתוֹ חִנָּם עַל לֹא דָבָר כוּ'. וְלִפְעָמִים יֵשׁ בָּזֶה גַּם כֵּן אֵיזֶה פְּרָטִים, דְּהַיְינוּ שֶׁיֵּשׁ לוֹ אֵיזֶה טַעֲנָה לָמָה הוּא שׂוֹנֵא אוֹתוֹ כוּ', אֲבָל זֶהוּ שֶׁבָּא אַחַר כָּךְ. וְהַיְינוּ שֶׁלֹּא שֶׁהַטְּעָמִים הַפְּרָטִים הֵם סִבַּת הַשִּׂנְאָה, רַק שֶׁמָּצָא לוֹ תוֹאֲנָה וַעֲלִילָה לְהַצְדִּיק אֶת עַצְמוֹ לִפְנֵי זוּלָתוֹ לְבַד . . .

וְהַסִּבָּה הוּא הַיֵּשׁוּת שֶׁלּוֹ, שֶׁהוּא חָשׁוּב בְּעֵינֵי עַצְמוֹ . . . דְּמִפְּנֵי הַיֵּשׁוּת שֶׁלּוֹ אֵינוֹ נוֹתֵן מָקוֹם לְזוּלָתוֹ, דְּהַזּוּלָת בְּהֶכְרֵחַ מְמַעֵט מְצִיאוּתוֹ וְלָכֵן אֵינוֹ יָכוֹל לִסְבּוֹל אוֹתוֹ.

RABBI SHALOM DOVBER SCHNEERSOHN (RASHAB) 1860–1920

Chasidic rebbe. Rabbi Shalom Dovber became the fifth leader of the Chabad movement upon the passing of his father, Rabbi Shmuel of Lubavitch. He established the Lubavitch network of *yeshivot* called Tomchei Temimim. He authored many volumes of chasidic discourses and is renowned for his lucid and thorough explanations of kabbalistic concepts.

[Ultimately, all] strife, conflict, and hatred . . . are not for any particular reason, but because a person cannot tolerate the other person's existence . . . and is incapable of joining with the other. This is what is called "baseless hatred": he hates him for no reason. At times, there may also be particular factors, meaning that he has some sort of explanation why he hates him, but this explanation came later. The particular factors are not the cause of the hatred; he has only found an excuse to justify himself . . .

The reason for this is his own *yeshut* (egotism) and self-importance. . . . His ego does not leave room for anyone else. The mere existence of another person detracts from his own existence; he therefore finds it impossible to tolerate others.

※ EGO desensitises us to a higher truth.

TEXT **13**

TALMUD, BERACHOT 40A

כְּלִי רֵיקָן מַחֲזִיק מָלֵא אֵינוֹ מַחֲזִיק.

An empty vessel can receive; a full vessel cannot receive.

The Crowded Mind/The Void (detail), Forrest Clemenger Bess, oil on canvas, 1947.

TEXT 14

RABBI SHNE'UR ZALMAN OF LIADI, *TANYA*, CHAPTER 29

לִפְעָמִים וְעִתִּים רַבִּים יֵשׁ לָהֶם טִמְטוּם הַלֵּב שֶׁנַּעֲשָׂה כָּאֶבֶן, וְלֹא יָכוֹל
לִפְתּוֹחַ לִבּוֹ בְּשׁוּם אוֹפֶן לַעֲבוֹדָה שֶׁבַּלֵּב זוֹ תְּפִלָּה. וְגַם לִפְעָמִים לֹא יוּכַל
לְהִלָּחֵם עִם הַיֵּצֶר . . . מִפְּנֵי כְּבֵדוּת שֶׁבְּלִבּוֹ . . . וְאַף שֶׁמֵּבִין וּמִתְבּוֹנֵן בְּשִׂכְלוֹ
בִּגְדֻלַּת ה', אֵינוֹ נִתְפָּס וְנִדְבָּק בְּמוֹחוֹ כָּל כַּךְ שֶׁיִּיכַל לִמְשׁוֹל עַל חוּמְרִיּוּת
הַלֵּב, מֵחֲמַת חוּמְרִיּוּתָן וְגַסּוּתָן. וְהַסִּיבָּה הִיא גַּסּוּת הַקְּלִיפָּה שֶׁמַּגְבִּיהַּ
עַצְמָהּ עַל אוֹר קְדֻשַּׁת נֶפֶשׁ הָאֱלֹקִית וּמַסְתֶּרֶת וּמַחְשִׁיכָה אוֹרָהּ.

Often a person suffers from a "blockage of the heart," that the heart becomes like a stone, and the person is unable, by any means, to open it to the "service of the heart," namely, prayer. At times, the person is also unable to combat the evil impulse . . . because of this heaviness in their heart. . . . Although they understand and meditate on the greatness of God intellectually, [this understanding] is not grasped and does not attach itself to the mind sufficiently for the person to gain control over the coarseness of the heart, due to its coarseness and crassness. The reason for this is the arrogance of the [Animal Soul], which exalts itself over the holiness of the Godly Soul, obscuring and darkening its light.

TEXT **15** *calling out ego in self regard.*
very source of Negativity.

RABBI SHNE'UR ZALMAN OF LIADI, *TANYA*, CHAPTER 6

שֶׁזֶּהוּ פֵּירוּשׁ לְשׁוֹן "סִטְרָא אַחֲרָא", פֵּירוּשׁ צַד אַחֵר, שֶׁאֵינוֹ צַד הַקְּדֻשָּׁה.

וְצַד הַקְּדֻשָּׁה אֵינוֹ אֶלָּא הַשְׁרָאָה וְהַמְשָׁכָה מִקְּדֻשָּׁתוֹ שֶׁל הַקָּדוֹשׁ בָּרוּךְ הוּא, וְאֵין הַקָּדוֹשׁ בָּרוּךְ הוּא שׁוֹרֶה אֶלָּא עַל דָּבָר שֶׁבָּטֵל אֶצְלוֹ יִתְבָּרֵךְ . . . אֲבָל כָּל מַה שֶׁאֵינוֹ בָּטֵל אֶצְלוֹ יִתְבָּרֵךְ, אֶלָּא הוּא דָּבָר נִפְרָד בִּפְנֵי עַצְמוֹ, אֵינוֹ מְקַבֵּל חַיּוּת מִקְּדֻשָּׁתוֹ שֶׁל הַקָּדוֹשׁ בָּרוּךְ הוּא מִבְּחִינַת פְּנִימִית הַקְּדֻשָּׁה וּמַהוּתָהּ וְעַצְמוּתָהּ בִּכְבוֹדָהּ וּבְעַצְמָהּ, אֶלָּא מִבְּחִינַת אֲחוֹרַיִים, שֶׁיּוֹרְדִים מִמַּדְרֵגָה לְמַדְרֵגָה, רִבְבוֹת מַדְרֵגוֹת בְּהִשְׁתַּלְשְׁלוּת הָעוֹלָמוֹת . . . וְצִמְצוּמִים רַבִּים, עַד שֶׁנִּתְמַעֵט כָּל כַּךְ הָאוֹר וְהַחַיּוּת . . . עַד שֶׁיָּכוֹל לְהִתְצַמְצֵם וּלְהִתְלַבֵּשׁ בִּבְחִינַת גָּלוּת תּוֹךְ אוֹתוֹ דָּבָר הַנִּפְרָד לְהַחֲיוֹתוֹ וּלְקַיְּמוֹ מֵאַיִן לְיֵשׁ, שֶׁלֹּא יַחֲזוֹר לִהְיוֹת אַיִן וָאֶפֶס כְּבַתְּחִלָּה מִקֹּדֶם שֶׁנִּבְרָא.

וְלָכֵן נִקְרָא עוֹלָם הַזֶּה וּמְלוֹאוֹ עוֹלַם הַקְּלִיפּוֹת וְסִטְרָא אַחֲרָא. וְלָכֵן כָּל מַעֲשֵׂה עוֹלָם הַזֶּה קָשִׁים וְרָעִים, וְהָרְשָׁעִים גּוֹבְרִים בּוֹ.

This is the meaning of the term *sitra achra*—literally, "the other side"—i.e., not the side of holiness.

The side of holiness is nothing but the indwelling and extension of God's holiness; and God dwells only in that which abnegates itself to Him. . . . Anything, however, that does not abnegate itself to God, but [considers itself] something separate unto itself, does not receive its vitality from the inner essence and substance of the holiness of God; only from its external aspect. [Namely, from the divine vitality] that descends from level to level, in myriads of levels in the chain of worlds . . . undergoing numerous contractions, until the light and life is so diminished . . . that it can be condensed and incorporated, in a state of exile as it were, within that separated thing, to impart life and existence to it *ex nihilo* ["something from nothing"], so that it does not revert to nothingness and nonexistence as it was before it was created.

Something from Nothing

It is for this reason that our physical world is called the world of "husks" and of "the other side." This is why all affairs of this world are severe and evil, and the wicked prevail in it.

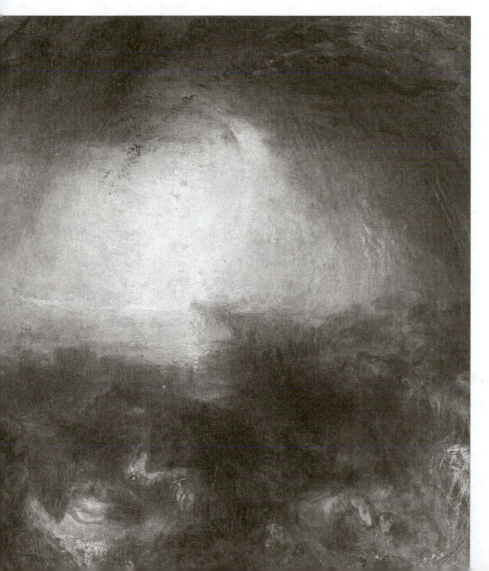

Shade and Darkness—The Evening of the Deluge, Joseph Mallord William Turner, oil on canvas, 1843. (The Tate Gallery, London)

TEXT **16**

RABBI SHNE'UR ZALMAN OF LIADI, *TANYA*, CHAPTER 27

וּבְכָל דְּחִיָּה וּדְחִיָּה שֶׁמַּדְחֵהוּ מִמַּחֲשַׁבְתּוֹ, אִתְכַּפְיָא סִטְרָא אַחֲרָא לְתַתָּא. וּבְאִתְעֲרוּתָא דִלְתַתָּא, אִתְעֲרוּתָא דִלְעֵילָא, וְאִתְכַּפְיָא סִטְרָא אַחֲרָא דִלְעֵילָא . . .

וְלָכֵן אַל יִפּוֹל לֵב אָדָם עָלָיו, וְלֹא יֵרַע לְבָבוֹ מְאֹד, גַּם אִם יִהְיֶה כֵּן כָּל יָמָיו בְּמִלְחָמָה זוֹ. כִּי אוּלַי לְכָךְ נִבְרָא, וְזֹאת עֲבוֹדָתוֹ, לְאַכְפְיָא לְסִטְרָא אַחֲרָא תָּמִיד . . .

וּשְׁנֵי מִינֵי נַחַת רוּחַ לְפָנָיו יִתְבָּרֵךְ לְמַעֲלָה. א' מִבִּיטוּל הַסִּטְרָא אַחֲרָא לְגַמְרֵי וְאִתְהַפְּכָא מִמְּרִירוּ לְמִתְקָא וּמֵחֲשׁוֹכָא לִנְהוֹרָא עַל יְדֵי הַצַּדִּיקִים. וְהַשֵּׁנִית כַּד אִתְכַּפְיָא הַסִּטְרָא אַחֲרָא בְּעוֹדָהּ בְּתָקְפָּהּ וּגְבוּרָתָהּ וּמַגְבִּיהַּ עַצְמָהּ כַּנֶּשֶׁר וּמִשָּׁם מוֹרִידָהּ ה' בְּאִתְעֲרוּתָא דִלְתַתָּא עַל יְדֵי הַבֵּינוֹנִים.

With each and every act of rejection by which a person thrusts away [the negative impulse] from their mind, the "other side" down in this world is conquered; and because a "stimulus from below causes a stimulus from above" (*ZOHAR* 2:135B), the [cosmic] "other side" above is suppressed as a result. . . .

Therefore, a person should not feel dejected, nor should their heart be distressed, even if they are engaged in this battle all their life. For perhaps it is for this that they were created, and this is their task—to constantly conquer the other side.

For there are two types of satisfaction before God. The first is from the complete obliteration of evil and its transformation from bitterness into sweetness and from darkness into light by the perfectly righteous. The second is when evil is suppressed while still at its strongest and mightiest, and exalts itself as an eagle, and God takes it down as a result of the stimulus generated by the efforts of the ordinary person.

Beyond There, Jae Sam Lee, South Korea, charcoal on cotton canvas, 1999. (Korean Art Museum Association, South Korea)

TEXT **17**

RABBI SHNE'UR ZALMAN OF LIADI, *TANYA*, CHAPTER 32 🕎

וְהִנֵּה עַל יְדֵי קִיּוּם הַדְּבָרִים הַנִּזְכָּרִים לְעֵיל לִהְיוֹת גּוּפוֹ נִבְזֶה וְנִמְאָס בְּעֵינָיו
רַק שִׂמְחָתוֹ תִּהְיֶה שִׂמְחַת הַנֶּפֶשׁ לְבַדָּהּ הֲרֵי זוֹ דֶּרֶךְ יְשָׁרָה וְקַלָּה לָבֹא לִידֵי
קִיּוּם מִצְוַת וְאָהַבְתָּ לְרֵעֲךָ כָּמוֹךָ ... בְּשֶׁגַּם שֶׁכֻּלָּן מַתְאִימוֹת וְאָב אֶחָד
לְכֻלָּנָה וְלָכֵן נִקְרְאוּ כָּל יִשְׂרָאֵל אַחִים מַמָּשׁ מִצַּד שׁוֹרֶשׁ נַפְשָׁם בַּה' אֶחָד
רַק שֶׁהַגּוּפִים מְחֻלָּקִים.

וְלָכֵן הָעוֹשִׂים גּוּפָם עִקָּר וְנַפְשָׁם טְפֵלָה אִי אֶפְשָׁר לִהְיוֹת אַהֲבָה וְאַחֲוָה
אֲמִתִּית בֵּינֵיהֶם אֶלָּא הַתְּלוּיָה בְּדָבָר לְבַדָּהּ.

וְזֶהוּ שֶׁאָמַר הִלֵּל הַזָּקֵן עַל קִיּוּם מִצְוָה זוֹ זֶהוּ כָּל הַתּוֹרָה כּוּלָהּ וְאִידַךְ
פֵּירוּשָׁא הוּא כו'. כִּי יְסוֹד וְשׁוֹרֶשׁ כָּל הַתּוֹרָה הוּא לְהַגְבִּיהַּ וּלְהַעֲלוֹת הַנֶּפֶשׁ
עַל הַגּוּף מַעֲלָה מַעֲלָה עַד עִיקָּרָא וְשָׁרְשָׁא דְכָל עָלְמִין.

When a person regards the body with disdain and rejoices only in the joy of the soul—this provides a direct
and easy path to the fulfillment of the mitzvah, "Love
your fellow as yourself" (LEVITICUS 19:18). . . . Because all [souls] are equal, having one father; which is
why all Jews are called true brothers, due to their common source in the one God. It is only the bodies that
are separate.

Indeed, those for whom the body is the primary thing
and the soul is secondary cannot achieve true love and
brotherhood among themselves, only a love that is dependent on something [i.e., some personal gain].

This is why Hillel the Elder said in regard to the fulfillment of this mitzvah, "This is the entire Torah; the rest

is commentary" (TALMUD, SHABBAT 31A). For the basis and root of the entire Torah is to raise up and exalt the soul above the body, reaching unto the source and root of all the worlds.

TEXT 18

RABBI YOSEF YITSCHAK SCHNEERSOHN, *IGROT KODESH*, VOL. 6, P. 270

כְּשֵׁם שֶׁצָּרִיךְ לֵידַע חֶסְרוֹנוֹת עַצְמוֹ, צָרִיךְ לֵידַע מַעֲלוֹת עַצְמוֹ.

Just as a person needs to know their own deficiencies, they also need to know their own virtues.

RABBI YOSEF YITSCHAK SCHNEERSON (RAYATS, FRIERDIKER REBBE, PREVIOUS REBBE) 1880–1950

Chasidic rebbe, prolific writer, and Jewish activist. Rabbi Yosef Yitschak, the sixth leader of the Chabad movement, actively promoted Jewish religious practice in Soviet Russia and was arrested for these activities. After his release from prison and exile, he settled in Warsaw, Poland, from where he fled Nazi occupation, and arrived in New York in 1940. Settling in Brooklyn, Rabbi Schneerson worked to revitalize American Jewish life. His son-in law, Rabbi Menachem Mendel Schneerson, succeeded him as the leader of the Chabad movement.

Learning Exercise 5.2

The square below contains sixteen "self" words. With a pencil, draw a line from top to bottom, separating the positive from the negative, so that the positive words are to the right of the line and the negative words to the left. You may make the line curve as much as you need to in order to achieve this result.

I am me + I am Not me.

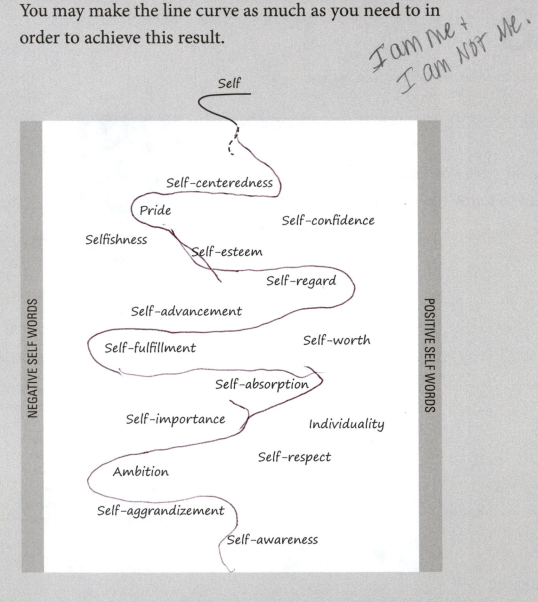

Self

Self-centeredness

Pride

Selfishness

Self-confidence

Self-esteem

Self-regard

Self-advancement

NEGATIVE SELF WORDS

Self-fulfillment

Self-worth

Self-absorption

Self-importance

Individuality

Self-respect

Ambition

Self-aggrandizement

Self-awareness

POSITIVE SELF WORDS

Figure 5.2

Hierarchy of Creation—Conventional Model

GOD

SPIRITUAL
WORLDS
"I'm not me"
consciousness

PHYSICAL
WORLD
"I am me"
consciousness

all the good
stuff

the most
Godly thing
I have.

the spiritual realms
recognize there is
nothing else but G-d

Figure 5.3

Hierarchy of Creation—Alternative Model

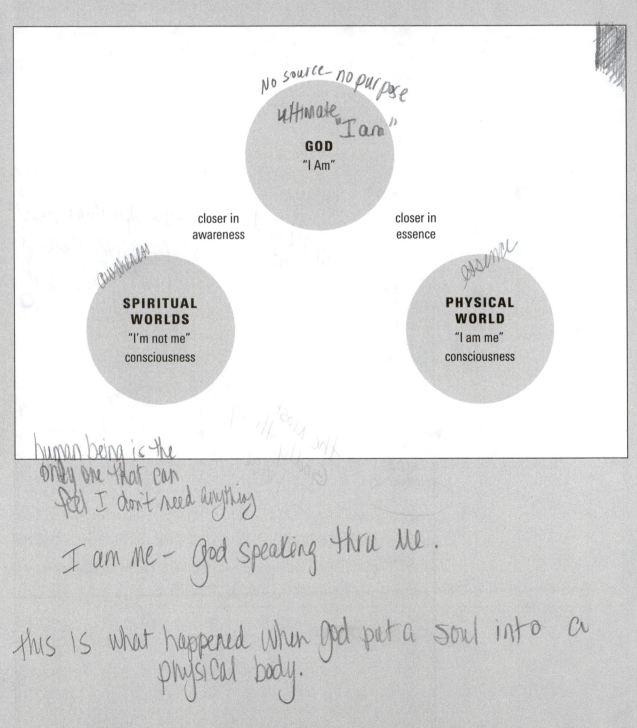

Handwritten annotations:

No source–no purpose
ultimate "I am"

closer in awareness   awareness

closer in essence   essence

human being is the only one that can feel I don't need anything

I am me – God speaking thru me.

this is what happened when god put a soul into a physical body.

QUESTION FOR DISCUSSION

How do we get *both* advantages—the advantage of divine awareness, and the advantage of expressing the divine essence?

Illusion of Male and Female, Carlotta M. Corpron, c. 1946.
(Amon Carter Museum of American Art, Fort Worth, Tex.)

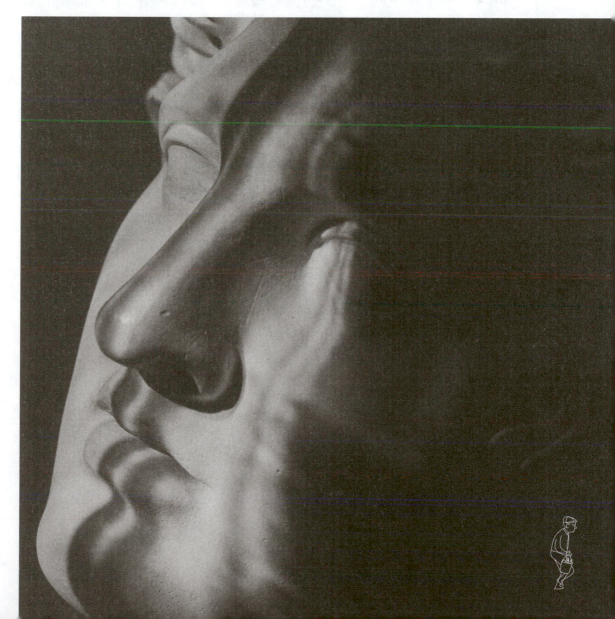

TEXT 19

THE REBBE, RABBI MENACHEM MENDEL SCHNEERSON,
SEFER HAMAAMARIM 5730, P. 143

דַּאֲמִתִּית הַמְּצִיאוּת שֶׁל הַיֵּשׁ הַנִּבְרָא דַּוְקָא הוּא הַיֵּשׁ הָאֲמִתִּי. כִּי דַוְקָא
בְּיֵשׁ הַנִּבְרָא יֶשְׁנָהּ הַהַרְגָּשָׁה שֶׁמְּצִיאוּתוֹ מֵעַצְמוּתוֹ וְאֵינוֹ עָלוּל מֵאֵיזוֹ
סִבָּה. שֶׁהֶרְגֵּשׁ זֶה שָׁרְשׁוֹ רַק בְּעַצְמוּתוֹ וּמַהוּתוֹ יִתְבָּרֵךְ שֶׁאֵינוֹ עָלוּל
מֵאֵיזוֹ עִילָּה שֶׁקָּדְמָה לוֹ . . .

הַטַּעַם שֶׁנִּשְׁתַּנָּה יְצִירַת גּוּף הָאָדָם מִשְּׁאָר כָּל הַנִּבְרָאִים. שֶׁדַּוְקָא בִּבְרִיאַת
הָאָדָם הֲרֵי הַגּוּף הוּא בְּאוֹפֶן שֶׁל דּוֹמֵם מַמָּשׁ. וְכַאֲשֶׁר הַנְּשָׁמָה מִתְלַבֶּשֶׁת
בַּגּוּף וְנֶפֶשׁ הַבַּהֲמִית, וְעַד שֶׁהַנְּשָׁמָה נַעֲשֵׂית לְדָבָר אֶחָד עִם הַגּוּף
וְנֶפֶשׁ הַבַּהֲמִית, דְּאָז הֲרֵי לִפְנֵי הָעֲבוֹדָה יֵשׁ אֶצְלוֹ הַהַרְגָּשָׁה שֶׁמְּצִיאוּתוֹ
מֵעַצְמוּתוֹ, וְאֵינוֹ עָלוּל מֵאֵיזוֹ עִילָּה שֶׁקָּדְמָה לוֹ.

וְזֶהוּ תַּכְלִית הָעֲבוֹדָה, שֶׁיְּגַלֶּה, בָּזֶה גוּפָא שֶׁיֵּשׁ לוֹ הַהֶרְגֵּשׁ דִּמְצִיאוּתוֹ
מֵעַצְמוּתוֹ, דְּהֶרְגֵּשׁ זֶה הוּא לִהְיוֹתוֹ חַד עִם הַיֵּשׁ הָאֲמִתִּי . . . דְּאָז הֲרֵי
דַּוְקָא בַּנְּשָׁמָה כְּפִי שֶׁהִיא לְמַטָּה וּמְלוּבֶּשֶׁת בַּגּוּף, מִתְגַּלֶּה בָּהּ שָׁרְשָׁהּ
הָאֲמִתִּי בְּעַצְמוּתוֹ יִתְבָּרֵךְ, שֶׁהִיא חַד מַמָּשׁ עִם הָעַצְמוּת.

RABBI MENACHEM MENDEL SCHNEERSON
1902–1994

The towering Jewish leader of
the 20th century, known as "the
Lubavitcher Rebbe," or simply as "the
Rebbe." Born in southern Ukraine,
the Rebbe escaped Nazi-occupied
Europe, arriving in the U.S. in June
1941. The Rebbe inspired and guided
the revival of traditional Judaism
after the European devastation,
impacting virtually every Jewish
community the world over. The
Rebbe often emphasized that the
performance of just one additional
good deed could usher in the era
of Mashiach. The Rebbe's scholarly
talks and writings have been printed
in more than 200 volumes.

The essence of the physical self is the divine Self. For only
the physical self possesses a consciousness that its own
existence is self-defined and has no cause or source. This
consciousness can derive only from the very essence of
G-d, which has no cause or source that preceded it. . . .

[This is] the reason why the creation of human body was
different from all other creations. Only in the creation
of the human was the body formed out of inanimate
matter. The soul then invests itself within the body and
the animal soul, to the extent that they form a single

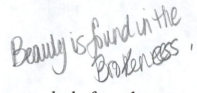
Beauty is found in the Brokenness!

entity. As a result, before the person begins to work on themselves, they feel that their existence is self-defined and does not derive from any preceding cause.

This, then, is the goal of one's service of G-d: to reveal that this very feeling of self-existence is one and the same with the true Self-Existence of G-d. . . . So it is specifically when the soul descends into the physical world and invests itself within the body, that its true source in the divine essence comes to light, and it is revealed that it is one with the Essence.

Der Turm (The Tower), Wolfgang Lettl, oil painting, Augsburg, 1963. (Lettl Collection, Augsburg, Germany)

KEY POINTS

1 The enigma of consciousness and self-awareness has occupied philosophers and scientists for centuries. What is it that makes the human being a "self"? Is our sense of self real, or perhaps just an illusion?

2 The Torah's account of God's creation of the first human being reveals a dichotomy of lowliness and loftiness: a body that was fashioned of the "soil of the earth," and a soul formed in the "image of God." Chasidic teaching adds another dimension to the dichotomy of body and soul. The body has its own consciousness—the Animal Soul—which parallels the divine consciousness of the Godly Soul.

3 In contrast to the "I am me" consciousness of the Animal Soul, the Godly Soul is defined by an "I'm not me" consciousness. Its striving is not to perpetuate its own existence, but to serve the greater truth of its Source.

4 The egotism of the physical self has many negative expressions. It is the root of many negative traits in a person's character; it is the ultimate source of all interpersonal conflict; and it deadens a person's spiritual sensitivity, making them less receptive to Godliness. Chasidic teaching goes so far as to define self-regard as the very the antithesis of holiness.

5 One reason why we have both an egocentric consciousness and an altruistic consciousness is that there is purpose in the struggle itself, as God derives great satisfaction from the conquest of evil.

6 A deeper reason relates to the very essence of our selfhood. The only true "I am" is God; a created being can possess this sensibility only when God chooses to impart something of His own self-awareness to it. Thus, our own sense of self is the imprint of the absolute self of God. When we lead a Godly life, the "I'm not me" awareness of our spiritual soul and the "I am me" consciousness of our physical body together express the ultimate truth of God.

Additional Readings

DO CHABAD TEACHINGS SAY ANYTHING ABOUT THE MIND-BODY PROBLEM?

BY RABBI ELI RUBIN AND MAX ARIEL ABUGOV

Introduction: Philosophical Questions

As human beings we are constantly confronted by the mind-body problem. On the one hand we have physical bodies, complete with arms, legs, a heart and a brain. On the other hand we have mental states: we think, we become emotional, we desire things, we understand things, we enjoy sunsets and the scent of flowers. This led the 17th-century René Descartes to a conclusion that schisms the mind from the body. He postulated that there is a mental substance, *res cogitans*, and a physical substance, *res extensa*. He understood G-d to be a third substance that is neither mental nor physical, and which chooses to make these created substances exist.[1]

From a philosophical point of view Descartes' position, known as dualism, is deeply problematic. If mind and body exist independently of each other, if the mental and the physical are in fact two completely different substances, how do they interact with one another? How does the brain, a physical lump of grey meat, apprehend ethereal mental concepts?[2]

The question of how the mind, or the soul, and the body, relate to each other has concerned philosophers from ancient times till today. But Descartes' dualism has often been rejected, usually in favor of monistic theories positing that mental and physical phenomena actually consist of the same substance. There is

physicalism, claiming that all is matter. There is *idealism*, claiming all is mind. There is *neutral monism*, which suggests that all is neither one nor the other, but a third, unified substance that is the combination of both.[3]

Today, many people assume that everything is physical, that there is no mental state independent of the physical brain. Accordingly, there is no mind and no soul, and hence no mind-body problem. But rather than solving the mind-body problem, this simply replaces it with a problem of a different name. A leading contemporary philosopher thinking about this new conundrum is David Chalmers, and he calls it the "hard" problem of consciousness: Chalmers wants to understand how and why we have subjective experiences.[4]

A computer, for example, processes large quantities of information—apparently without having any mental awareness or subjective experience of those processes. But when humans process information something happens besides the physical, electronic or chemical changes happening in the body and in the brain: We experience these processes subjectively; there is a feeling of "what it is like." Philosophers call these subjective experiences qualia.[5]

Chalmers argues:

RABBI ELI RUBIN

Researcher, writer. Rubin studied Chasidic literature and Jewish Law at the Rabbinical College of America and at *yeshivot* in the U.K., the U.S., and Australia. He has been a research writer and editor at Chabad.org since 2011, focusing on the social and intellectual history of Chabad Chasidism. His work has also appeared in *Hakirah* and *Mosaic Magazine*.

MAX ARIEL ABUGOV

Abugov graduated with a B.A. in psychology from the University of Pennsylvania, where he worked at the Boundaries of Anxiety and Depression Lab. He also attended Yeshivas Kol Yakov Yehudah Hadar HaTorah in Crown Heights, where he developed an appreciation of *Chasidus*. He is passionate about the interdisciplinary study of psychology, philosophy, and religion.

It is undeniable that some organisms are subjects of experience. But the question of how it is that these systems are subjects of experience is perplexing. Why is it that when our cognitive systems engage in visual and auditory information-processing, we have visual or auditory experience: the quality of deep blue, the sensation of middle C? How can we explain why there is something it is like to entertain a mental image, or to experience an emotion? It is widely agreed that experience arises from a physical basis, but we have no good explanation of why and how it so arises. Why should physical processing give rise to a rich inner life at all? It seems objectively unreasonable that it should, and yet it does.[6]

This line of thinking has led Chalmers away from physicalism and persuaded him to consider the view that all physical substance—including rocks and electrons—fundamentally possesses some kind of mental quality.[7] Today this line of thinking is seen as innovative and controversial, but in truth it is one of the most ancient and persistent ideas in the history of philosophy. Similar theories can be found both among early Greek thinkers, and in the Jewish philosophical, kabalistic and midrashic traditions. Philosophers refer to this as panpsychism, which means that everything (*pan*) has a mind or a soul (*psyche*).

It is important to note, however, that not all panpsychic theories are the same. As with other complex philosophical questions, we should realize that different thinkers often fit similar ideas into vastly different systems of thought, and we should always be weary of false equivalences and conflations.[8]

Chabad: A Parallel Conceptual Universe

As a counterpoint to the prevalent assumption that everything is physical, the Chabad view is that everything is divine.[9]

The Chabad intellectual tradition might be described as a conceptual universe that runs parallel to the Western one. It engages with many of the questions raised in the Western philosophical tradition to which Descartes, Chalmers and their interlocutors belong, but brings a different set of concepts, assumptions

and goals, and a different terminology to the table. This is true of the mind-body problem and the "hard" problem of consciousness, and it is true of many other philosophical quandaries as well.[10]

In Chabad thought these questions are made all the more problematic because we are not simply talking about the interface of the mind—or the soul—and the body, but also about the interface of G-d and the world. As the Talmudic sages put it, "just as the soul fills the body, so G-d fills the world."[11] This is taken to a whole new level of difficulty when we consider that G-d is infinite and the world seems to be composed of finite matter. How can the finitude of creation possibly be filled with infinite divinity? The crucial point for the present discussion is that in Chabad thought these paradoxes are all resolved by what can be described as a panentheistic false-dualism: Chabad does not subscribe to a monistic idealism ("everything is ideas") according to which our experience of the physical is some kind of mirage. The physical is at least as real as the spiritual. But both physicality and spirituality are refractions of singular divinity. From this perspective, the designation of the physical realm as a "world of falsehood" (עלמא דשיקרא) should not be understood as a denial of the reality of its existence. The falsehood lies in the impression that the utter singularity of all-encompassing divinity is compromised by the dual modes of divine manifestation.

The unavoidable reality of the physical universe is emphasized in an oft cited discourse by the fourth rebbe of Chabad-Lubavitch, Rabbi Shmuel Schneersohn ("Maharash," 1834–1888):

The existence of the world, and all that is created, is a reality. . . . For if we say it is only that it so appears to us, if so what is the meaning of the verse "In the beginning of G-d's creation" (Genesis 1:1)? Did not no creation occur at all, but rather it was made to appear to us as if it was so? Therefore we must say that the world does exist as a substantive reality (yesh ve-davar). . . .[12]

In the same breath, R. Shmuel also emphasizes that the physical reality of creation is not something other than G-d:

In truth there is no physical existence other than divinity, for in truth the capacity for concealment is also divinity like the capacity for revelation. . . . All the physical things that are created are themselves literally divinity.[13]

Even more radical than the equation of physicality with divinity is a phrase oft repeated by the seventh rebbe of Chabad-Lubavitch, Rabbi Menachem M. Schneerson of righteous memory, which emphasizes that physical existence is ultimately a deeper expression of divine reality and truth than spirituality: "The created being is itself [an unmediated manifestation of] the true being [of G-d]. . . ." For the most part, however, this truth remains concealed by the very facade of otherness and duality that most gives it expression. It is only "through the work in this world to remove the concealments and veils" . . . that "it will be revealed in the created being that it itself is [an unmediated manifestation of] the true being."[14] As will be further explained below, it is precisely in the most abject sphere of cosmic being—or more precisely, in the transformation of the abject into the exalted—that the greatest expression of divine transcendence is found.

Hasidic Panpsychism

There are many relevant texts that could be cited as examples of the different ways in which Chabad teachings approach the problem, its solution, and various resulting implications. Already in the first generation of Chabad we find that panpsychism was an issue of particular interest and controversy. One early chassidic work, titled "Testament of the Baal Shem Tov," records the following "major principle": "In everything that exists in the world there are holy sparks, there is nothing empty of the sparks, even wood and stones, and even all the actions that a person executes". . . .[15] Rabbi Schneur Zalman of Liadi similarly cites the Lurianic teaching that "even in the literally inanimate—like stones, dust and water—there is a soul and spiritual life . . . which enlivens and creates the inanimate, that it may emerge as an existence from nothing". . . .[16]

In a direct attack on this concept, Rabbi Eliyahu—the famed Gaon of Vilna—wrote that the chassidim "proclaim of every stick and every stone, 'These are your gods, Israel!'" By borrowing a phrase from the biblical episode of the golden calf, he equated chassidism with Judaism's worst example of public idolatry.[17] The Gaon apparently sought to uphold a dualistic schism between the spiritual and the physical, between G-d and the world. Elsewhere, he explicitly argued that G-d transcends the world, and that it is only divine knowledge and superintendence that extends into the created realm.[18]

The Gaon's attack was countered by R. Schneur Zalman with a sharp argument proving that divine superintendence could not be accounted for without resort to a form of divine panpsychism. Following the Maimonidean principle that divine knowledge is self-knowledge—G-d being the knower, the subject of knowledge, and the knowledge itself[19]—R. Schneur Zalman concludes that G-d's knowledge of the world entails that the world itself is not in any way separate from G-d. Implicitly referring to those who shared the Gaon's position, he wrote:

Since they believe that G-d knows all created beings in this lowly world and superintends them, they are compelled to accept that His knowledge of them does not add to Him any plurality or novelty, for He knows all through knowing His self. It is as if His being and essence and knowledge are all one.[20]

Aristotle famously described *G-d* as "thought thinking itself." But the Maimonidean view, as interpreted by R. Schneur Zalman, is that *all reality* is divine thought thinking itself. In technical philosophical terminology the complexity of the Chabad position might be captured with the designation "theological panpsychic false-dualism." But even as we speak of panpsychism we must also recall that "G-d's thoughts are not as our thoughts" (Isaiah 55:8). G-d's thoughts extend beyond the realm of ideas to animate and encompass physical reality as well.[21] We must also recall that G-d ultimately transcends the category of thought altogether.[22] However central the principle of divine panpsychism is to the Chabad system of thought, it must always be considered in terms of what Elliot Wolfson has designated "the logic inherent" to Chabad thought: "a way of thinking that begets an annihilation of thinking."[23]

The Mitzvah: Fusing Body and Soul

From the Chabad perspective there is no "hard" problem of consciousness. Consciousness is not an anomalous product of the physical universe. Rather, the physical universe is an anomalous product of divine consciousness. The "hard" problem of Chabad thought is: How does the finite universe exist without compromising the infinite singularity of G-d?[24]

Rather than an outright rejection of dualism, Chabad teachings constantly affirm that G-d at once fills the finite realm immanently (*memale kol almin*) and infinitely transcends it (*sovev kol almin*). Yet G-d's essential being (*atzmuto u-mahuto*) is neither finite nor infinite. Nor can G-d's essential being simply be reduced to that which encompasses those poles. G-d is instead understood to transcend all definable categories and limitations, and can therefore be equally manifest in the finite and the physical as in the infinite and the spiritual. The result of this false-duality is the impression that the finite world is something other than the infinite G-d. But the truth is that G-d is the immanent core of all reality.[25]

Moving from the cosmic to the microcosmic, a similar model of false dualism—or more precisely, false multiplicity—is applied to the relationship between the soul and the body. In the second chapter of *Likutei Amarim—Tanya*, R. Schneur Zalman describes a hierarchy of souls, but emphasizes that "all of them, from the beginning of all levels to the end of all levels . . . are drawn from the supernal mind [of G-d]." The difference between one soul and another is only in the degree to which they *openly reveal* G-dliness in their own lives and actions, and in the world around them. But all souls are fundamentally bound up in the circle of divine consciousness. Here too, R. Schneur Zalman cites Maimonides' principle that G-d is the knower, the subject of knowledge, and knowledge itself.

The divine quality of the soul extends to the physical body as well, but it only becomes overtly revealed therein through the performance of mitzvot, divinely mandated commandments. In *Likutei Amarim—Tanya*, chapter twenty-three, R. Schneur Zalman explains that when a person performs a commandment "the lowest faculty of their divine soul (*levush ha-hitzon shel nefesh ha-elokit*), which is its capacity for action, is vested in the animation of that mitzvah performance. . . . Therefore, also the limbs of the person's body that are performing the mitzvah . . . become a literal vehicle for the supernal will [of G-d]. By way of example, the hand that distributes charity to the poor . . . the feet that walk in the cause of a mitzvah, and likewise the mouth that speaks words of Torah, and the brain that thinks of Torah matters, fear of heaven, and the greatness of G-d." These limbs and organs, R. Schneur Zalman explains, are themselves "sanctified" because they have become transparent to their divine core.[26]

The divine nature of the body can only be openly revealed through mitzvah observance and Torah study. But in truth, the Baal Shem Tov taught, even the body's most mundane cravings are identical with the cravings of the soul. "Hungry as well as thirsty, their soul enwraps itself within them" (Psalms 107:5). In its original context this is a poetic image describing wanderers lost in the desert, whose souls contract as their hunger and thirst intensifies. But the Baal Shem Tov decontextualized the verse and reinterpreted it to mean that the divine soul is enwrapped within the hunger and thirst of the physical body. Externally the body's cravings seem mundane, even crass, but in truth they stem from the soul's craving to raise up the divine sparks that are concealed throughout all reality. Not only is the body not the enemy of the soul, on the contrary, the body and the soul are actually in sync. They function as one, yet mirror the false-duality of the cosmic singularity.[27] The soul's mission on earth, accordingly, is to make the body—and all aspects of earthly life—transparent to the divine core of all reality.[28]

Yehidah: The Singular Substance of Everything

The above passages allude to another oft discussed theme in Chabad teachings. Drawing on earlier rabbinic sources, each individual soul is understood to have five general levels.[29] The lowest, *nefesh*, corresponds to the soul's capacity for action, which is channeled through the body to have a transformative impact in the physical world. The highest is referred to as *yehidah*, meaning singularity, because it is utterly bound up with the singular essence of G-d. The *yehidah* transcends the false dualism that distinguishes between the physical and the spiritual, and therefore cannot even be associated with the loftiest of spiritual soul faculties. Yet it is precisely the transcendence of the *yehidah* that is the immanent core of all levels of soul expression, including the lowest, which animates the actions of the body.

Though the *yehidah* is discussed in many Chabad teachings, its significance is most fully articulated and emphasized in a treatise by the seventh rebbe of Chabad-Lubavitch, Rabbi Menachem M. Schneerson of righteous memory. In this treatise, *On the Essence of Chassidus*, the essential core of divine being and the essential core of the soul are described in precisely the same terms. In both cases, the disclosure of the essence is synonymous with the dissolution of the false opposition between spirituality and physicality, light and darkness, good and evil:

> All [spiritual] revelations, even the very loftiest, are bound in the category of light and revelation. . . . Consequently, the existence of evil . . . is in opposition to them, and it is therefore not in their power to transform it to good (only to battle with it till it is effaced). Only the essence of G-d . . . which is uncontained by any form and which can have nothing in opposition to it . . . has the power to transform it to good.[30]

The essential transcendence of G-d, in other words, is such that spirituality and physicality alike—and even good and evil—are equally inadequate to give it expression. It is axiomatic that the physical realm conceals the all-encompassing presence of G-d. But here it emerges that the same is true of the spiritual realm, of spiritual experience and activity as well. The only way in which the essence can be tangibly disclosed is in the overcoming of binaries, through transforming evil into good, through infusing physical reality with the spirit of divinity.

Paradoxically, Chabad's radical conception of divine transcendence leads us to find the greatest expression of that transcendence in the most abject sphere of cosmic being, or more precisely, in the transformation of the abject into the exalted. The same applies on the microcosmic plane—the essential potency of the soul is only expressed in transformative activities that overcome the divide between body and soul, revealing the G-dly core even of physical existence. But once the essence is revealed it illuminates all faculties of the soul and all aspects of reality:

> Only when the [soul] faculties come to refine a physical object beyond the individual self... (using it for the sake of heaven)—specifically then is the yehidah *revealed in them.*[31]

In the final paragraph of his treatise on *yehidah*—which he also associates with the essence of chassidic teaching itself—the Rebbe cites the messianic vision articulated by R. Schneur Zalman of Liadi in *Tanya*, chapters thirty-six and thirty-seven:

> The physicality of the body and the world will be purified . . . as it is written, "all flesh [shall see] together, etc." "all dwellers of your universe". . . . This ultimate wholeness of the messianic era . . . is dependent on our actions and work throughout the era of exile. . . .[32]

In philosophical language we might say that the ultimate goal of all human endeavor is to overcome the false sense of dualism that leads us to the mind-body problem in the first place.[33] We achieve this through Torah study and mitzvah observance, through serving G-d in all aspects of earthly life, and through transforming evil into good.[34] We are not simply bodies, nor are we minds, nor do we merely combine the two. Ultimately, there is but one single substance, uncompromised by the mind-body duality. The multiple dimensions of existence are real. Yet they are all refractions of the singular substance of G-d.

Reprinted with permission from Chabad.org

Endnotes

[1] See Justin Skirry, "*René Descartes: The Mind-Body Distinction*," in *The Internet Encyclopedia of Philosophy*.

[2] See Howard Robinson, "*Dualism*," in *The Stanford Encyclopedia of Philosophy* (Spring 2016 Edition), Edward N. Zalta (ed.). A classical Jewish reference to the mind-body problem, often referenced in Chabad teachings, is the remark of Rabbi Moshe Isserles ("Rema," 1520–1572), in his gloss to *Shulkhan Arukh, Orakh Hayim* 6:1. Rema suggests that the liturgical formulation praising G-d as "the one who acts wondrously" (*ha-maphlia la'asot*) can be understood as an allusion to the fact that G-d "preserves the spirit of man within him, *binding something spiritual to something physical*, all through Him being the healer of all flesh, for then man is healthy and his soul is preserved within him." (Emphasis added.)

[3] See Leopold Stubenberg, "*Neutral Monism*," in *The Stanford Encyclopedia of Philosophy* (Fall 2014 Edition), Edward N. Zalta (ed.).

[4] See also Thomas Nagel, *Mind and Cosmos: Why the Materialist Neo-Darwinian Conception of Nature Is Almost Certainly False* (Oxford University Press: New York and Oxford, 2012), 45–46: "On a purely materialist understanding of biology, consciousness would have to be regarded as a tremendous and inexplicable brute fact about the world. If it is to be explained in any sense naturalistically, through the understanding of organic life, something fundamental must be changed in our conception of the natural order that gave rise to life."

[5] See Michael Tye, "*Qualia*," in *The Stanford Encyclopedia of Philosophy* (Fall 2015 Edition), Edward N. Zalta (ed.).

[6] David J. Chalmers, "*Facing Up to the Problem of Consciousness*," in the *Journal of Consciousness Studies* 2(3): 200–19, 1995.

[7] See David J. Chalmers, *The Conscious Mind: In Search of a Fundamental Theory* (Oxford University Press: New York and Oxford, 1996), 299: "I hope to have said enough to show that we at least ought to take the possibility of some sort of panpsychism seriously: there seem to be no knockdown arguments against the view, and there are various positive reasons why one might embrace it." See also the relevant discussions of panpsychism in Thomas Nagel, *Mind and Cosmos: Why the Materialist Neo-Darwinian Conception of Nature Is Almost Certainly False* (Oxford University Press: New York and Oxford, 2012), 57–58 and 61–63.

[8] For an overview of some important proponents of various forms of panpsychism throughout the history of Western philosophy, see William Seager and Sean Allen-Hermanson, "*Panpsychism*," in *The Stanford Encyclopedia of Philosophy* (Fall 2015 Edition), Edward N. Zalta (ed.). For a classical rabbinic example of panpsychism that is often cited in Chabad literature, see *Bereishit Rabbah*, 10:6: "There isn't a single blade of grass that does not have an angel in heaven that smites it and tells it to grow. . . ." For more direct examples from kabbalistic and chassidic teachings—including the particulars of Chabad's panpsychic conception, which is rooted in a Maimonidean axiom—see below.

[9] See Rabbi Yosef Yitzchak Schneersohn, *Sefer Hasichos 5690* (Kehot Publication Society: New York, 1995), 86, (עד איז אלץ, אלץ איז עד) and further sources cited there, n. 10. Also notable are the words of Rabbi DovBer Schneuri (the "Mitteler Rebbe"), son and successor of Rabbi Schneur Zalman of Liadi, founder of Chabad (the "Alter Rebbe"): "The central object of my father's teachings, was to fix the simple singularity of G-d—that is, the essence of the infinite—in the mind and heart of each individual according to what they can conceive, each according to their ability. . . ." (Introduction to *Imrei Binah*.) The singular existence of G-d is a topic that is dealt with in great richness and depth throughout the Chabad corpus, but its locus classicus is the second section of *Likutei Amarim—Tanya, Shaar Hayikhud Ve-ha-emunah*. For a more succinct treatment see the first section of *Likutei Amarim—Tanya*, chapters 20–21.

[10] For more on the relationship between Chabad teachings and the Western tradition of philosophy, touching on the work of William James, Isaiah Berlin, Hilary Putnam et al., see Eli Rubin, *Can You Square the Circle of Faith? How to preserve an open mind and a unified core of cohesive meaning*, http://www.chabad.org/library/article_cdo/aid/2849758/jewish/Can-You-Square-the-Circle-of-Faith.htm .

[11] *Midrash Tehillim*, 103a.

[12] Rabbi Shmuel Schneersohn of Lubavitch ("the Rebbe Maharash"), "*Mi Komokhah*," in *Likutei Torah—Torat Shmuel, Sefer 5629* (Kehot Publication Society: New York, 1992), 161–162.

[13] Rabbi Shmuel Schneersohn of Lubavitch, *Ibid.*, 163. See also Rabbi Shalom DovBer Schneersohn, *Torat Shalom* (Kehot Publication Society: New York, 1970), 198: "All is encompassed in G-d's essence, accordingly no other being exists at all. Yet, this implies that nothing was created, which is impossible to say, since creation is itself the divine name *Elokim*. It is a divine name and therefore true. That is, *Elokim* exists, and accordingly there is concealment (that is, there is otherly existence, which is the concealment). However the concealment is encompassed in the essence, because the divine name *Elokim*—which is the divine power that contracts—is also of the essence. . . ."

[14] Rabbi Menachem Mendel Schneerson ("the Rebbe"), "*Vehit'halakhti*," in *Torat Menachem 3, Shnat 5711*, 115. The word manifestation is inserted into my translation of this passage to emphasize that it is not to be taken as a reductive description of divine being, but rather as an apotheosistic description of physical being: In contrast to the revelation of G-d via the medium of spirituality, physicality is a direct manifestation of divine being. While this idea was most emphasized by the seventh rebbe it has a long history in Chabad thought. For a discussion of the concealing and concrete dimension of reality as the more unmediated embodiment of divine being in the thought of the third rebbe, the Tzemach Tzedek (1789–1866), see Eli Rubin, "*Covert Luminosity: The reshimu, the kav, and the concretization of creativity*," http://www.chabad.org/library/article_cdo/aid/3201311/jewish/Covert-Luminosity.htm.

[15] *Tzavaat ha-Rivash* #141. page 71 in the Kehot Publication Society, 1998 edition.

[16] *Likutei Amarim—Tanya, Shaar Hayikhud Ve-ha-emunah*, Chapter 1.

[17] See Mordecai Wilenski, *Hasidim and Mitnaggedim*, vol. 1 (Bialik: Jerusalem, 1990), 188–189.

[18] *Aderet Eliyahu* to Isaiah 6:3; Supplementary notes in *Be'ur ha-Gra* to *Sifra di-Tzeni'uta, Sod ha-Tzimtzum*, p. 75 [38a in Hebrew pagination]. For a more detailed discussion of these sources see Eli Rubin, "*Immanent Transcendence: Chassidim, mitnagdim, and the debate about tzimtzum*," http://www.chabad.org/library/article_cdo/aid/2306809/jewish/Immanent-Transcendence.htm.

[19] *Mishneh Torah, Hilchot Yesodei ha-Torah* 2:10.

[20] *Shaar ha-Yichud veha-Emunah*, ch. 7, pp. 165–166 [83a–b in the Hebrew pagination].

21 See *Likutei Amarim—Tanya*, end of Chapter 48: "His thought and knowledge, with which He knows all the creations, encompasses each one of them from top to bottom, and its interior and innermost being, all literal actuality . . ." On the distinctions and similarities between thought and speech as applied to the concept of divine creation see *Likutei Amarim—Tanya*, chapters 20 and 21, see also the relevant discussion of those chapters in Eli Rubin, *'The Pen Shall Be Your Friend': Intertextuality, Intersociality, and the Cosmos—Examples of the Tzemach Tzedek's Way in the Development of Chabad Chassidic Thought,*" § on "Speech, Externalization, and Divine Singularity," http://www.chabad.org/library/article_cdo/aid/3286179/jewish/The-Pen-Shall-Be-Your-Friend.htm.

22 See *Shaar Ha-yikhud Ve-ha-emunah*, note to chapter 9, p. 173 [87a in Hebrew pagination]: "After the infinite light is vested in the receptacles of *chabad*, then it is possible to say what Maimonides writes: 'He is the knower, the subject of knowledge, and the knowledge itself, and in knowledge of himself, etc.' . . . But without the *tsimtsum* and investment mentioned above it is not possible at all to say, 'He is the knower, and He is the subject of knowledge, etc.' For he is not in the category of knowing and knowledge at all, but entirely transcendent without limit beyond the category of wisdom, to the extent that wisdom [even divine wisdom] is considered in comparison to Him as [the realm of] physical action."

23 Elliot R. Wolfson, *"Nequddat ha-Reshimu—The Trace of Transcendence and the Transcendence of Trace: The Paradox of Simsum in the RaShaB's Hemshekh Ayin Beit,"* in *Kabbalah 30* (2013), p. 94. The idea that the ultimate goal of Chabad thought is to go beyond the entire category of thought altogether is given explicit expression by Rabbi Yosef Yitzchak Schneersohn in *Likutei Dibburim, Vol. 1* (Yiddish Edition, Kehot Publication Society 2009), 305 [153a in Hebrew pagination]. Commenting on the biblical prophecy that in the messianic era divinity will be revealed so that "all flesh shall see," he argues that this signifies a fundamental shift in the way we apprehend divinity: "We will see, and the seer will be the body. . . . In the present era, the soul allows the body to understand an intellectual concept. This means that the soul is the communicator [of divine revelation] and the body the recipient. But when the messiah will come the body itself will apprehend; it will see divinity with the sight of its physical eyes literally; and it will be the communicator [of divine revelation] while the soul will receive [that revelation] from the body." Our current mode of apprehending G-d is conceptual and spiritual, and therefore chiefly mediated by the soul. But in the messianic era we will apprehend G-d somatically and physically, and the soul will receive this more essential form of revelation through the mediation of the body. This passage is particularly relevant given the present discussion centering on the relationship between body and soul, and the relationship between singular divinity and physical reality.

24 See the closing passage of *Shaar Ha-yikhud Ve-ha-emunah*, chapter 3.

25 See for example, Rabbi Schneur Zalman of Liadi, *Maamarei Admur Hazaken 5569* (Kehot Publication Society: New York, 2005), 262: "Such is the immense exaltedness of the essence of the infinite . . . just as He is not grasped and limited in the physicality of the created realms (*b'ya*) so He is not grasped in the spirituality of the realm of emanation (*olam ha-atsilut*), for before Him are literally equal spirituality and physicality, [the realms of] emanation and action, as it is written, 'as dark, as light' (Psalms 139:12), and up and down are equal. . . ."; Rabbi Menachem Mendel Schneerson, "*Patach Eliyahu 5715,*" in *Sefer Ha-maamarim Melukat, Vol. 2* (Kehot Publication Society: New York, 2002), 106: "The binding of nature and that which transcends nature is through the revelation of the [divine] essence, which transcends both of them." See further sources discussed and cited below.

26 See also Rabbi Yosef Yitzchak Schneersohn, *Likutei Dibburim, Vol. 1* (Yiddish Edition, Kehot Publication Society 2009), 310 [155b in Hebrew pagination]: "The hidden power [namely, the essence of divine being] that is in the physical is only revealed when the physical is used for the purpose for which the creator created it." This concept will be further elaborated below.

27 *Keter Shem Tov* (Kehot Publication Society: New York, 2004), section 194, in the name of the Baal Shem Tov, also discussed and elucidated by Rabbi Menachem Mendel Schneerson, *Likutei Sichot, vol. 19* (Kehot Publication Society: New York, 2006), 295–297.

28 See also Rabbi Menachem Mendel Schneerson, "*Veshavti Beshalom 5738,*" in *Sefer Ha-maamarim Melukat, Vol. 2* (Kehot Publication Society: New York, 2002), 17–38.

29 See *Bereishit Rabbah*, 10:9 and *Devarim Rabbah*, 2:37. See also *Zohar, Vol. 1*, 81a and 206a; *Zohar Vol. 3*, 152a.

30 Rabbi Menachem Mendel Schneerson, "*Inyannah Shel Torat Ha-chassidut,*" in *Sefer Ha-erchim Habad, vol. 1* (Kehot Publication Society: New York, 1970) section 19, p. 5771. The present translations are all my own, for a full English translation of this treatise see *On the Essence of Chassidus* (Kehot Publication Society: New York, 1986), viewable here.

31 Rabbi Menachem Mendel Schneerson, *Ibid.*, section 20, p. 5772–5773.

32 Rabbi Menachem Mendel Schneerson, *Ibid.*, section 21, p. 5773; Rabbi Schneur Zalman of Liadi, *Likutei Amarim—Tanya*, chapters 36 and 37. In a footnote to the main body of the text in "*Inyannah Shel Torat Ha-chassidut,*" the Rebbe takes the opportunity to further underscore Rabbi Schneur Zalman's inclusion of the non-Jewish nations in his vision of universal transformation. The latter writes that "from the overwhelming revelation to the Jewish people the darkness of the nations will also be reached (יגי' חשך האומות ג'כ)." Drawing on a text from Rabbi DovBer Schneuri ("the Mitteler Rebbe") the Rebbe suggests that this can be read to mean "the darkness of the nations will also be transformed," adding that this is "similar to what was explained above that [through the revelation of the *yehidah*] bad itself is turned to good." This remark is particularly significant as it complicates the assumption that Chabad discussions of the soul and its relationship to G-d, and discussions of the *yehidah* in particular, apply uniquely to Jews. In this definitive treatise, which consciously lays bare the essence of Chabad chassidic teaching through the central motif of the *yehidah*, the Rebbe concludes with a statement implying that this transformative vision must ultimately overcome the distinctions between Jew and non-Jew as well. For an important and illuminating discussion of the highly complex discourse in Chabad texts on this issue, see Elliot R. Wolfson, "*Apocalyptic Crossing: Beyond the (Non-)Jewish Other*" in *Open Secret: Postmessianic Messianism and the Mystical Revision of Menachem Mendel Schneerson*" (Columbia University Press: New York, 2009), pages 224–264. See also Jonathan Garb, *Yearnings of the Soul: Psychological Thought in Modern Kabbalah* (The University of Chicago Press: Chicago and London, 2015), 200, n. 12; Wojciech Tworek, *Time in the Teachings of Rabbi Shneur Zalman of Liadi*

(Unpublished PhD dissertation, University College London, September 2014), 126–136. Here it is also worth citing a related passage by Rabbi Levi Yitzchak of Berditchev, *Kedushat Levi Ha-Shalom*, Vol. 2 (Jerusalem, 1958), 413–414, as recently discussed by Shaul Magid, "*Jewish Ethics Through A Hasidic Lens*," in *Hasidism Incarnate* (Stanford University Press, 2015), 62–66, and by Eli Rubin, "'*The Pen Shall Be Your Friend': Intertextuality, Intersociality, and the Cosmos—Examples of the Tzemach Tzedek's Way in the Development of Chabad Chassidic Thought*."

33 For more on the overcoming, or overturning, of the mind body duality in the messianic era, see *Likutei Dibburim, Vol. 1* (Yiddish Edition, Kehot Publication Society 2009), 305 [153a in Hebrew pagination], and the relevant discussion above, n. 23.

34 For an extended exposition on why the sanctification of the mundane, and the transformation of evil into good through a fundamental process of return to G-d (*teshuvah*), provides the ultimate expression of the transcendent essence, see Rabbi Menachem Mendel Schneerson, "*Veshavti Be-shalom 5738*," in *Sefer Ha-maamarim Melukot Vol. 2* (Kehot Publication Society: New York, 2002), 17–38.

Lesson

IS CHOICE REAL?

If God already knows what we will do tomorrow, is "free choice" nothing more than an illusion? And with so many factors outside of our control influencing our choices, how "free" could they possibly be? Ultimately, to fully experience choice, we need to better understand the source of our deepest desires, as well as the nature of the choices we face in our lives.

La Fortune, Man Ray, oil on linen, 1938.
(Whitney Museum of American Art, New York)

TEXT 1

DEUTERONOMY 30:15–19

רְאֵה נָתַתִּי לְפָנֶיךָ הַיּוֹם אֶת הַחַיִּים וְאֶת הַטּוֹב. וְאֶת הַמָּוֶת וְאֶת הָרָע . . .
הַחַיִּים וְהַמָּוֶת נָתַתִּי לְפָנֶיךָ, הַבְּרָכָה וְהַקְּלָלָה. וּבָחַרְתָּ בַּחַיִּים.

See, I have given before you, this day, life and good, and
death and evil. . . .

Life and death I have set before you, blessing and curse;
and you shall choose life.

Locks (detail), Inshō Dōmoto, pigment on paper, 1951. (Kyoto
Prefectural Domoto-Insho Museum of Fine Arts, Kyōto-shi, Japan)

Fundamental to any Moral system.

Choice. Fundamental of the Torah.

TEXT 2

MAIMONIDES, *MISHNEH TORAH*, LAWS OF REPENTANCE 5:1–4

רְשׁוּת לְכָל אָדָם נְתוּנָה. אִם רָצָה לְהַטּוֹת עַצְמוֹ לְדֶרֶךְ טוֹבָה וְלִהְיוֹת צַדִּיק, הָרְשׁוּת בְּיָדוֹ, וְאִם רָצָה לְהַטּוֹת עַצְמוֹ לְדֶרֶךְ רָעָה וְלִהְיוֹת רָשָׁע, הָרְשׁוּת בְּיָדוֹ . . .

וְדָבָר זֶה עִיקָר גָּדוֹל הוּא וְהוּא עַמּוּד הַתּוֹרָה וְהַמִּצְוָה. שֶׁנֶּאֱמַר, "רְאֵה נָתַתִּי לְפָנֶיךָ הַיּוֹם אֶת הַחַיִּים" . . . אִילּוּ הָאֵ-ל הָיָה גּוֹזֵר עַל הָאָדָם לִהְיוֹת צַדִּיק אוֹ רָשָׁע, אוֹ אִילּוּ הָיָה שָׁם דָּבָר שֶׁמּוֹשֵׁךְ אֶת הָאָדָם בְּעִיקָר תּוֹלַדְתּוֹ לְדֶרֶךְ מִן הַדְּרָכִים, אוֹ לְמַדָּע מִן הַמַּדָּעוֹת, אוֹ לְדֵעָה מִן הַדֵּעוֹת, אוֹ לְמַעֲשֶׂה מִן הַמַּעֲשִׂים . . . הֵיאַךְ הָיָה מְצַוֶּה לָנוּ עַל יְדֵי הַנְּבִיאִים עֲשֵׂה כָּךְ וְאַל תַּעֲשֶׂה כָּךְ . . . ? וּמַה מָּקוֹם הָיָה לְכָל הַתּוֹרָה כֻּלָּהּ? וּבְאֵי זֶה דִין וְאֵי זֶה מִשְׁפָּט נִפְרַע מִן הָרָשָׁע אוֹ מְשַׁלֵּם שָׂכָר לַצַּדִּיק . . . ?

RABBI MOSHE BEN MAIMON (MAIMONIDES, RAMBAM) 1135–1204

Halachist, philosopher, author, and physician. Maimonides was born in Córdoba, Spain. After the conquest of Córdoba by the Almohads, he fled Spain and eventually settled in Cairo, Egypt. There, he became the leader of the Jewish community and served as court physician to the vizier of Egypt. He is most noted for authoring the *Mishneh Torah*, an encyclopedic arrangement of Jewish law, and for his philosophical work, *Guide for the Perplexed*. His rulings on Jewish law are integral to the formation of halachic consensus.

Freedom of choice has been granted to every person. If a person wants to turn to the path of good and be righteous, the choice is theirs; and if a person wants to turn to the path of evil and be wicked, the choice is theirs. . . .

This concept is a fundamental principle and a pillar of the Torah and its commandments. As it is written, "See, I have given before you, this day, life [and good, and death and evil]." . . . Were God to decree that a person should be righteous or wicked, of if there were to be something in a person's primary nature that would compel them toward a particular path, a particular conviction, a particular character trait, or a particular deed . . . how could God command us through the prophets, "do this" and "do not do this" . . . ? What place would the entire Torah have? And by what measure of justice would God punish the wicked and reward the righteous . . . ?

TEXT 3

RAAVAD, GLOSS ON *MISHNEH TORAH*, LAWS OF REPENTANCE 5:5

> וְהַדָּבָר יָדוּעַ שֶׁכָּל מִקְרֵה הָאָדָם, קָטָן וְגָדוֹל, מְסָרוֹ הַבּוֹרֵא בְּכֹחַ הַמַּזָּלוֹת.
> אֶלָּא שֶׁנָּתַן בּוֹ הַשֵּׂכֶל לִהְיוֹתוֹ מַחֲזִיקוֹ לָצֵאת מִתַּחַת הַמַּזָּל. וְהוּא הַכֹּחַ
> הַנָּתוּן בָּאָדָם לִהְיוֹתוֹ טוֹב אוֹ רַע.

As is known, everything that happens to a person, whether a major event or a minor one, the Creator placed in the hands of the constellations. However, God gave a person a mind that is empowered to overcome the influence of the constellations. This is the power given to a person to be good or bad.

Forces of nature that impacts our lives.

RABBI AVRAHAM BEN DAVID (RAAVAD III) CA. 1125–1198

Mystic and author. Rabbi Avraham served as rabbi of Posquieres (today Vauvert) in Provence. He is most famous for his critical notes on Rambam's *Mishneh Torah;* he also wrote commentaries on the Talmud, *Sifra,* and *Rif,* and authored *Baalei Hanefesh,* a compilation of laws relating to Jewish family law. Raavad was wealthy and served as a patron for the charity institutions in Posquieres.

TEXT 4

TALMUD, SHABBAT 156A

> הַאי מַאן דִּבְמַאֲדִים יְהִי גְּבַר אֵשֵׁיד דְּמָא. אָמַר רַב אַשִׁי: אִי אוּמָנָא, אִי
> גַּנָּבָא, אִי טַבָּחָא, אִי מוֹהֲלָא.

One who is born under the influence of Mars will be a person who sheds blood. Said Rav Ashi: Either a surgeon, or a robber, or a butcher, or a *mohel*.

BABYLONIAN TALMUD

A literary work of monumental proportions that draws upon the legal, spiritual, intellectual, ethical, and historical traditions of Judaism. The 37 tractates of the Babylonian Talmud contain the teachings of the Jewish sages from the period after the destruction of the Second Temple through the fifth century CE. It has served as the primary vehicle for the transmission of the Oral Law and the education of Jews over the centuries; it is the entry point for all subsequent legal, ethical, and theological Jewish scholarship.

— Fate is the hand of the cards we have been dealt
Choice is how we play that hand.

TEXT 5

ETHICS OF THE FATHERS 3:15

הַכֹּל צָפוּי, וְהָרְשׁוּת נְתוּנָה.

All is foreseen, and free choice is granted.

ETHICS OF THE FATHERS
(*PIRKEI AVOT*)

A six-chapter work on Jewish ethics that is studied widely by Jewish communities, especially during the summer. The first five chapters are from the Mishnah, tractate Avot. Avot differs from the rest of the Mishnah in that it does not focus on legal subjects; it is a collection of the sages' wisdom on topics related to character development, ethics, healthy living, piety, and the study of Torah.

? QUESTION FOR DISCUSSION

What is the connection between the two statements, "all is foreseen" and "free choice is granted"?

2 truths —

➤ God Knows everything that is going to happen.

on the other hand ...

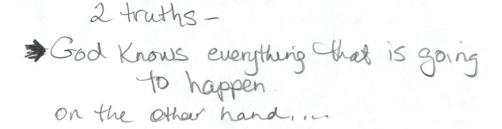

TEXT 6

MAIMONIDES, *MISHNEH TORAH,* LAWS OF REPENTANCE 5:5

שֶׁמָּא תֹּאמַר: וַהֲלֹא הַקָּדוֹשׁ בָּרוּךְ הוּא יוֹדֵעַ כָּל מַה שֶׁיִּהְיֶה. וְקוֹדֶם שֶׁיִּהְיֶה,
יָדַע שֶׁזֶּה יִהְיֶה צַדִּיק אוֹ רָשָׁע אוֹ לֹא יָדַע? אִם יָדַע שֶׁהוּא יִהְיֶה צַדִּיק, אִי
אֶפְשָׁר שֶׁלֹּא יִהְיֶה צַדִּיק. וְאִם תֹּאמַר שֶׁיָּדַע שֶׁיִּהְיֶה צַדִּיק וְאֶפְשָׁר שֶׁיִּהְיֶה
רָשָׁע, הֲרֵי לֹא יָדַע הַדָּבָר עַל בּוּרְיוֹ!

One may ask: God certainly knows all that will transpire. Now, before it happened, did God know whether the person will be righteous or wicked, or did He not know? If God knew that the person would be righteous, then it was not possible for that person to not be righteous. And if you will say that God knew that the person would be righteous, but it was nevertheless possible that the person might be wicked, then God did not fully know it!

Limitations of God

TEXT **7**

MAIMONIDES, *MISHNEH TORAH*, LAWS OF REPENTANCE 5:5

דַּע שֶׁתְּשׁוּבַת שְׁאֵלָה זוֹ אֲרֻכָּה מֵאֶרֶץ מִדָּה וּרְחָבָה מִנִּי יָם, וְכַמָּה עִקָּרִים גְּדוֹלִים וַהֲרָרִים רָמִים תְּלוּיִים בָּהּ. אֲבָל צָרִיךְ אַתָּה לֵידַע וּלְהָבִין בְּדָבָר זֶה שֶׁאֲנִי אוֹמֵר.

כְּבָר בֵּאַרְנוּ בְּפֶרֶק שֵׁנִי מֵהִלְכוֹת יְסוֹדֵי הַתּוֹרָה שֶׁהַקָּדוֹשׁ בָּרוּךְ הוּא אֵינוֹ יוֹדֵעַ מִדֵּעָה שֶׁהִיא חוּץ מִמֶּנּוּ, כִּבְנֵי אָדָם שֶׁהֵם וְדַעְתָּם שְׁנַיִם, אֶלָּא הוּא יִתְעַלֶּה שְׁמוֹ וְדַעְתּוֹ אֶחָד. וְאֵין דַּעְתּוֹ שֶׁל אָדָם יְכוֹלָה לְהַשִּׂיג דָּבָר זֶה עַל בֻּרְיוֹ. וּכְשֵׁם שֶׁאֵין כֹּחַ בָּאָדָם לְהַשִּׂיג וְלִמְצוֹא אֲמִתַּת הַבּוֹרֵא . . . אֵין כֹּחַ בָּאָדָם לְהַשִּׂיג וְלִמְצוֹא דַּעְתּוֹ שֶׁל בּוֹרֵא. הוּא שֶׁהַנָּבִיא אָמַר, "כִּי לֹא מַחְשְׁבוֹתַי מַחְשְׁבוֹתֵיכֶם וְלֹא דַרְכֵיכֶם דְּרָכָי."

וְכֵיוָן שֶׁכֵּן הוּא, אֵין בָּנוּ כֹּחַ לֵידַע הֵיאַךְ יֵדַע הַקָּדוֹשׁ בָּרוּךְ הוּא כָּל הַבְּרוּאִים וְהַמַּעֲשִׂים. אֲבָל נֵדַע בְּלֹא סָפֵק שֶׁמַּעֲשֵׂה הָאָדָם בְּיַד הָאָדָם, וְאֵין הַקָּדוֹשׁ בָּרוּךְ הוּא מוֹשְׁכוֹ וְלֹא גוֹזֵר עָלָיו לַעֲשׂוֹת כָּךְ.

Know that the answer to this question, "longer than the land is its measure, and broader than the sea," and that many great foundations and lofty mountains hang upon it. But you need to know and understand what I am going to say.

We have already explained in the second chapter of *The Laws of the Torah's Foundations* that God does not know with a "mind" that is distinct from His being, as is the case with the human being, whose being and mind are two distinct entities. Rather, God and His "mind" are one and the same—a concept that is impossible for the human mind to fully comprehend. Thus, just as man cannot discover and grasp the being of the Creator . . . so, too, man cannot discover and grasp the "mind" of the Creator. In the words of the prophet (ISAIAH 55:8), "My thoughts are not as your thoughts, nor are your ways as My ways."

Therefore, we lack the capacity to know the nature of God's knowledge of all creations and all actions. But this we know without doubt: that the deeds of man are in the hands of man, and God does not induce or coerce a person to do anything.

Two Designs for Ewer-Shaped Ornaments (detail), Franz Xaver Habermann, etching and engraving on white laid paper, c. 1750. (Cooper Hewitt, Smithsonian Design Museum, New York)

QUESTION FOR DISCUSSION

What are the difficulties in Maimonides's answer?

TEXT **8**

RAAVAD, GLOSS ON *MISHNEH TORAH*, LAWS OF REPENTANCE 5:5

אָמַר אַבְרָהָם: לֹא נָהַג זֶה הַמְחַבֵּר מִנְהַג הַחֲכָמִים, שֶׁאֵין אָדָם מַתְחִיל בְּדָבָר
וְלֹא יֵדַע לְהַשְׁלִימוֹ. וְהוּא הֵחֵל בִּשְׁאֵלוֹת קֻשְׁיוֹת, וְהִנִּיחַ הַדָּבָר בְּקֻשְׁיָא
וְהֶחֱזִירוֹ לֶאֱמוּנָה. וְטוֹב הָיָה לוֹ לְהַנִּיחַ הַדָּבָר בִּתְמִימוּת הַתְּמִימִים וְלֹא
יְעוֹרֵר לִבָּם וְיַנִּיחַ דַּעְתָּם בְּסָפֵק.

Says Abraham: The author did not act in the manner of the wise, as one ought not to begin something that one is incapable of concluding. He begins by posing a difficult question, then remains with the difficulty, and reverts to faith. It would have been better for him to have left it as a matter of faith for the innocent, instead of making them aware [of the contradiction] and leaving their minds in doubt.

TEXT **9**

RAAVAD, GLOSS ON *MISHNEH TORAH*, LAWS OF REPENTANCE 5:5

וְאַף עַל פִּי שֶׁאֵין תְּשׁוּבָה נִצַּחַת עַל זֶה, טוֹב הוּא לִסְמוֹךְ לוֹ קְצָת תְּשׁוּבָה. וְאוֹמֵר: אִם הָיוּ צִדְקַת הָאָדָם וְרִשְׁעָתוֹ תְּלוּיִים בִּגְזֵירַת הַבּוֹרֵא יִתְ׳, הָיִינוּ אוֹמְרִים שֶׁיְּדִיעָתוֹ הִיא גְזֵירָתוֹ, וְהָיְתָה לָנוּ הַשְּׁאֵלָה קָשָׁה מְאֹד. וְעַכְשָׁיו שֶׁהַבּוֹרֵא הֵסִיר זוֹ הַמֶּמְשָׁלָה מִיָּדוֹ וּמְסָרָהּ בְּיַד הָאָדָם עַצְמוֹ, אֵין יְדִיעָתוֹ גְזֵירָה, אֲבָל הִיא כִּידִיעַת הָאִצְטַגְנִינִים שֶׁיּוֹדְעִים מִכֹּחַ אַחֵר מַה יִּהְיוּ דְּרָכָיו שֶׁל זֶה. . . . וְהַבּוֹרֵא יוֹדֵעַ כֹּחַ הַמַּזָּל וּרְגָעָיו אִם יֵשׁ כֹּחַ בַּשֵּׂכֶל לְהוֹצִיאוֹ לְזֶה מִיָּדוֹ אִם לֹא. וְזוֹ הַיְדִיעָה אֵינָהּ גְזֵירָה. וְכָל זֶה אֵינֶנּוּ שָׁוֶה.

Although there is no conclusive answer for this question, one had best give some sort of answer. I would therefore say: If a person's righteousness and wickedness were forced by divine decree, then we would say that God's knowledge is His decree, and we would indeed have a very difficult question. But because God relinquished this authority and handed it over to the person, God's knowledge does not coerce. Rather, it is like the knowledge of a fortune-teller, who knows, by some other means, what a particular person's path will be. . . . The Creator knows how strong the influence of the constellations is at any given moment, and if the person will muster the strength to overcome this influence or not. This knowledge does not coerce the person's choice. All this, however, is not a worthy explanation.

Knowledge is the
result of
choice
not the cause of the choice

TEXT 10

RABBI YOM TOV LIPMANN HELLER, *TOSAFOT YOM TOV,*
ETHICS OF THE FATHERS 3:15

דְּמֵעִיקָרָא לָאו קֻשְׁיָא. לְפִי שֶׁיְּדִיעַת הַשֵּׁם יִתְבָּרֵךְ הִיא כְּצוֹפֶה וּמַבִּיט הָעֲשִׂיָּיה שֶׁעוֹשֶׂה הָאָדָם... וְאֵין שַׁיָּךְ לוֹמַר מַה שֶׁיּוֹדֵעַ מַה שֶׁעָתִיד יַעֲשֶׂה הָאָדָם וְאִם כֵּן מֻכְרָח שֶׁיַּעֲשֶׂה, כִּי לְפָנָיו יִתְבָּרֵךְ אֵין קְדִימָה וְאִיחוּר, שֶׁאֵינוֹ בְּחוֹק הַזְּמַן... וְאֵין עָתִיד לְפָנָיו יִתְבָּרֵךְ, אֲבָל הַכֹּל הֹוֶה. וּכְמוֹ שֶׁבְּעֶרְכֵּינוּ יְדִיעַת הַהֹוֶה אֵינָהּ מַכְרַחַת, כֵּן יְדִיעָתוֹ תְּמִידִי בַּהֹוֶה וְאֵינָהּ מַכְרַחַת.

RABBI YOM TOV LIPPMAN HELLER
1579–1654

Authority on Jewish law; author; flourished in Poland and Germany; often called the *Tosafot Yom Tov* after the title of this most famous work on the Mishnah. In his youth, he was a student of the Maharal of Prague. In addition to his profound mastery of the Talmud and post-Talmudic commentaries, he was engaged in the study of kabbalah, philosophy, and grammar, and had a broad grasp of mathematics, astronomy, and natural science. At 18, he was appointed rabbinic judge in Prague, and served there for almost 28 years. Later, he served as rabbi in Nikolsburg, Vienna, Lublin, Brisk, Ludmir, and other communities.

There is no contradiction in the first place. God's knowledge of the future is the result of His observing the deed that the person is doing. . . . One cannot argue that because God knows the future actions of man He therefore compels them, because for God there is no "before" and "after," as God is not governed by the laws of time. . . . There is no future in God's reality; rather, the whole of time is present to Him. So just like our knowledge of the present has no compelling effect, so, too, God's knowledge is always in the present and is non-compelling.

TEXT **11**

MAIMONIDES, *MISHNEH TORAH*, LAWS OF THE TORAH'S FOUNDATIONS 2:9–10 🔊

כָּל הַנִּמְצָאִים חוּץ מִן הַבּוֹרֵא, מִצּוּרָה הָרִאשׁוֹנָה עַד יַתּוּשׁ קָטָן שֶׁיִּהְיֶה בְּטַבּוּר הָאָרֶץ, הַכֹּל מִכֹּחַ אֲמִתָּתוֹ נִמְצְאוּ. וּלְפִי שֶׁהוּא יוֹדֵעַ עַצְמוֹ . . . הוּא יוֹדֵעַ הַכֹּל . . .

הַקָּדוֹשׁ בָּרוּךְ הוּא מַכִּיר אֲמִתּוֹ וְיוֹדֵעַ אוֹתָהּ כְּמוֹ שֶׁהִיא. וְאֵינוֹ יוֹדֵעַ בְּדֵעָה שֶׁהִיא חוּץ מִמֶּנּוּ, כְּמוֹ שֶׁאָנוּ יוֹדְעִין. שֶׁאֵין אָנוּ וְדַעְתֵּנוּ אֶחָד. אֲבָל הַבּוֹרֵא יִתְבָּרֵךְ, הוּא וְדַעְתּוֹ וְחַיָּיו אֶחָד מִכָּל צַד וּמִכָּל פִּנָּה וּבְכָל דֶּרֶךְ יִחוּד. שֶׁאִלְמָלֵי הָיָה חַי בַּחַיִּים וְיוֹדֵעַ בְּדֵעָה חוּץ מִמֶּנּוּ, הָיוּ שָׁם אֱלוֹהוּת הַרְבֵּה: הוּא וְחַיָּיו וְדַעְתּוֹ . . . נִמְצֵאת אַתָּה אוֹמֵר: הוּא הַיּוֹדֵעַ וְהוּא הַיָּדוּעַ וְהוּא הַדֵּעָה עַצְמָהּ, הַכֹּל אֶחָד. וְדָבָר זֶה אֵין כֹּחַ בַּפֶּה לְאוֹמְרוֹ וְלֹא בָאֹזֶן לְשָׁמְעוֹ וְלֹא בְּלֵב הָאָדָם לְהַכִּירוֹ עַל בֻּרְיוֹ . . .

לְפִיכָךְ אֵינוֹ מַכִּיר הַבְּרוּאִים וְיוֹדְעָם מֵחֲמַת הַבְּרוּאִים, כְּמוֹ שֶׁאָנוּ יוֹדְעִין אוֹתָם, אֶלָּא מֵחֲמַת עַצְמוֹ יָדָעָם. לְפִיכָךְ, מִפְּנֵי שֶׁהוּא יוֹדֵעַ עַצְמוֹ יוֹדֵעַ הַכֹּל, שֶׁהַכֹּל נִסְמָךְ לוֹ בַּהֲוָיָתוֹ.

All existences aside of the Creator, from the highest [spiritual] form to a tiny gnat in the belly of the earth, all exist by virtue of God's reality. So, in knowing Himself . . . God knows everything. . . .

God is aware of His own reality and knows it as it is. He does not know with a mind that is distinct from Himself, as we know. We and our minds are not one; but God, His mind, and His life are one from every side and from every angle and in every manner of unity. For if God were to be animated by a life-force, and know with a knowledge, that are external to Him, there would exist several "gods": He, His vitality, and His knowledge. . . .

One must therefore conclude that He is the knower, He is the subject of the knowledge, and He is the knowledge itself, all in one. This concept is beyond the capacity of the mouth to articulate, the ear to hear, and the human heart to fully comprehend. . . .

Therefore, God does not know the creations because the creations exist—as we know them—but rather, God knows them from Himself. By knowing Himself He knows everything, as everything derives from His being.

TEXT 12

RABBI MENACHEM MENDEL OF LUBAVITCH, *DERECH MITZVOTECHA* 94B

וְהָעִנְיָן דִּכְתִיב "אֵ-ל דֵּעוֹת ה'" (שְׁמוּאֵל א' ב' ג'). שֶׁכּוֹלֵל ב' דֵּעוֹת.

הָא' הַדֵּעָה שֶׁלְּמַעֲלָה הוּא הַיֵּשׁ הָאֲמִיתִּי, וְכָל מַה שֶּׁלְּמַטָּה כְּלָא חָשִׁיב, כִּי הוּא רַק הֶאָרָה בְּעָלְמָא . . . וְזוֹהִי הַדֵּעָה שֶׁלּוֹ דִּהַיְינוּ כְּמוֹ שֶׁהוּא קַמֵּי' יִתְבָּרֵךְ.

הַב' הִיא כְּמוֹ שֶׁנִּרְאֶה לְגַבֵּי הַנִּבְרָאִים. שֶׁנִּדְמֶה לָהֶם שֶׁהֵם בְּחִינַת יֵשׁ וְדָבָר. וְאוֹמְרִים שֶׁהַבְּרִיאָה "יֵשׁ מֵאַיִן". וְרוֹצֶה לוֹמַר שֶׁהָאֱלֹקוּת הוּא בְּחִינַת אַיִן עַל שֵׁם שֶׁאֵינוֹ מוּשָּׂג, וְהַנִּבְרָאִים הֵם בְּחִינַת יֵשׁ וְדָבָר . . .

וְהִנֵּה אָנוּ אוֹמְרִים, "מוֹדִים אֲנַחְנוּ לָךְ" (דִּבְרֵי הַיָּמִים א' כ"ט ט"ז). פֵּירוּשׁ, שֶׁאֲנַחְנוּ מוֹדִים שֶׁהָאֱמֶת כְּמוֹ שֶׁהוּא קַמֵּי' יִתְבָּרֵךְ . . . וּמַה שֶּׁהָעוֹלָם וּמְלוֹאוֹ נִרְאֶה לְיֵשׁ וְדָבָר, זֶהוּ מִצַּד הַצִּמְצוּמִים וְהֶעָלֵמוֹת, כְּדִכְתִיב, "אֵ-ל מִסְתַּתֵּר" (יְשַׁעְיָ' מ"ה ט"ו). שֶׁעַל יְדֵי צִמְצוּם זֶה נִרְאֶה הַנִּבְרָא לְיֵשׁ, וְעַל פִּי צִמְצוּמִים אֵלּוּ הוּא הַדֵּעָה הַב' . . . וּבֶאֱמֶת הַצִּמְצוּמִים אֵינָן אֶלָּא לְפָנֵינוּ. אֲבָל קַמֵּי' יִתְבָּרֵךְ, אֵין הַצִּמְצוּמִים אֲמִיתִּיִּים כְּלָל . . .

שֶׁהֲרֵי הוּא לְמַעֲלָה מִן הַצִּמְצוּמִים, וְגַם הוּא הַמְצַמְצֵם הַצִּמְצוּמִים. וְנִמְצָא הוּא כּוֹלֵל ב' הַדֵּעוֹת. וְזֶהוּ שֶׁכָּתוּב "אֵ-ל דֵּעוֹת ה'".

RABBI MENACHEM MENDEL SCHNEERSOHN OF LUBAVITCH *(TSEMACH TSEDEK)* 1789–1866

Chasidic rebbe and noted author. The *Tsemach Tsedek* was the third leader of the Chabad Chasidic movement and a noted authority on Jewish law. His numerous works include halachic responsa, Chasidic discourses, and kabbalistic writings. Active in the plight of Russian Jewry, he worked to alleviate the plight of the cantonists, Jewish children kidnapped to serve in the Czar's army. He passed away in Lubavitch, leaving seven sons and two daughters.

It is written (1 SAMUEL 2:3), "God is the God of minds." This implies the existence of two "minds."

The first "mind" is that God is the true reality, and all that is here below is regarded as naught, as it is nothing but a reflection [of God's reality]. . . . This is how it is from God's perspective.

The second "mind" is how it appears from the perspective of the creations. To them, it seems that they are real and "something." They describe the creation [of the world] as "something from nothing"—meaning, that

mind
minds (opinions דֵּעוֹת*)*

Godliness is "nothing," as it is not graspable, and the creations are real and "something." . . .

Now we say (I CHRONICLES 29:13), "We concede to You." Meaning, we concede that the truth is how it is from God's perspective. . . . The fact that the world and all it contains appears to be real and "something" is only due to the "constrictions" (*tsimtsumim*) and conceal-ments, as it is written (ISAIAH 45:15), "God hides Him-self." It is by means of this constriction that a created thing appears to be "something," and these constrictions generate the "second mind." . . . Yet the constrictions are only from our perspective. From God's perspective, the constrictions are not real at all. . . .

God is beyond these constrictions, and is also the source of these constrictions. So in the end result, God includes both "minds." Hence the verse states, "God is the God of minds."

G-d is the source of the constrictions

TEXT 13

RASHI, COMMENTARY ON DEUTERONOMY 30:19

"וּבָחַרְתָּ בַּחַיִּים"–אֲנִי מוֹרֶה לָכֶם שֶׁתִּבְחֲרוּ בְּחֵלֶק הַחַיִּים. כְּאָדָם הָאוֹמֵר לִבְנוֹ, "בְּחַר לְךָ חֵלֶק יָפֶה בְּנַחֲלָתִי", וּמַעֲמִידוֹ עַל חֵלֶק הַיָּפֶה וְאוֹמֵר לוֹ: "אֶת זֶה בְּרוֹר לְךָ".

וְעַל זֶה נֶאֱמַר (תְּהִלִּים טז, ה): "ה' מְנָת חֶלְקִי וְכוֹסִי אַתָּה תּוֹמִיךְ גּוֹרָלִי". הִנַּחְתָּ יָדִי עַל גּוֹרַל הַטּוֹב, לוֹמַר: "אֶת זֶה קַח לְךָ".

RABBI SHLOMO YITSCHAKI (RASHI) 1040–1105

Most noted biblical and Talmudic commentator. Born in Troyes, France, Rashi studied in the famed *yeshivot* of Mainz and Worms. His commentaries on the Pentateuch and the Talmud, which focus on the straightforward meaning of the text, appear in virtually every edition of the Talmud and Bible.

"Choose life"—I am directing you to choose the portion of life. This is like a person who says to his son, "Choose for yourself a fine portion of my estate," and then stands him upon the fine portion, and says to him: "Select this for yourself."

not manipulate but appreciate

Regarding this, the verse (PSALMS 16:5) says: "God is my allotted portion and my cup; You support my lot." You laid my hand upon the good lot, saying: "Take this for yourself.'"

how we experience choice (multiple options)

options or desire

① select for yourself
② take for yourself

satisfaction @ your desire.

TEXT 14

THE REBBE, RABBI MENACHEM MENDEL SCHNEERSON,
LIKUTEI SICHOT, VOL. 19, PP. 279–281

שְׁנֵי עִנְיָנִים אֵלּוּ - "חֵלֶק הַיָּפֶה . . . בְּרוֹר לְךָ", וְ"גוֹרָל הַטּוֹב . . . קַח לְךָ",
הֵם שְׁנֵי אוֹפַנִּים שֶׁבָּהֶם יָכוֹל יְהוּדִי לְהַגִּיעַ לְ"וּבָחַרְתָּ בַּחַיִּים":

דֶּרֶךְ אַחַת הִיא: בְּחִירָה עַל-יְדֵי חִישׁוּב שִׂכְלִי, שֶׁלְּפִי טַעַם וָדַעַת . . . בְּחִירָה
זוֹ הִיא בְּאוֹפֶן שֶׁל "בְּרוֹר לְךָ" - יֶשְׁנָם שְׁנֵי דְרָכִים וַחֲלָקִים, שֶׁבְּכָל אֶחָד
מֵהֶם יֵשׁ יִתְרוֹן עַל פְּנֵי הָאַחֵר (שֶׁלּוּלֵא זֹאת לֹא יִתָּכֵן כַּאן מַצָּב שֶׁל
"בְּרוֹר"), וּבוֹחֲרִים חֵלֶק אֶחָד, וְלֹא אֶת הָאַחֵר.

הַדֶּרֶךְ הַשְּׁנִיָּה הִיא: בְּחִירָה בְּטוֹב וּבַחַיִּים בִּבְחִירָה שֶׁלְּמַעְלָה מִטַּעַם
וָדַעַת . . . בְּחִירָה זוֹ מִתְבַּטֵּאת רַק בְּ"קַח לְךָ" - הַחֵלֶק הַשֵּׁנִי אוֹ הַדֶּרֶךְ
הַשֵּׁנִי אֵין לָהֶם מָקוֹם מִלְּכַתְּחִילָה . . .

הַשּׁוֹרֶשׁ שֶׁל בְּחִירַת הַיְּהוּדִי בֶּאֱלֹקוּת נוֹבֵעַ מִכַּךְ שֶׁעֶצֶם הַנְּשָׁמָה שֶׁל יְהוּדִי
מְאֻחֶדֶת, כִּבְיָכוֹל, עִם עַצְמוּת . . . [וְ]אֵינֶנָּה נוֹבַעַת מִסִּבָּה וְיִתְרוֹן . . .
אֶלָּא מִפְּנֵי שֶׁזֶּהוּ הָרָצוֹן שֶׁל עֶצֶם הַנְּשָׁמָה מִצַּד עַצְמָהּ . . . הֲרֵי שֶׁבְּחִירָה
זוֹ הִיא בְּאוֹפֶן הַשּׁוֹלֵל לְגַמְרֵי כָּל דָּבָר זוּלַת אֱלֹקוּת.

**RABBI MENACHEM MENDEL SCHNEERSON
1902–1994**

The towering Jewish leader of the 20th century, known as "the Lubavitcher Rebbe," or simply as "the Rebbe." Born in southern Ukraine, the Rebbe escaped Nazi-occupied Europe, arriving in the U.S. in June 1941. The Rebbe inspired and guided the revival of traditional Judaism after the European devastation, impacting virtually every Jewish community the world over. The Rebbe often emphasized that the performance of just one additional good deed could usher in the era of Mashiach. The Rebbe's scholarly talks and writings have been printed in more than 200 volumes.

These two formulas—"select for yourself the fine portion" and "take for yourself the good lot"—are two ways that a Jew can achieve the objective to "choose life."

The first way is a logical choice, employing reasoning and knowledge. . . . This type of choice is described as "select for yourself." There are two paths or portions, each of which has an advantage over the other—otherwise, we would not call it *selecting*—and the person chooses one portion rather than the other.

The second way is that the person chooses good and life with a suprarational choice. . . . This type of choosing is described simply as "take for yourself," as the other portion or path is not an option in the first place. . . .

[This is because] the ultimate source of a Jew's choice of G-dliness is the fact that the essence of his or her soul is one with the essence of G-d . . . not because of any reason or advantage. . . . Rather, this is what the soul, in and of itself, desires and chooses. . . . When a person chooses with this type of choice, anything other than G-dliness is not an option at all.

Figure 6.1

Free Choice — Lower Perspective

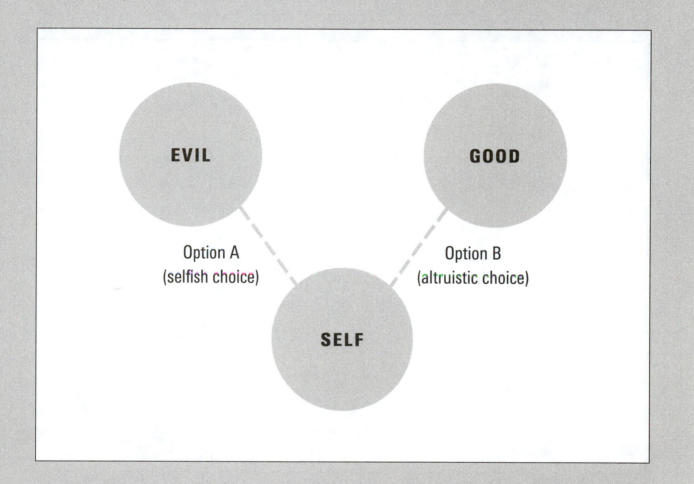

EVIL

GOOD

Option A
(selfish choice)

Option B
(altruistic choice)

SELF

Figure 6.2

Free Choice — Higher Perspective

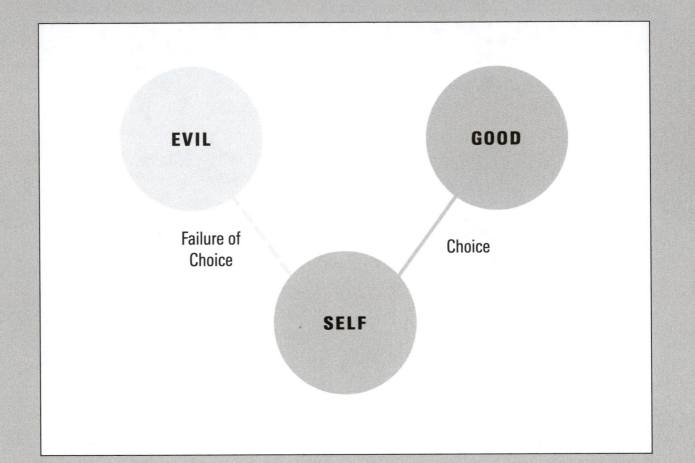

KEY POINTS

1 Free choice is a fundamental principle of Judaism. Unless a person is free to choose between good and evil, the entire concept of a "Torah" or "divine commandments"—or, for that matter, of any religion or moral system—is essentially meaningless.

2 Our choices are influenced by our inborn traits, as well as by environmental influences. Nevertheless, we possess an autonomous mind and will that are capable of overriding these influences and choosing good over evil.

3 There are two fundamental principles of Judaism—(a) God knows everything that will happen; (b) the human being has absolute freedom to choose between good and evil—that seem to contradict each other. If God already knows what I will do tomorrow, how is it possible that I will be free to choose what to do?

4 The paradox of divine knowledge and human choice is discussed extensively in Jewish sources, and a number of logical resolutions are offered. The "Fortune-Teller Model" posits that knowledge of a future choice is merely the *result* of the person's choice, not its cause. Furthermore, because God exists outside of time and the whole of time is an open book to Him, God can observe our future actions without influencing them. Maimonides, however, maintains that a true understanding of God's unity necessitates the conclusion that the paradox cannot be resolved logically.

5   Chasidic teaching explains that there are two perspectives on reality, both originating from God: (1) A "Higher Perspective," in which God is the only true reality, and the whole of creation is but a reflection of God's self-expression. (2) A "Lower Perspective," in which the divine self-concealment creates a reality that is distinct—at least in its own perception—from the divine reality. While our daily existence is defined by the Lower Perspective, we also carry a consciousness of the Higher Perspective.

6   Freedom of choice is experienced on two levels. On one level, free choice is the ability to select one out of two or more options. But the deeper and truer definition of "free choice" is the ability to freely actualize the unadulterated desire of our core self. When true choice is exercised, there is only one option: the option representing the chooser's true will.

7 We usually think of free choice as a triangle whose three points are: our self, good, and bad. The bad choice is typically the selfish option, and the good choice is usually the selfless option. This is choice as experienced within the reality of the Lower Perspective. A higher level of choice is experienced when we recognize that our core self is Godly and quintessentially good, and that the choice we face in our every action is the choice to actualize our true self, or fail to actualize it.

Additional Readings

FREE CHOICE

BY RABBI YANKI TAUBER

See, I have set before you life and goodness, and death and evil; in that I command you this day to love G-d, to walk in His ways and to keep His commandments . . .
Life and death I have set before you, blessing and curse. And you shall choose life.
Deuteronomy 30:15-19

With these verses, the Torah establishes what Maimonides calls "a fundamental principle [of the Jewish faith] and a pillar of the Torah and its commandments"[1]—the concept that the human being possesses the capacity to freely choose their path through life.

However, the concept of "free choice" seems to contradict another fundamental principle of the Jewish faith—the belief in the ultimate triumph of good. Indeed, this apparent contradiction can be discerned in the very verses that establish the concept of free choice.

After stating, "I have set before you life and goodness, and death and evil," and "Life and death I have set before you, blessing and curse," the Torah proclaims: "And you shall choose life." What is meant by these concluding words? Are they a commandment? A promise? A statement of fact? In any case, the Torah has no doubts about the ultimate outcome of man's choice between good and evil. "In the end of days," prophesies Moses, "you will return to the L-rd your G-d and you will obey His voice."[2] No matter to what

RABBI YANKI TAUBER, 1965–

Chasidic scholar and author. A native of Brooklyn, NY, Rabbi Tauber is an internationally renowned author who specializes in adapting the teachings of the Lubavitcher Rebbe. He is a member of the JLI curriculum development team, and has written numerous articles and books, including *Once Upon a Chassid* and *Beyond the Letter of the Law*.

moral and spiritual depths we may fall, no matter how far we may stray from the fulfillment of our purpose, "G-d . . . devises means that the forsaken one be not forsaken."[3] Ultimately, we will all rectify our wrongs and restore the innate perfection of our soul. How is this to be reconciled with the "fundamental principle" of free choice?

The same question could be asked on the cosmic level. The purpose of creation is that mankind should bring to light the innate goodness and perfection that has been invested within the human soul and within all of existence by the Creator. The ultimate realization of this purpose is the era of Moshiach, described by the prophets as a world free of evil and strife—a world in which humanity has overcome ignorance, jealousy, and hatred to bring about the harmonious world that G-d envisioned at creation and outlined in the Torah.

A basic principle of the Jewish faith[4] is the belief in Moshiach as an absolute eventuality—the belief that we not only can, but actually will, attain this goal. Indeed, can the possibility exist that G-d's purpose in creation will not be realized? But if the human being has been granted freedom of choice, how can we be certain of man's eventual election of good? Does not "free choice" mean that it can go either way?

Choice in Three Dimensions

Because a choice, by definition, is not coerced, it would seem that the word "free" in the phrase "free choice" is superfluous. But there are various degrees of freedom that a chooser may possess in making their choice.

All told, there are three levels of choice: *compelled choice, random choice,* and *quintessential choice.*

1) Compelled choice: The first level of choice relates to the conventional, everyday usage of the term. We each make countless "choices" every day: Will you have coffee or tea? Should you paint the picket fence white or green? Should you take the job in New York City or the one in Missoula, Montana?

As long as no one is forcing your decision, yours can be said to be a "free" choice. But are you truly choosing freely? Each of the options confronting you is armed with an array of qualities to sway your choice. The taste of coffee draws you to it, while your sense of decorum dictates tea, which everyone else is having. White will liven up your gloomy backyard, but it will also show the dirt sooner than the green. The pay in New York is higher, but so is the crime rate.

You will weigh all the factors and make your decision. But have *you* chosen? Or have the chosen thing's qualities, together with elements of your upbringing, personality, and past experiences, conspired to compel your choice? Ultimately, you chose what you did because there is something about the thing that you chose that made you need it or want it. Even if the reasons for both options were equally compelling, the one that you *did* choose was chosen because of its particular qualities. You made a choice as to which set of influences to succumb to—hardly the epitome of freedom.

2) *Random choice:* But suppose that you are above it all. Suppose that nothing about any of the choices has the power to hold you or sway you. That, to you, the taste of coffee and social niceties are equally irrelevant, and white and green are simply two cans of paint. That you are utterly immune to salary figures and the threats of a violent city.

Inasmuch as the advantages and shortcomings of all the options are of no significance to you, you are in a position to make a "free" (i.e., non-influenced) choice: to select one option or the other for no reason other than that that is the one you have chosen.

Nevertheless, this is still not the ultimate in choice and freedom. True, you are free of the attractions and rationalizations that ordinarily influence the choices of men. But how *did* you choose? By a mental throw of dice? By some completely arbitrary surge of will? The choice could have gone either way, correct? So where were *you* in all this? In what way have you exercised your freedom to choose? You have merely surrendered to something that is beyond your comprehension and control.

3) *Quintessential choice:* We seem to be in a catch-22 situation. Is there ever a free choice between A and B? If you choose A for a reason—if there is something about it that attracts you—then it is not really you who is doing the choosing; your "choice" has been swayed by its qualities and by your own biases and behavior patterns. And if you choose it for no reason, again you are not choosing, only serving as a pawn to the capricious turns of fate.

But what if your choice is determined by the very essence of what you are? What about the choice to live, the choice to be free, the choice to have a child? Certainly, these choices are motivated by a reason. But theirs is not an external reason, nor is it a reason that is related to your "external" self (i.e., your mindset, your emotional makeup, your personality). The reason for these choices is *you*. For what is "life" but the desire to be? And what is "freedom" if not the opportunity to express your most deep-seated potentials? And what are children if not the continuity of self? The quintessence of your being is what dictates that you choose life, liberty, and parenthood.

The fact that the outcome of these choices is determined makes them no less free. On the contrary: this is the ultimate proof of their freedom. Because when a choice is truly free, when the quintessence of self asserts itself, then the other, anti-self option (death, enslavement, childlessness) is obviously rejected.

In other words, we usually see the existence of more than one option as the hallmark of "choice"—choice, in the conventional definition of the term, means the ability to choose between A and B. But when it comes to the ultimate definition of choice, the very opposite is true. When your choice is free of all constraints and inhibitions, external or internal, there is no "other" option—any more than there is another you.

To summarize: On the first and lowest level of choice, our choices are determined by external factors—the qualities of the chosen thing and the mental and emotional baggage we lug through life. The only thing that makes this any sort of choice at all is the existence of more than one option: we can resist one set of influences to succumb to another.

A second, higher level of choice is one that is free of compulsion—at least, there are no identifiable factors, conscious or otherwise, that influence our decision. Again, there are two or more options (if there weren't, it wouldn't be a choice). But the very fact that the choice can go either way indicates that, ultimately, it is not the person himself—that is, his singular essence—who is doing the choosing.

On the third, highest level of choice there is only one option: the course that represents the uninhibited choice of one's deepest self. The ultimate criterion of free choice is not "Is it determined?" but "What determines it?" *Every* choice is determined by something, be it a rational motive or an intuitive flash of no traceable origins. True choice is when one's course of action is determined by, and only by, the very essence of self.

Layers

These three degrees of choice are actually three aspects of the same phenomenon. Often, we experience only the most external layer of our power to choose. But there are also points in our life in which this outer layer is peeled away and we are in touch with a deeper—and freer—dimension of our choices. Finally, there are those rare moments when our most deeply rooted drives assert themselves, effecting a decision that is the very essence of choice.

Let us take the example of a choice we make countless times, and in countless different ways, every day—the choice to live. No matter how difficult and tiresome the effort may become, we continue to elect life and survival.

As we generally experience it (if and when we think about it at all), this is firstly a "choice" in the most commonplace sense of the term. We are faced with two options: to live, or not to live (G-d forbid). On the one hand, we have the reasons for life: its joys and rewards, our commitments to our loved ones, and so on. On the other hand, we have its burdens and heartaches. We decide that it's worth the effort. We have been swayed by the many compulsions for life.

But then there are those circumstances under which all the conventional "reasons" to live no longer apply. When life and death, stripped bare of their advantages and faults, are seen as equally significant (or non-significant). Yet something inside us says, "Live!" Why? There is no why, only the simple fact

that a choice has been made—a choice free of all the motives that compel it in its lower, lesser incarnation.

On this level, we experience choice as a completely arbitrary throw of dice, which could just as easily have fallen on the other, negative side. The chooser can offer no reason, no explanation for their choice. "This is what I chose," is all they can say.

In truth, these two experiences of choice are two perspectives on one reality. Also one who chooses life because of its positive qualities is, on a deeper level of self (—a level of self to which the life's "benefits" are irrelevant), really making a "blind" supra-rational choice. Their "compelled" choice is but an expression, on a more external level of consciousness and experience, of the "arbitrary" choice that transcends the external reasons for life.

Ultimately, however, *both* these dimensions of a person's choice are outgrowths of a third, even deeper dimension that lies at their core: choice as the uninhibited assertion of their quintessential self. A person experiences choice on this level when they recognize that, ultimately, their desire for life is not caused by its particular benefits, nor is it the lot they have drawn from the blue yonder of arbitrary impulse. Rather, it is an expression of their very "I"—an expression of a definitive, unequivocal choice to project their being and potentials into the arena of physical existence.

So when we choose life in many "little" and "ordinary" ways every day, we are actually making this choice on three different levels. On the rational and emotional level, we choose life because of its rewards. On a deeper level of self, where such mundane considerations are irrelevant, it is a "blind" supra-rational choice. Simultaneously, the very core of our being is choosing life, and it is this very choice that is being reiterated by the more external layers of our self.

Choosing Good

In light of the above, we can understand that there is no contradiction between the freedom of choice granted to man and the Torah's certainty that we will indeed choose "life and goodness."

As we said, choice is a three-tiered affair, consisting of three dimensions or experiences of the same act of choice. The same applies to our choice to pursue good and reject evil by following the commandments of the Torah.

On the most elementary, everyday level, we choose the path of Torah as the most beneficial course to life. We see how Torah refines a person's character, establishes a harmonious social order, and imbues our lives with meaning and purpose. After all, G-d is the designer and creator of life; it stands to reason that His instructions on to how to live it are the surest path toward spiritual and material fulfillment. Not that a selfish and hedonistic life, unencumbered by morals and responsibilities, doesn't have its enticements. Indeed, this is what makes our choice between good and evil a *choice*: we are faced with two options, each with its own attractions and compulsions. Our choice of good is because of its virtues: because we understand that "I have set before you life and goodness, and death and evil"— that good is synonymous with life while evil ultimately spells its destruction.

But not always are the advantages of good perceivable. There are times when "darkness covers the earth and a fog envelops the nations"[5]—when a world gone amok eclipses the vitality of good and the goodness of life. When "the way of the wicked prospers"[6] while the righteous suffer. When our sensitivity to the spiritual rewards of fulfilling the divine will is deadened. Such conditions serve to elevate our choice of good to a higher, freer level: no longer is our commitment to G-d advantageous in any perceivable way; no longer is it compelled by our reason and by our perception of reality. When we choose good under such conditions, it is a pure choice: beyond motive, beyond rationale, beyond anything save our "blind" faith in G-d and the fact that we have cast our lot with the fulfillment of His will.

What both these levels of choice have in common is that they share the "conventional" definition of choice: the existence of two options (good and evil). On both these levels, we could have conceivably chosen otherwise—we could have opted for the "advantages" of evil, or we could have failed to make the "leap of faith" that the second level of choice requires.

But on the highest level of choice there is no other option. Our quintessential identity as G-d's chosen people breaks through all our secondary and superimposed personas, and freely translates into the unequivocal commitment to the fulfillment of the divine will in our daily lives.

This is the deeper significance of the three separate sentences, quoted above, in which the Torah sets down the principle of "free choice." Indeed, there is a level of which G-d says "See, I have set before you life and goodness, and death and evil"—a choice that is based on the fact that we see goodness as beneficial, and evil as detrimental, to life. There is also a higher level of choice on which "Life and death I have set before you"—when "life" and "death" are simply set before us as equals. But both these choices are but echoes of the ultimate choice: "You *shall* choose life." When you truly choose, that choice will be life.

But also when we choose life because of its virtues, or when we choose it without apparent cause or reason, the true source of our choice is the fact that *we* are choosing—and our real "I" always chooses life. And because this is the choice dictated by our quintessential self, it is the choice that will eventually assert itself in *all* our decisions. For our true self can only remain suppressed for so long: ultimately, inevitably, it must come to light.

So it is with absolute certainty that the we believe that there will come a time when the quintessential truth of every created thing will assert itself and opt for life. This is not in contradiction with the concept of "free choice"—it is its ultimate expression.

Based on the Lubavitcher Rebbe's talks, Shabbat Nitzavim and Rosh Hashanah 1965 (*Likutei Sichot*, vol. 19, pp. 274-282) Republished with permission of the Meaningful Life Center, meaningfullife.com.

Endnotes

[1] Mishneh Torah, *Laws of Repentance* 5:1.

[2] Deuteronomy 4:30; In the words of Maimonides, "The Torah has already promised that Israel is destined to repent at the end of their exile and will immediately be redeemed" (Mishneh Torah, *Laws of Repentance* 7:5).

[3] II Samuel 14:14.

[4] The twelfth of Maimonides's "Thirteen Principles of the Jewish Faith."

[5] Isaiah 60:2.

[6] Jeremiah 12:1.

Puzzle Solutions

Figure 1.4—Solution

Nine-Dot Challenge

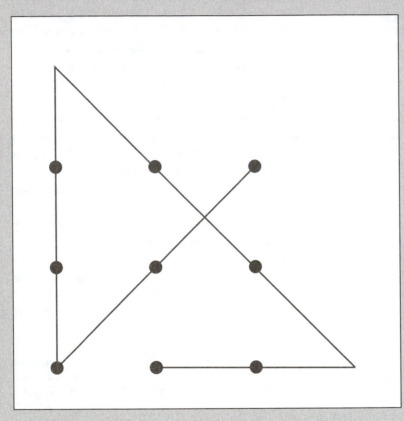

Figure 1.7—Solution

Hiding in Plain Sight

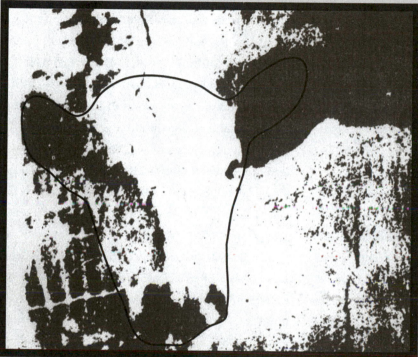

Acknowledgments

"G-d founded the earth with wisdom; He established the heavens with understanding; with His knowledge the depths were split."

—PROVERBS 3:19–20

Wisdom, understanding, and knowledge are the pillars of Chabad Chasidism, which defines "wisdom" as the acquisition of new ideas, "understanding" as their analysis and comprehension, and "knowledge" as their assimilation into one's consciousness and character. Rabbi Shne'ur Zalman of Liadi, the founder of Chabad, insisted that these three intellectual activities are key to a G-dly life. When the G-dly wisdom of Torah is integrated into the thinking and feeling self, the positive behaviors it inspires are impactful and enduring.

Seven generations of Chabad Rebbes labored to bring Rabbi Shne'ur Zalman's vision to fruition. They penned and delivered thousands of *maamarim* (discourses) distilling the deepest, most esoteric concepts contained in the Torah. Their objective: to enable those who would study these texts to see the world around them, the inner universe of their own minds and hearts, and the relationship between creation and its Creator in an entirely new light; to enable the human mind to see reality as G-d sees reality.

It is toward this aim that the Rohr Jewish Learning Institute has create this course: *What Is?: Rethinking Everything We Know about the Universe*. We have attempted to take some of the most revolutionary and mind-transforming ideas of Chabad Chasidism and present them to our students.

We are grateful to the following individuals for helping shape this innovative course:

We extend our thanks to **Rabbi Yanki Tauber** for authoring and editing this course, and to the team of researchers and writers who assisted in the drafting of some of the lessons: **Rabbi Benyomin Walters** (Lessons 1 and 2), **Rabbi Lazer Gurkow** (Lesson 2), **Rabbi Yosi Wolf** (Lesson 4), and **Rabbi Yisrael Rice** (Lesson 5).

We extend our appreciation to **Rabbis Mordechai Dinerman and Naftali Silberberg**, who direct the JLI Curriculum Department and the Flagship editorial team; to **Rabbi Dr. Shmuel Klatzkin**, JLI's senior editor; and to **Rabbi Zalman Abraham**, who skillfully provides the vision for strategic branding and marketing of JLI course offerings.

JLI Editorial Board members **Rabbi Sholom Raichik, Rabbi Shraga Sherman, Mrs. Rivkah Slonim**, and **Rabbi Ari Sollish** reviewed the course and provided many useful suggestions that enhanced the course material and ensured its suitability for a wide range of students.

Curriculum administrator **Rivki Mockin** and project manager **Chana Dechter** oversaw the course's production with unflagging grace, patience, and professionalism. **Zelda Abelsky, Rabbi Yakov Gershon**, and **Rabbi Michoel Shapiro** provided research and editorial assistance, and **Sarah Hinda Appelbaum, Shmuel Telsner, Ya'akovah Weber,** and **Rachel Witty** enhanced the quality and accuracy of the writing with their proofreading. **Shternie Morozow** designed the textbooks with taste and expertise, and the textbook images were researched and selected by **Rabbi Zalman Abraham** and **Chany Tauber**. **Mendel Sirota** directed the book publication and distribution.

Mushka Minsky oversaw multimedia production for the course. **Baila Pruss, Mushka Druk,** and **Rivka Rapoport** designed the aesthetically pleasing Power-Points, and **Moshe Raskin** and **Getzy Raskin** produced the videos; the video scripts were masterfully written by **Rabbi Yaakov Paley**.

We are immensely grateful for the encouragement of JLI's visionary chairman, and vice-chairman of Merkos L'Inyonei Chinuch—Lubavitch World Headquarters, **Rabbi Moshe Kotlarsky**. Rabbi Kotlarsky has been highly instrumental in building the infrastructure for the expansion of Chabad's international network, and is the architect of scores of initiatives and services to help Chabad representatives across the globe succeed in their mission. We are blessed to have the unwavering support of JLI's principal benefactor, **Mr. George Rohr**, who is fully invested in our work, continues to be instrumental in JLI's monumental growth and expansion, and is largely responsible for the Jewish renaissance that is being spearheaded by JLI and its affiliates across the globe.

The commitment and sage direction of JLI's dedicated Executive Board—**Rabbis Chaim Block, Hesh Epstein, Ronnie Fine, Yosef Gansburg, Shmuel Kaplan, Yisrael Rice**, and **Avrohom Sternberg**—and the countless hours they devote to the development of JLI, are what drive the vision, growth, and tremendous success of the organization.

Finally, JLI represents an incredible partnership of more than 1,400 *shluchim* and *shluchot* in more than one thousand locations across the globe, who contribute their time and talent to further Jewish adult education. We thank them for generously sharing feedback and making suggestions that steer JLI's development and growth. They are our most valuable critics and our most cherished contributors.

Inspired by the call of the **Lubavitcher Rebbe**, of righteous memory, it is the mandate of the Rohr JLI to **provide a community of learning** for all Jews throughout the world, where they can participate in their precious heritage of Torah learning and experience its rewards. May this course succeed in fulfilling this sacred charge!

On behalf of the Rohr Jewish Learning Institute,

RABBI EFRAIM MINTZ
Executive Director

RABBI YISRAEL RICE
Chairman, Editorial Board

11 Nisan, 5778

The Rohr Jewish Learning Institute

**AN AFFILIATE OF MERKOS L'INYONEI CHINUCH,
THE EDUCATIONAL ARM OF THE CHABAD-LUBAVITCH MOVEMENT**

822 EASTERN PARKWAY, BROOKLYN, NY 11213

JLI INTERNATIONAL

Rabbi Avrohom Sternberg
CHAIRMAN

Rabbi Dubi Rabinowitz
DIRECTOR

Rabbi Berry Piekarski
ADMINISTRATOR

Rabbi Levi Kaplan
PROJECT MANAGER

Rabbi Yosef Yitzchok Noyman
ADMINISTRATOR, JLI ISRAEL
IN PARTNERSHIP WITH
MIVTZA TORAH—ISRAEL

Rabbi Eli Wolf
ADMINISTRATOR, JLI IN THE CIS
IN PARTNERSHIP WITH
THE FEDERATION OF JEWISH
COMMUNITIES OF THE CIS

Rabbi Shevach Zlatopolsky
EDITOR, JLI IN THE CIS

Dr. Arye Olman
TRANSLATOR, RUSSIAN

Rabbi Nochum Schapiro
REGIONAL REPRESENTATIVE,
AUSTRALIA

Rabbi Avraham Golovacheov
REGIONAL REPRESENTATIVE,
GERMANY

Rabbi Shmuel Katzman
REGIONAL REPRESENTATIVE,
NETHERLANDS

Rabbi Avrohom Steinmetz
REGIONAL REPRESENTATIVE,
BRAZIL

Rabbi Bentzi Sudak
REGIONAL REPRESENTATIVE,
UNITED KINGDOM

Rabbi Mendel Edelman
LIAISON TO FRENCH SPEAKING
COUNTRIES

NATIONAL JEWISH RETREAT

Rabbi Hesh Epstein
CHAIRMAN

Mrs. Shaina B. Mintz
DIRECTOR

Mrs. Mushka Minsky
PROJECT MANAGER

Bruce Backman
HOTEL LIAISON

Rabbi Menachem Klein
PROGRAM COORDINATOR

Rabbi Shmuly Karp
SHLUCHIM LIAISON

Rabbi Mendel Rosenfeld
LOGISTIC COORDINATOR

Aliza Landes
Mrs. Mussie Sputz
SERVICE AND SUPPORT

JLI LAND & SPIRIT
ISRAEL EXPERIENCE

Rabbi Shmuly Karp
DIRECTOR

Mrs. Shaina B. Mintz
ADMINISTRATOR

Rabbi Yechiel Baitelman
Rabbi Dovid Flinkenstein
Rabbi Chanoch Kaplan
Rabbi Levi Klein
Rabbi Mendel Lifshitz
Rabbi Mendy Mangel
Rabbi Sholom Raichik
Rabbi Ephraim Silverman
STEERING COMMITTEE

SHABBAT IN THE HEIGHTS

Rabbi Shmuly Karp
DIRECTOR

Mrs. Shulamis Nadler
SERVICE AND SUPPORT

Rabbi Chaim Hanoka
CHAIRMAN

Rabbi Mordechai Dinerman
Rabbi Zalman Marcus
STEERING COMMITTEE

MYSHIUR
ADVANCED LEARNING INITIATIVE

Rabbi Shmuel Kaplan
CHAIRMAN

Rabbi Levi Kaplan
DIRECTOR

TORAHCAFE.COM
ONLINE LEARNING

Rabbi Levi Kaplan
DIRECTOR

Rabbi Mendy Elishevitz
WEBSITE DEVELOPMENT

Moshe Levin
CONTENT MANAGER

Avrohom Shimon Ezagui
FILMING

MACHON SHMUEL
THE SAMI ROHR RESEARCH INSTITUTE

Rabbi Avrohom Bergstein
DEAN

Rabbi Zalman Korf
ADMINISTRATOR

Rabbi Gedalya Oberlander
Rabbi Chaim Rapoport
Rabbi Levi Yitzchak Raskin
Rabbi Chaim Schapiro
Rabbi Moshe Miller
RABBINIC ADVISORY BOARD

Rabbi Yakov Gershon
RESEARCH FELLOW

FOUNDING DEPARTMENT HEADS

Rabbi Mendel Bell
Rabbi Zalman Charytan
Rabbi Mendel Druk
Rabbi Menachem Gansburg
Rabbi Meir Hecht
Rabbi Yoni Katz
Rabbi Chaim Zalman Levy
Rabbi Benny Rapoport
Dr. Chana Silberstein
Rabbi Elchonon Tenenbaum
Rabbi Mendy Weg

Faculty Directory

ALABAMA

BIRMINGHAM
Rabbi Yossi Friedman......................205.970.0100

MOBILE
Rabbi Yosef Goldwasser......................251.265.1213

ALASKA

ANCHORAGE
Rabbi Yosef Greenberg
Rabbi Mendy Greenberg......................907.357.8770

ARIZONA

FLAGSTAFF
Rabbi Dovie Shapiro......................928.255.5756

ORO VALLEY
Rabbi Ephraim Zimmerman......................520.477.8672

PHOENIX
Rabbi Zalman Levertov
Rabbi Yossi Friedman......................602.944.2753

SCOTTSDALE
Rabbi Yossi Levertov......................480.998.1410

TUCSON
Rabbi Yehuda Ceitlin......................520.881.7956

ARKANSAS

LITTLE ROCK
Rabbi Pinchus Ciment......................501.217.0053

CALIFORNIA

AGOURA HILLS
Rabbi Moshe Bryski
Rabbi Yisroel Levine......................818.991.0991

BAKERSFIELD
Rabbi Shmuli Schlanger
Mrs. Esther Schlanger......................661.331.1695

BEL AIR
Rabbi Chaim Mentz......................310.475.5311

BERKELEY
Rabbi Yosef Romano......................510.396.4448

BURBANK
Rabbi Shmuly Kornfeld......................818.954.0070

CARLSBAD
Rabbi Yeruchem Eilfort
Mrs. Nechama Eilfort......................760.943.8891

CHATSWORTH
Rabbi Yossi Spritzer......................818.718.0777

CONTRA COSTA
Rabbi Dovber Berkowitz......................925.937.4101

CORONADO
Rabbi Eli Fradkin......................619.365.4728

ENCINO
Rabbi Aryeh Herzog......................818.784.9986
Chapter founded by Rabbi Joshua Gordon, OBM

FOLSOM
Rabbi Yossi Grossbaum......................916.608.9811

FREMONT
Rabbi Moshe Fuss......................510.300.4090

GLENDALE
Rabbi Simcha Backman......................818.240.2750

HUNTINGTON BEACH
Rabbi Aron Berkowitz......................714.846.2285

LA JOLLA
Rabbi Baruch Shalom Ezagui......................858.455.5433

LAGUNA BEACH
Rabbi Elimelech Gurevitch......................949.499.0770

LOMITA
Rabbi Eli Hecht
Rabbi Sholom Pinson......................310.326.8234

LONG BEACH
Rabbi Abba Perelmuter......................562.621.9828

LOS ANGELES
Rabbi Leibel Korf......................323.660.5177

MALIBU
Rabbi Levi Cunin......................310.456.6588

MARINA DEL REY
Rabbi Danny Yiftach-Hashem
Rabbi Dovid Yiftach....................310.859.0770

NORTH HOLLYWOOD
Rabbi Nachman Abend....................818.989.9539

NORTHRIDGE
Rabbi Eli Rivkin....................818.368.3937

OJAI
Rabbi Mordechai Nemtzov....................805.613.7181

PACIFIC PALISADES
Rabbi Zushe Cunin....................310.454.7783

PALO ALTO
Rabbi Yosef Levin
Rabbi Ber Rosenblatt....................650.424.9800

PASADENA
Rabbi Chaim Hanoka
Rabbi Sholom Stiefel....................626.539.4578

RANCHO MIRAGE
Rabbi Shimon H. Posner....................760.770.7785

RANCHO PALOS VERDES
Rabbi Yitzchok Magalnic....................310.544.5544

RANCHO S. FE
Rabbi Levi Raskin....................858.756.7571

REDONDO BEACH
Rabbi Yossi Mintz
Rabbi Zalman Gordon....................310.214.4999

S. CLEMENTE
Rabbi Menachem M. Slavin....................949.489.0723

S. CRUZ
Rabbi Yochanan Friedman....................831.454.0101

S. DIEGO
Rabbi Rafi Andrusier....................619.387.8770
Rabbi Motte Fradkin....................858.547.0076

S. FRANCISCO
Rabbi Shlomo Zarchi....................415.752.2866

S. LUIS OBISPO
Rabbi Chaim Leib Hilel....................805.229.1836

S. MATEO
Rabbi Yossi Marcus....................650.341.4510

S. MONICA
Rabbi Boruch Rabinowitz....................310.394.5699

S. RAFAEL
Rabbi Yisrael Rice....................415.492.1666

SOUTH LAKE TAHOE
Rabbi Mordechai Richler....................530.314.7677

THOUSAND OAKS
Rabbi Chaim Bryski....................805.493.7776

TUSTIN
Rabbi Yehoshua Eliezrie....................714.508.2150

VENTURA
Rabbi Yakov Latowicz....................805.658.7441

WEST HOLLYWOOD
Rabbi Mordechai Kirschenbaum....................310.275.1215

WEST LOS ANGELES
Rabbi Mordechai Zaetz....................424.652.8742

YORBA LINDA
Rabbi Dovid Eliezrie....................714.693.0770

COLORADO

ASPEN
Rabbi Mendel Mintz....................970.544.3770

DENVER
Rabbi Yossi Serebryanski....................303.744.9699

FORT COLLINS
Rabbi Yerachmiel Gorelik....................970.407.1613

HIGHLANDS RANCH
Rabbi Avraham Mintz....................303.694.9119

LONGMONT
Rabbi Yakov Borenstein....................303.678.7595

VAIL
Rabbi Dovid Mintz....................970.476.7887

WESTMINSTER
Rabbi Benjy Brackman....................303.429.5177

CONNECTICUT

FAIRFIELD
Rabbi Shlame Landa....................203.373.7551

GREENWICH
Rabbi Yossi Deren
Rabbi Menachem Feldman....................203.629.9059

NEW LONDON
Rabbi Avrohom Sternberg....................860.437.8000

STAMFORD
Rabbi Yisrael Deren
Rabbi Levi Mendelow 203.3.CHABAD

WEST HARTFORD
Rabbi Shaya Gopin 860.232.1116

WESTPORT
Rabbi Yehuda L. Kantor 203.226.8584

DELAWARE

WILMINGTON
Rabbi Chuni Vogel 302.529.9900

DISTRICT OF COLUMBIA

WASHINGTON
Rabbi Levi Shemtov
Rabbi Shua Hecht 202.332.5600

FLORIDA

ALTAMONTE SPRINGS
Rabbi Mendy Bronstein 407.280.0535

BAL HARBOUR
Rabbi Dov Schochet 305.868.1411

BOCA RATON
Rabbi Zalman Bukiet
Rabbi Arele Gopin 561.994.6257
Rabbi Moishe Denburg 561.526.5760
Rabbi Ruvi New 561.394.9770

BOYNTON BEACH
Rabbi Yosef Yitzchok Raichik 561.732.4633

BRADENTON
Rabbi Menachem Bukiet 941.388.9656

SOUTHWEST BROWARD COUNTY
Rabbi Aryeh Schwartz 954.252.1770

CAPE CORAL
Rabbi Yossi Labkowski 239.963.4770

CORAL GABLES
Rabbi Avrohom Stolik 305.490.7572

CORAL SPRINGS
Rabbi Yankie Denburg 954.471.8646

DELRAY BEACH
Rabbi Sholom Ber Korf 561.496.6228

FLEMING ISLAND
Rabbi Shmuly Feldman 904.290.1017

FORT LAUDERDALE
Rabbi Yitzchok Naparstek 954.568.1190

FORT MYERS
Rabbi Yitzchok Minkowicz
Mrs. Nechama Minkowicz 239.433.7708

HALLANDALE BEACH
Rabbi Mordy Feiner 954.458.1877

HOLLYWOOD
Rabbi Leizer Barash 954.965.9933
Rabbi Leibel Kudan 954.801.3367

KENDALL
Rabbi Yossi Harlig 305.234.5654

LAKELAND
Rabbi Moshe Lazaros 863.510.5968

LONGWOOD
Rabbi Yanky Majesky 407.636.5994

MAITLAND
Rabbi Sholom Dubov
Rabbi Levik Dubov 470.644.2500

MIAMI
Rabbi Chaim Lipskar 786.368.9040
Rabbi Yakov Fellig 305.445.5444

MIAMI BEACH
Rabbi Yisroel Frankforter 305.534.3895

N. MIAMI BEACH
Rabbi Eily Smith 786.247.7222

OCALA
Rabbi Yossi Hecht 352.291.2218

ORLANDO
Rabbi Yosef Konikov 407.354.3660

ORMOND BEACH
Rabbi Shmuel Konikov 386.672.9300

PALM BEACH GARDENS
Rabbi Dovid Vigler 561.624.2223

PALM CITY
Rabbi Shlomo Uminer 772.288.0606

PALMETTO BAY
Rabbi Zalman Gansburg 786.282.0413

PEMBROKE PINES
Rabbi Mordechai Andrusier 954.874.2280

PLANTATION
Rabbi Pinchas Taylor 954.644.9177

PONTE VEDRA BEACH
Rabbi Nochum Kurinsky 904.543.9301

SARASOTA
Rabbi Chaim Shaul Steinmetz 941.925.0770

SATELLITE BEACH
Rabbi Zvi Konikov 321.777.2770

SOUTH PALM BEACH
Rabbi Leibel Stolik 561.889.3499

SOUTH TAMPA
Rabbi Mendy Dubrowski 813.922.1723

SUNNY ISLES BEACH
Rabbi Alexander Kaller 305.803.5315

S. AUGUSTINE
Rabbi Levi Vogel 904.521.8664

TALLAHASSEE
Rabbi Schneur Oirechman 850.523.9294

VENICE
Rabbi Sholom Ber Schmerling 941.493.2770

WESTON
Rabbi Yisroel Spalter 954.349.6565

WEST PALM BEACH
Rabbi Yoel Gancz 561.659.7770

GEORGIA

ALPHARETTA
Rabbi Hirshy Minkowicz 770.410.9000

ATLANTA
Rabbi Yossi New
Rabbi Isser New 404.843.2464

ATLANTA: INTOWN
Rabbi Eliyahu Schusterman
Rabbi Ari Sollish 404.898.0434

CUMMING
Rabbi Levi Mentz 310.666.2218

GWINNETT
Rabbi Yossi Lerman 678.595.0196

MARIETTA
Rabbi Ephraim Silverman 770.565.4412

HAWAII

PRINCEVILLE
Rabbi Michoel Goldman 808.647.4293

IDAHO

BOISE
Rabbi Mendel Lifshitz 208.853.9200

ILLINOIS

CHAMPAIGN
Rabbi Dovid Tiechtel 217.355.8672

CHICAGO
Rabbi Meir Hecht 312.714.4655
Rabbi Yosef Moscowitz 773.772.3770
Rabbi Levi Notik 773.274.5123

DES PLAINES
Rabbi Lazer Hershkovich 224.392.4442

ELGIN
Rabbi Mendel Shemtov 847.440.4486

GLENVIEW
Rabbi Yishaya Benjaminson 847.910.1738

HIGHLAND PARK
Mrs. Michla Schanowitz 847.266.0770

NAPERVILLE
Rabbi Mendy Goldstein 630.778.9770

NORTHBROOK
Rabbi Meir Moscowitz 847.564.8770

OAK PARK
Rabbi Yitzchok Bergstein 708.524.1530

PEORIA
Rabbi Eli Langsam 309.692.2250

ROCKFORD
Rabbi Yecheskel Rothman 815.596.0032

SKOKIE
Rabbi Yochanan Posner 847.677.1770

VERNON HILLS
Rabbi Shimmy Susskind 847.984.2919

WILMETTE
Rabbi Dovid Flinkenstein 847.251.7707

INDIANA

INDIANAPOLIS
Rabbi Avraham Grossbaum
Rabbi Dr. Shmuel Klatzkin 317.251.5573

IOWA

BETTENDORF
Rabbi Shneur Cadaner 563.355.1065

KANSAS

OVERLAND PARK
Rabbi Mendy Wineberg 913.649.4852

KENTUCKY

LOUISVILLE
Rabbi Avrohom Litvin 502.459.1770

LOUISIANA

METAIRIE
Rabbi Yossie Nemes
Rabbi Mendel Ceitlin 504.454.2910

MARYLAND

ANNAPOLIS
Rabbi Nochum Light 443.321.9859

BALTIMORE
Rabbi Velvel Belinsky 410.764.5000
Classes in Russian

BEL AIR
Rabbi Kushi Schusterman 443.353.9718

BETHESDA
Rabbi Sender Geisinsky 301.913.9777

COLUMBIA
Rabbi Hillel Baron
Rabbi Yosef Chaim Sufrin 410.740.2424

FREDERICK
Rabbi Boruch Labkowski 301.996.3659

GAITHERSBURG
Rabbi Sholom Raichik 301.926.3632

OLNEY
Rabbi Bentzy Stolik 301.660.6770

OWINGS MILLS
Rabbi Nochum H. Katsenelenbogen 410.356.5156

POTOMAC
Rabbi Mendel Bluming 301.983.4200
Rabbi Mendel Kaplan 301.983.1485

ROCKVILLE
Rabbi Moishe Kavka 301.836.1242

MASSACHUSETTS

BOSTON
Rabbi Yosef Zaklos 617.297.7282

CAPE COD
Rabbi Yekusiel Alperowitz 508.775.2324

LONGMEADOW
Rabbi Yakov Wolff 413.567.8665

NEWTON
Rabbi Shalom Ber Prus 617.244.1200

SUDBURY
Rabbi Yisroel Freeman 978.443.0110

SWAMPSCOTT
Rabbi Yossi Lipsker
Rabbi Yisroel Baron 781.581.3833

MICHIGAN

ANN ARBOR
Rabbi Aharon Goldstein 734.995.3276

BLOOMFIELD HILLS
Rabbi Levi Dubov 248.949.6210

GRAND RAPIDS
Rabbi Mordechai Haller 616.957.0770

WEST BLOOMFIELD
Rabbi Elimelech Silberberg 248.855.6170

MINNESOTA

MINNETONKA
Rabbi Mordechai Grossbaum
Rabbi Shmuel Silberstein 952.929.9922

S. PAUL
Rabbi Shneur Zalman Bendet 651.998.9298

MISSOURI

CHESTERFIELD
Rabbi Avi Rubenfeld 314.258.3401

S. LOUIS
Rabbi Yosef Landa 314.725.0400

NEVADA

LAS VEGAS
Rabbi Yosef Rivkin 702.217.2170

SUMMERLIN
Rabbi Yisroel Schanowitz
Rabbi Tzvi Bronchtain 702.855.0770

NEW JERSEY

BASKING RIDGE
Rabbi Mendy Herson
Rabbi Mendel Shemtov 908.604.8844

CLINTON
Rabbi Eli Kornfeld 908.623.7000

FAIR LAWN
Rabbi Avrohom Bergstein 201.362.2712

FORT LEE
Rabbi Meir Konikov 201.886.1238

FRANKLIN LAKES
Rabbi Chanoch Kaplan 201.848.0449

HASKELL
Rabbi Mendy Gurkov 201.696.7609

HOLMDEL
Rabbi Shmaya Galperin 732.772.1998

MADISON
Rabbi Shalom Lubin 973.377.0707

MANALAPAN
Rabbi Boruch Chazanow
Rabbi Levi Wolosow 732.972.3687

MOUNTAIN LAKES
Rabbi Levi Dubinsky 973.551.1898

MULLICA HILL
Rabbi Avrohom Richler 856.733.0770

OLD TAPPAN
Rabbi Mendy Lewis 201.767.4008

PASSAIC - CLIFTON
Rabbi Yitzchak Sebbag 973.246.5251

RANDOLPH
Rabbi Avraham Bekhor 973.895.3070

ROCKAWAY
Rabbi Asher Herson
Rabbi Mordechai Baumgarten 973.625.1525

RUTHERFORD
Rabbi Yitzchok Lerman 347.834.7500

SCOTCH PLAINS
Rabbi Avrohom Blesofsky 908.790.0008

TEANECK
Rabbi Ephraim Simon 201.907.0686

TENAFLY
Rabbi Mordechai Shain 201.871.1152

TOMS RIVER
Rabbi Moshe Gourarie 732.349.4199

WEST ORANGE
Rabbi Mendy Kasowitz 973.325.6311

NEW YORK

BEDFORD
Rabbi Arik Wolf 914.666.6065

BINGHAMTON
Mrs. Rivkah Slonim 607.797.0015

BRIGHTON BEACH
Rabbi Moshe Winner 718.946.9833

BROOKVILLE
Rabbi Mendy Heber 516.626.0600

CEDARHURST
Rabbi Zalman Wolowik 516.295.2478

COMMACK
Rabbi Mendel Teldon 631.543.3343

DOBBS FERRY
Rabbi Benjy Silverman..................................914.693.6100

EAST HAMPTON
Rabbi Leibel Baumgarten
Rabbi Mendy Goldberg..................................631.329.5800

ELLENVILLE
Rabbi Shlomie Deren....................................845.647.4450

FOREST HILLS
Rabbi Yossi Mendelson..................................917.861.9726

GREAT NECK
Rabbi Yoseph Geisinsky..................................516.487.4554

KINGSTON
Rabbi Yitzchok Hecht....................................845.334.9044

LARCHMONT
Rabbi Mendel Silberstein..................................914.834.4321

LONG BEACH
Rabbi Eli Goodman....................................516.897.2473

NYC KEHILATH JESHURUN
Rabbi Elie Weinstock....................................212.774.5636

NYACK
Rabbi Chaim Zvi Ehrenreich..................................845.356.6686

OCEANSIDE
Rabbi Levi Gurkow....................................516.764.7385

OSSINING
Rabbi Dovid Labkowski..................................914.923.2522

OYSTER BAY
Rabbi Shmuel Lipszyc
Rabbi Shalom Lipszyc..................................347.853.9992

PARK SLOPE
Rabbi Menashe Wolf..................................347.957.1291

PORT WASHINGTON
Rabbi Shalom Paltiel..................................516.767.8672

PROSPECT HEIGHTS
Rabbi Mendy Hecht....................................347.622.3599

RIVERDALE
Rabbi Levi Shemtov....................................718.549.1100

ROCHESTER
Rabbi Nechemia Vogel..................................585.271.0330

ROSLYN
Rabbi Yaakov Reiter....................................516.484.8185

SEA GATE
Rabbi Chaim Brikman..................................917.975.2792

SOUTHAMPTON
Rabbi Chaim Pape....................................917.627.4865

STATEN ISLAND
Rabbi Mendy Katzman..................................718.370.8953

STONY BROOK
Rabbi Shalom Ber Cohen..................................631.585.0521

SUFFERN
Rabbi Shmuel Gancz....................................845.368.1889

YORKTOWN HEIGHTS
Rabbi Yehuda Heber....................................914.962.1111

NORTH CAROLINA

ASHEVILLE
Rabbi Shaya Susskind..................................828.505.0746

CARY
Rabbi Yisroel Cotlar....................................919.651.9710

CHAPEL HILL
Rabbi Zalman Bluming..................................919.630.5129

CHARLOTTE
Rabbi Yossi Groner
Rabbi Shlomo Cohen....................................704.366.3984

GREENSBORO
Rabbi Yosef Plotkin....................................336.617.8120

RALEIGH
Rabbi Pinchas Herman
Rabbi Lev Cotlar....................................919.637.6950

WILMINGTON
Rabbi Moshe Lieblich..................................910.763.4770

OHIO

BEACHWOOD
Rabbi Shmuli Friedman..................................216.282.0112

BLUE ASH
Rabbi Yisroel Mangel....................................513.793.5200

COLUMBUS
Rabbi Yitzi Kaltmann....................................614.294.3296

DAYTON
Rabbi Nochum Mangel
Rabbi Shmuel Klatzkin..................................937.643.0770

OKLAHOMA

OKLAHOMA CITY
Rabbi Ovadia Goldman 405.524.4800

TULSA
Rabbi Yehuda Weg 918.492.4499

OREGON

PORTLAND
Rabbi Mordechai Wilhelm 503.977.9947

SALEM
Rabbi Avrohom Yitzchok Perlstein 503.383.9569

PENNSYLVANIA

AMBLER
Rabbi Shaya Deitsch 215.591.9310

BALA CYNWYD
Rabbi Shraga Sherman 610.660.9192

LAFAYETTE HILL
Rabbi Yisroel Kotlarsky 484.533.7009

LANCASTER
Rabbi Elazar Green 717.368.6565

MONROEVILLE
Rabbi Mendy Schapiro 412.372.1000

NEWTOWN
Rabbi Aryeh Weinstein 215.497.9925

PHILADELPHIA: CENTER CITY
Rabbi Yochonon Goldman 215.238.2100

PITTSBURGH
Rabbi Yisroel Altein .... 412.422.7300 EXT. 269

PITTSBURGH: SOUTH HILLS
Rabbi Mendy Rosenblum 412.278.3693

RYDAL
Rabbi Zushe Gurevitz 267.536.5757

WYNNEWOOD
Rabbi Moishe Brennan 610.529.9011

PUERTO RICO

CAROLINA
Rabbi Mendel Zarchi 787.253.0894

RHODE ISLAND

WARWICK
Rabbi Yossi Laufer 401.884.7888

SOUTH CAROLINA

COLUMBIA
Rabbi Hesh Epstein
Rabbi Levi Marrus 803.782.1831

MYRTLE BEACH
Rabbi Doron Aizenman 843.448.0035

TENNESSEE

CHATTANOOGA
Rabbi Shaul Perlstein 423.490.1106

MEMPHIS
Rabbi Levi Klein 901.754.0404

TEXAS

ARLINGTON
Rabbi Levi Gurevitch 817.451.1171

AUSTIN
Rabbi Mendy Levertov 512.905.2778

BELLAIRE
Rabbi Yossi Zaklikofsky 713.839.8887

DALLAS
Rabbi Mendel Dubrawsky
Rabbi Moshe Naparstek 972.818.0770

FORT WORTH
Rabbi Dov Mandel 817.263.7701

FRISCO
Rabbi Mendy Kesselman 214.460.7773

HOUSTON
Rabbi Dovid Goldstein
Rabbi Zally Lazarus 281.589.7188
Rabbi Moishe Traxler 713.774.0300

HOUSTON: RICE UNIVERSITY AREA
Rabbi Eliezer Lazaroff 713.522.2004

LEAGUE CITY
Rabbi Yitzchok Schmukler 281.724.1554

MISSOURI CITY
Rabbi Mendel Feigenson 832.758.0685

PLANO
Rabbi Mendel Block
Rabbi Yehudah Horowitz 972.596.8270

S. ANTONIO
Rabbi Chaim Block
Rabbi Levi Teldon 210.492.1085

THE WOODLANDS
Rabbi Mendel Blecher 281.719.5213

UTAH

SALT LAKE CITY
Rabbi Benny Zippel 801.467.7777

VERMONT

BURLINGTON
Rabbi Yitzchok Raskin 802.658.5770

VIRGINIA

ALEXANDRIA/ARLINGTON
Rabbi Mordechai Newman 703.370.2774

FAIRFAX
Rabbi Leibel Fajnland 703.426.1980

NORFOLK
Rabbi Aaron Margolin
Rabbi Levi Brashevitzky 757.616.0770

TYSONS CORNER
Rabbi Chezzy Deitsch 703.829.5770
Chapter founded by Rabbi Levi Deitsch, OBM

WASHINGTON

BELLINGHAM
Rabbi Yosef Truxton 617.640.8841

MERCER ISLAND
Rabbi Elazar Bogomilsky 206.527.1411

SPOKANE COUNTY
Rabbi Yisroel Hahn 509.443.0770

WISCONSIN

KENOSHA
Rabbi Tzali Wilschanski 262.359.0770

MADISON
Rabbi Avremel Matusof 608.231.3450

MILWAUKEE
Rabbi Mendel Shmotkin 414.961.6100

WAUKESHA
Rabbi Levi Brook 925.708.4203

ARGENTINA

BUENOS AIRES
Mrs. Chani Gorowitz 54.11.4865.0445
Rabbi Mendi Mizrahi 54.11.4963.1221
Rabbi Mendy Grunblatt 54.11.4771.8228
Rabbi Mendy Gurevitch 55.11.4545.7771
Rabbi Pinhas Sudry 54.1.4822.2285
Rabbi Shloimi Setton 549.11.5325.0849
Rabbi Yaakov Birman 54.11.4774.5071
Rabbi Yoel Migdal 54.11.4961.0621

SALTA
Rabbi Rafael Tawil 54.387.421.4947

AUSTRALIA

NEW SOUTH WALES

DOUBLE BAY
Rabbi Yanky Berger
Rabbi Yisroel Dolnikov 612.9327.1644

QUEENSLAND

BRISBANE
Rabbi Levi Jaffe 617.3843.6770

DOVER HEIGHTS
Rabbi Motti Feldman 612.9387.3822

NORTH SHORE
Rabbi Nochum Schapiro
Mrs. Fruma Schapiro 612.9488.9548

VICTORIA

ELSTERNWICK
Rabbi Chaim Cowen 614.3330.8584

MOORABBIN
Rabbi Elisha Greenbaum 614.0349.0434

WESTERN AUSTRALIA

PERTH
Rabbi Shalom White......................618.9275.2106

AZERBAIJAN

BAKU
Mrs. Chavi Segal......................994.12.597.91.90

BELARUS

BOBRUISK
Mrs. Mina Hababo......................375.29.104.3230

MINSK
Rabbi Shneur Deitsch
Mrs. Bassie Deitsch......................375.29.330.6675

BELGIUM

BRUSSELS
Rabbi Shmuel Pinson......................375.29.330.6675

BRAZIL

CURITIBA
Rabbi Mendy Labkowski......................55.41.3079.1338

S. PAULO
Rabbi Avraham Steinmetz......................55.11.3081.3081

CANADA

ALBERTA

CALGARY
Rabbi Mordechai Groner......................403.281.3770

EDMONTON
Rabbi Ari Drelich
Rabbi Mendy Blachman......................780.200.5770

BRITISH COLUMBIA

RICHMOND
Rabbi Yechiel Baitelman......................604.277.6427

VANCOUVER
Rabbi Dovid Rosenfeld......................604.266.1313

VICTORIA
Rabbi Meir Kaplan......................250.595.7656

MANITOBA

WINNIPEG
Rabbi Shmuel Altein......................204.339.8737

ONTARIO

LAWRENCE/EGLINTON
Rabbi Menachem Gansburg......................416.546.8770

MISSISSAUGA
Rabbi Yitzchok Slavin......................905.820.4432

NIAGARA FALLS
Rabbi Zalman Zaltzman......................905.356.7200

OTTAWA
Rabbi Menachem M. Blum......................613.843.7770

RICHMOND HILL
Rabbi Mendel Bernstein......................905.770.7700

GREATER TORONTO REGIONAL OFFICE & THORNHILL
Rabbi Yossi Gansburg......................905.731.7000

THORNHILL WOODS
Rabbi Chaim Hildeshaim......................905.881.1919

WATERLOO
Rabbi Moshe Goldman......................226.338.7770

YORK MILLS
Rabbi Levi Gansburg......................416.551.9391

QUEBEC

HAMPSTEAD
Rabbi Moshe New
Rabbi Berel Bell......................514.739.0770

MONTREAL
Rabbi Ronnie Fine
Pesach Nussbaum......................514.738.3434

S. LAZARE
Rabbi Nochum Labkowski......................514.436.7426

TOWN OF MOUNT ROYAL
Rabbi Moshe Krasnanski
Rabbi Shneur Zalman Rader......................514.342.1770

WESTMOUNT
Rabbi Yossi Shanowitz
Mrs. Devorah Leah Shanowitz......................514.937.4772

SASKATCHEWAN

REGINA
Rabbi Avrohom Simmonds......................306.585.1359

SASKATOON
Rabbi Raphael Kats 306.384.4370

CAYMAN ISLANDS

GRAND CAYMAN
Rabbi Berel Pewzner 717.798.1040

COLOMBIA

BOGOTA
Rabbi Chanoch Piekarski 57.1.635.8251

COSTA RICA

S. JOSÉ
Rabbi Hershel Spalter
Rabbi Moshe Bitton 506.4010.1515

CROATIA

ZAGREB
Rabbi Pinchas Zaklas 385.1.4812227

DENMARK

COPENHAGEN
Rabbi Yitzchok Loewenthal 45.3316.1850

ESTONIA

TALLINN
Rabbi Shmuel Kot 372.662.30.50

FRANCE

BOULOGNE
Rabbi Michael Sojcher 33.1.46.99.87.85

CANNES
Rabbi Yehouda Lewin 33.4.92.98.67.51

MARSEILLE
Rabbi Eliahou Altabe 33.6.11.60.03.05
Rabbi Menahem Mendel Assouline 33.6.64.88.25.04
Rabbi Emmanuel Taubenblatt 33.4.88.00.94.85

PARIS
Rabbi Avraham Barou'h Pevzner 33.6.99.64.07.70

GEORGIA

TBILISI
Rabbi Meir Kozlovsky 995.32.2429770

GERMANY

BERLIN
Rabbi Yehuda Tiechtel 49.30.2128.0830

COLOGNE
Rabbi Menachem M. Schtroks 49.178.4444.770

DUSSELDORF
Rabbi Chaim Barkahn 49.173.2871.770

HAMBURG
Rabbi Shlomo Bistritzky 49.40.4142.4190

HANNOVER
Rabbi Binyamin Wolff 49.511.811.2822

GREECE

ATHENS
Rabbi Mendel Hendel 30.210.323.3825

GUATEMALA

GUATEMALA CITY
Rabbi Shalom Pelman 502.2485.0770

ISRAEL

ASHKELON
Rabbi Shneor Lieberman 054.977.0512

BALFURYA
Rabbi Noam Bar-Tov 054.580.4770

CAESAREA
Rabbi Chaim Meir Lieberman 054.621.2586

EVEN YEHUDA
Rabbi Menachem Noyman 054.777.0707

GANEI TIKVA
Rabbi Gershon Shnur 054.524.2358

GIV'ATAYIM
Rabbi Pinchus Bitton..................052.643.8770

KARMIEL
Rabbi Mendy Elishevitz..................054.521.3073

KFAR SABA
Rabbi Yossi Baitch..................054.445.5020

KIRYAT BIALIK
Rabbi Pinny Marton..................050.661.1768

KIRYAT MOTZKIN
Rabbi Shimon Eizenbach..................050.902.0770

KOCHAV YAIR
Rabbi Dovi Greenberg..................054.332.6244

MACCABIM-RE'UT
Rabbi Yosef Yitzchak Noiman..................054.977.0549

NES ZIYONA
Rabbi Menachem Feldman..................054.497.7092

NETANYA
Rabbi Schneur Brod..................054.579.7572

RAMAT GAN-KRINITZI
Rabbi Yisroel Gurevitz..................052.743.2814

RAMAT GAN-MAROM NAVE
Rabbi Binyamin Meir Kali..................050.476.0770

RAMAT YISHAI
Rabbi Shneor Zalman Wolosow..................052.324.5475

RISHON LEZION
Rabbi Uri Keshet..................050.722.4593

ROSH PINA
Rabbi Sholom Ber Hertzel..................052.458.7600

YEHUD
Rabbi Shmuel Wolf..................053.536.1479

JAPAN

TOKYO
Rabbi Mendi Sudakevich..................81.3.5789.2846

KAZAKHSTAN

ALMATY
Rabbi Shevach Zlatopolsky..................7.7272.77.59.49

KYRGYZSTAN

BISHKEK
Rabbi Arye Raichman..................996.312.68.19.66

LATVIA

RIGA
Rabbi Shneur Zalman Kot
Mrs. Rivka Glazman..................371.6720.40.22

LITHUANIA

VILNIUS
Rabb Sholom Ber Krinsky..................370.6817.1367

LUXEMBOURG

LUXEMBOURG
Rabbi Mendel Edelman..................352.2877.7079

MOROCCO

CASABLANCA
Rabbi Levi Banon..................212.5.22.26.90.37

NETHERLANDS

ALMERE
Rabbi Moshe Stiefel..................31.36.744.0509

AMSTERDAM
Rabbi Jaacov Zwi Spiero..................31.652.328.065

HAGUE
Rabbi Shmuel Katzman..................31.70.347.0222

HEEMSTEDE-HAARLEM
Rabbi Shmuel Spiero..................31.23.532.0707

NIJMEGEN
Rabbi Menachem Mendel Levine..................31.621.586.575

ROTTERDAM
Rabbi Yehuda Vorst..................31.10.265.5530

PANAMA

PANAMA CITY
Rabbi Ari Laine
Rabbi Gabriel Benayon 507.223.3383

PARAGUAY

ASUNCION
Rabbi Levi Feigelstock...................595.21.228.669

RUSSIA

ASTRAKHAN
Rabbi Yisroel Melamed 7.851.239.28.24

BRYANSK
Rabbi Menachem Mendel Zaklas...................7.483.264.55.15

CHELYABINSK
Rabbi Meir Kirsh...................7.351.263.24.68

MOSCOW: MARINA ROSHA
Rabbi Mordechai Weisberg...................7.495.645.50.00

NIZHNY NOVGOROD
Rabbi Shimon Bergman...................7.920.253.47.70

OMSK
Rabbi Osher Krichevsky...................7.381.231.33.07

PERM
Rabbi Zalman Deutch...................7.342.212.47.32

ROSTOV
Rabbi Chaim Danzinger...................7.8632.99.02.68

S. PETERSBURG
Rabbi Zvi Pinsky...................7.812.713.62.09

SAMARA
Rabbi Shlomo Deutch...................7.846.333.40.64

SARATOV
Rabbi Yaakov Kubitshek...................7.8452.21.58.00

TOGLIATTI
Rabbi Meier Fischer...................7.848.273.02.84

UFA
Rabbi Dan Krichevsky...................7.347.244.55.33

VORONEZH
Rabbi Levi Stiefel...................7.473.252.96.99

SINGAPORE

SINGAPORE
Rabbi Mordechai Abergel 656.337.2189
Rabbi Netanel Rivni...................656.336.2127
Classes in Hebrew

SOUTH AFRICA

CAPE TOWN
Rabbi Levi Popack...................27.21.434.3740

JOHANNESBURG
Rabbi Dovid Masinter
Rabbi Ari Kievman 27.11.440.6600

SWEDEN

MALMO
Rabbi Shneur Kesselman...................46.707.366.770

STOCKHOLM
Rabbi Chaim Greisman 468.679.7067

SWITZERLAND

BASEL
Rabbi Zalmen Wishedsky...................41.41.361.1770

LUZERN
Rabbi Chaim Drukman...................41.41.361.1770

THAILAND

BANGKOK
Rabbi Yosef C. Kantor 6681.822.9541

UKRAINE

DNEPROPETROVSK
Rabbi Dan Makagon 380.504.51.13.18

NIKOLAYEV
Rabbi Sholom Gotlieb 380.512.37.37.71

ODESSA
Rabbi Avraham Wolf
Rabbi Yaakov Neiman...................38.048.728.0770 EXT. 280

ZHITOMIR
Rabbi Shlomo Wilhelm 380.504.63.01.32

UNITED KINGDOM

BOURNEMOUTH
Rabbi Bentzion Alperowitz......................44.749.456.7177

CARDIFF
Rabbi Michoel Rose 44.792.866.9536

CHEADLE
Rabbi Peretz Chein 44.161.428.1818

LEEDS
Rabbi Eli Pink.......................................44.113.266.3311

LONDON
Rabbi Mendel Cohen 44.777.261.2661
Rabbi Nissan D. Dubov...........................44.208.944.1581
Rabbi Mendy Korer.................................44.794.632.5444
Rabbi Dovid Katz...................................44.207.624.2770
Rabbi Yisroel Lew..................................44.207.060.9770
Rabbi Gershon Overlander
Rabbi Hillel Gruber................................44.208.202.1600
Rabbi Shlomo Odze................................44.791.757.3558

MANCHESTER
Rabbi Levi Cohen 44.161.792.6335
Rabbi Shmuli Jaffe.................................44.161.766.1812

URUGUAY

MONTEVIDEO
Rabbi Menachem Shemtov 598.2628.6770

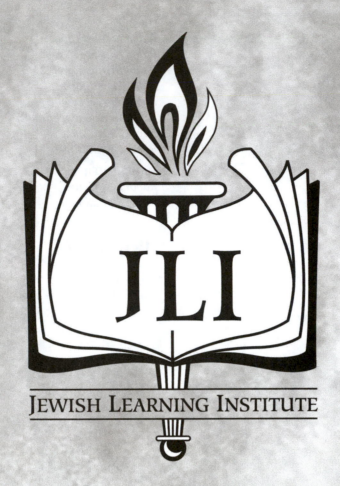

JEWISH LEARNING INSTITUTE

THE JEWISH LEARNING MULTIPLEX
Brought to you by the Rohr Jewish Learning Institute

In fulfillment of the mandate of the Lubavitcher Rebbe, of blessed memory,
whose leadership guides every step of our work,
the mission of the Rohr Jewish Learning Institute is to transform
Jewish life and the greater community through the study of Torah,
connecting each Jew to our shared heritage of Jewish learning.

While our flagship program remains the cornerstone of our organization,
JLI is proud to feature additional divisions catering to specific populations,
in order to meet a wide array of educational needs.

THE ROHR JEWISH LEARNING INSTITUTE,
a subsidiary of *Merkos L'Inyonei Chinuch*,
is the adult education arm of the Chabad-Lubavitch Movement.

Torah Studies provides a rich and nuanced
encounter with the weekly Torah reading.

MyShiur courses are designed to assist students in developing
the skills needed to study Talmud independently.

IN PARTNERSHIP WITH CHABAD ON CAMPUS

This rigorous fellowship program invites select college
students to explore the fundamentals of Judaism.

IN PARTNERSHIP WITH CTEEN: CHABAD TEEN NETWORK

Jewish teens forge their identity as they engage in
Torah study, social interaction, and serious fun.

The Rosh Chodesh Society gathers Jewish women
together once a month for intensive textual study.

TorahCafe.com provides an exclusive selection
of top-rated Jewish educational videos.

This yearly event rejuvenates mind, body, and spirit with
a powerful synthesis of Jewish learning and community.

Participants delve into our nation's rich past while
exploring the Holy Land's relevance and meaning today.

Select affiliates are invited to partner with peers and noted
professionals, as leaders of innovation and excellence.

THE SAMI ROHR
RESEARCH INSTITUTE

Machon Shmuel is an institute providing Torah
research in the service of educators worldwide.